# The BEATLES
# Get Back to Abbey Road

Compiled by Bruce Spizer

With additional contributions by

Bill King,
Al Sussman,
Frank Daniels,
Piers Hemmingsen
and other Beatles fans

www.imagineandwonder.com

## YOUR GUARANTEE OF QUALITY

As publishers, we strive to produce every book to the highest commercial standards. The printing and binding have been planned to ensure a sturdy, attractive publication which should give years of enjoyment. If your copy fails to meet our high standards, please inform us and we will gladly replace it. admin@imagineandwonder.com

www.beatle.net
498 Productions, L.L.C.
935 Gravier Street, Suite 707
New Orleans, Louisiana 70112
Fax: 504-299-1964
email: 498@beatle.net

Scan these QR codes with your phone camera for more titles from Imagine and Wonder and 498 Productions.

Copyright ©2019 by 498 Productions, LLC
This paperback edition first published 2021 by Imagine & Wonder under agreement with 498 Productions, LLC.
This book is not an official product of Capitol Records, Inc., Universal Music Group, Inc. or Apple Corps, Ltd.

The Billboard, Cash Box and Record World chart data used in this book were taken from books published by Record Research, including Billboard Pop Album Charts 1965-1969 and The Comparison Book 1954-1982. Images provided by: Eric Cash (page 167 drawing); Gary Deiter (page 63); Hope Juber (page 130); Vincent Ruello (page 135); Mark Galloway (page 143); and Jennifer Sandi (page 144). The Timothy Leary poster (page 156) is from the collection of C.W. Doran. The Canadian images (pages 59-69) were provided by Piers Hemmingsen. Most of the other collectibles shown in the book are from the collections of Bruce Spizer, Frank Daniels, Gary Hein and Perry Cox.

Paperback edition ISBN 9781637610008
Library of Congress Control Number 2021936185
Printed in China by Hung Hing Off-set Printing Co. Ltd.
1 2 3 4 5 6 7 8 9

# One Sweet Dream Came True

1968 had been a rough year in many ways, with constant news about the Vietnam War (with weekly dead and wounded tabulations on TV), civil rights unrest and the assassinations of Martin Luther King, Jr. and Robert Kennedy. But for me, a few key events made it magical. On a cool Sunday August night, as I lay on my bunk at Camp Zakelo in Harrison, Maine, I heard "Hey Jude" for the first time. When I bought the single five days later, every thing about it, from the classy Apple labels to the music in the grooves, left me spellbound. And then that November, the Beatles first album on Apple gave me 30 new recordings and over an hour and a half of incredible music. And, as if that wasn't enough for a Beatles fan, I saw the group's cartoon film *Yellow Submarine* at a downtown New Orleans theater on a mid-November Saturday afternoon.

It was also an exciting time for my other passion, the space program. In October, NASA bounced back from the tragic loss of the three Apollo 1 astronauts with the successful shakedown mission of Apollo 7. And on Christmas Eve, Apollo 8 circled the moon as its crew showed images of the lunar surface and read from the Book of Genesis. Another truly magical moment.

1969 was set to be the year where dreams came true. With the success of Apollo 8, America was in position to reach President Kennedy's goal, before the end of the decade, of landing a man on the moon and returning him safely to the Earth.

The release of the *Yellow Submarine* LP in January gave us four new Beatles songs and a side of George Martin instrumentals. But for me, the most tantalizing Beatles news since the release of *The White Album* appeared in an April issue of TV Guide, which told of an upcoming TV documentary on the recording of the new Beatles album. It also featured a cool picture of the Beatles performing on a London roof. I couldn't wait for the TV show and LP!

That same April week I heard the group's new "Get Back" single on the radio. It was pure rock 'n' roll. On Saturday, I bought the single at Studio A, where I learned that the Billy Preston listed on the label was an organist. I added that info and "APR. 69" to the label.

The last night in April gave me a taste of what the Beatles TV documentary would be like. The group was seen performing both sides of its fabulous new single in promotional films on the Glen Campbell Goodtime Hour. By the time the show aired, I had already taped the TV Guide two-page spread on the Beatles (shown on page 9) to my bedroom wall next to my Yellow Submarine light switch plate cover. That night I watched the picture of the band on the London roof come to life as they performed "Get Back." The promo clip of "Don't Let Me Down" showed the group in action, both indoors and outdoors.

As expected, "Get Back" received saturation air play in New Orleans and was soon at number one on the WTIX Boss Thirty chart. By June, school was on summer break, which gave me more time to go to the record store. There I saw a new Beatles 45, "The Ballad Of John And Yoko." It seemed strange that the group would issue a new single while "Get Back" had only been out a little over a month, but I certainly was not complaining. Another great rocker from the Beatles. The song's "Christ you know it ain't easy" refrain explained why I hadn't heard the song on the radio. I was pretty sure that WTIX wasn't gonna play a song that had John singing "They're gonna crucify me." Not in a Southern city with a large Catholic population.

Towards the end of June, I was back at Camp Zakelo, where I celebrated my 14th birthday. I had a subscription to the Boston Globe newspaper, so I was well informed about the upcoming flight of Apollo 11, which would be NASA's first attempt to land two men on the moon and return them safely home. Fortunately, the camp director, Zak Zarakov, allowed those interested in following the flight to watch its important moments on TV. We were all allowed to see one sweet dream come true as Neil Armstrong took those first steps on the moon. I persuaded Zak to let me stay up for the entire moon walk by promising to write a story about "Man's greatest moment" for the camp newspaper.

Upon returning from camp, I quickly made my way to Studio A to pick up some of the hot singles that came out while I was away. I purchased two Apple discs, "Give Peace A Chance" by the Plastic Ono Band and "That's The Way God Planned It" by Billy Preston, along with "Honky Tonk Women" by the Rolling Stones.

As September came to a close, I began hearing new Beatles songs on the radio again, although it wasn't quite the same domination that had occurred with *The White Album* the previous November. I bought *Abbey Road* on Friday, October 3, and played it all weekend long. I instantly fell in love with the first three songs and will never forget my surprise at the abrupt ending of the last track on Side One or at the sudden appearance of "Her Majesty" as I was getting ready to lift the needle off the turntable! "Here Comes The Sun" was an instant favorite and the vocal harmonies of "Because" blew my mind. But it was the medley that convinced me that the Beatles had somehow managed to create another sweet dream without repeating themselves.

That mid-November, NASA returned men to the moon with Apollo 12. For a science project, I build a tall Revelle plastic model of the mighty Saturn V rocket that was displayed for many years in the science building at Newman School. Then came the rumor that Paul was dead. I assured concerned girls in my class that he was still alive, although I found it freaky that "Number nine" played backwards really did sound like "Turn me on dead man." Towards the end of the year, an FM radio station that had Spanish programming during the day and "went hippie" at night played another batch of Beatles songs I had yet to hear, which I taped on my cassette player. But that is a story for another book.

# Carry That Weight

Well, here I am again writing my acknowledgments for yet another book on the Beatles. My initial offerings were tomes on the Beatles records released on various American record labels, augmented with the convoluted story of how Beatlemania developed in America: Vee-Jay, Capitol singles, Capitol albums, Apple, The Beatles Are Coming!, Apple Solo and Swan (a catch all collection). One, two, three, four, five, six, seven....

I honestly thought my seventh book, *The Beatles Swan Song*, would be my swan song. I had said all that could be said about the Beatles American records. The End. But then, Frank Daniels pointed out that something was missing and convinced me to come together with him to write a book on the Beatles British records. It was time to get back to where I once belonged, behind the computer writing about the Beatles. And so, *Beatles For Sale on Parlophone Records* came to be. Surely that would be The End. But no, it wasn't (and don't call me Shirley).

I wanted to write a special article for the 50th anniversary of *Sgt. Pepper's Lonely Hearts Club Band*. That project magically morphed into another book, *The Beatles and Sgt. Pepper: A Fans' Perspective*. As a historian, I enjoyed going back to 1967 with a little help from my friends. The book contained contributions from Bill King and Al Sussman of Beatlefan magazine, Professor Frank Daniels and Piers Hemmingsen, plus dozens of fan recollections from everyday people, as well as a gems from Beatles fans Billy Joel, Peter Tork of the Monkees and Pat Dinizio of the Smithereens. I had a lot of fun putting it together, loved the new format and knew, deep down, I wasn't done after all.

With *The White Album* being my favorite Beatles LP, I just had to do a book on *The Beatles White Album and the Launch of Apple*. I went with the same format and realized it would be cool to do an entire series on the Beatles albums. And so I'm gonna carry that weight a long time, at least long enough for me to write another six or so books, starting with *The Beatles Get Back to Abbey Road*. So no, this book isn't going to be The End.

Of course it's easier to carry that weight when you have so many people providing recollections, articles, images of memorabilia and support. I once again thank those who helped me and were named in prior books. For this project, I received extra help beyond the call of duty from Gary Hein, Perry Cox, Mark Lewisohn, Jason Cornthwaite, Hope Juber, Vincent Ruello, Mark Galloway, Mark Lapidos and Chris O'Dell. Once again I was able to compile a wonderful set of Fan Recollections. Jude Southerland Kessler's fan recollection on John was so long that I ran it as a separate chapter!

As always, Diana Thornton of Crescent Music Services served as my art director, graphic designer, pre-press, IT advisor and so much more. She's the one who makes it come together. Once again, Kaye Alexander coordinated matters with our printer. The book was proofed by Diana, Frank, Al and Beatle Tom Frangione. In the tradition, my thanks to my family, Sarah, Eloise, Barbara, Trish, Big Puppy and others too numerous and crazy to name.

And, in case you hadn't guessed, my next project shall be a book on the *Get Back/Let It Be* sessions. See you then!

# About Author

Bruce Spizer is a lifelong native of New Orleans, Louisiana, who was eight years old when the Beatles invaded America. He began listening to the radio at age two and was a die-hard fan of WTIX, a top forty AM station that played a blend of New Orleans R&B music and top pop and rock hits. His first two albums were *The Coasters' Greatest Hits*, which he permanently "borrowed" from his older sisters, and *Meet The Beatles!*, which he still occasionally plays on his vintage 1964 Beatles record player.

During his high school and college days, Bruce played guitar in various bands that primarily covered hits of the sixties, including several Beatles songs. He wrote numerous album and concert reviews for his high school and college newspapers, including a review of *Abbey Road* that didn't claim Paul was dead. He received his B.A., M.B.A. and law degrees from Tulane University. His legal and accounting background have proved valuable in researching and writing his books.

Bruce is considered one of the world's leading experts on the Beatles. A "taxman" by day, Bruce is a Board Certified Tax Attorney with his own practice. A "paperback writer" by night, Bruce is the author of ten critically acclaimed books on the Beatles, including *The Beatles Are Coming! The Birth of Beatlemania in America*, a series of six books on the group's American record releases, *Beatles For Sale on Parlophone Records*, which covers all of the Beatles records issued in the U.K. from 1962- 1970, and his new series of books on the Beatles albums. His articles have appeared in Beatlefan, Goldmine and American History magazines. He was selected to write the questions for the special Beatles edition of Trivial Pursuit. He maintains the popular website www.beatle.net.

Bruce has been a guest speaker at numerous Beatles conventions and at the Grammy Museum, the American Film Institute, New York's Lincoln Center and the Rock 'N' Roll Hall of Fame & Museum. He has appeared on Fox National News, CNN, ABC's Good Morning America and Nightline, CBS's The Early Show and morning shows in New York, Chicago, Los Angeles, New Orleans and other cities, and is a frequent guest on radio shows, including NPR, BBC and Beatle Brunch.

Bruce serves as a consultant to Universal Music Group, Capitol Records and Apple Corps Ltd. on Beatles projects. He has an extensive Beatles collection, concentrating on American, Canadian and British first issue records, promotional items and concert posters.

# contents

# LOVE ME DO

WRITTEN AND COMPOSED BY McCARTNEY AND LENNON

RECORDED BY **THE BEATLES** ON PAR R. 4949

**ARDMORE & BEECHWOOD LTD**
30 - 34 LANGHAM ST. LONDON W.I.
SOLE SELLING AGENTS
CAMPBELL CONNELLY & CO. LTD
10 DENMARK STREET LONDON W.C. 2

2/6

# Once There Was A Way
# To Get Back Home

On June 6, 1962, four scruffy young lads from Liverpool first set foot in a converted old residence located at 3 Abbey Road, London NW8. Built in 1830, the structure was originally a 16-room house prior to being purchased by The Gramophone Company Ltd. in 1929. The building, located in St. John's Wood, was converted into a recording studio and opened for business in 1931. By then, The Gramophone Company had merged with The Columbia Gramophone Company to form Electric and Musical Industries Ltd., more commonly known as EMI.

When the Beatles entered EMI Studios on Abbey Road for their commercial test that summer day, the band's lineup was John Lennon on rhythm guitar, Paul McCartney on bass, George Harrison on lead guitar and Pete Best on drums. The group's equipment was in deplorable condition. A string had to be tied around John's amplifier to keep it from rattling. The rumbling of Paul's bass amp was so severe that it is was deemed unusable. The engineers were forced to improvise, mixing parts of studio equipment to create a bass rig. The group recorded four songs, including three Lennon-McCartney originals. Although George Martin set up the session, his assistant, Ron Richards, initially served as producer because he was more familiar with rock 'n' roll than Martin, whose background encompassed classical and comedy recordings. But by the time the group ran through "Love Me Do," Martin was in the studio and taking charge. He reassigned the singing of the song's "Love me do" refrain from John to Paul and insisted that the tune be played at a faster tempo. Although none of the tracks recorded that day were deemed suitable for release, the exploratory session marked the beginning of the group's successful union with George Martin and Abbey Road.

When the Beatles returned to the studio three months later on September 4, Pete Best was gone, replaced by Ringo Starr. With Martin at the helm, the group recorded their first single, "Love Me Do." Photographer Dezo Hoffman shot several pictures of the group's first proper Abbey Road session, including a photo of the boys posing with their instruments, which appeared on the U.K. sheet music to "Love Me Do."

Not counting their BBC sessions, the Beatles recorded exclusively at Abbey Road in 1962 and 1963, knocking out five singles and two albums over a dozen or so sessions. "Please Please Me," "From Me To You," "She Loves You" and "I Want To Hold Your Hand" all hit number one on the singles charts published by the British music magazines. The albums "Please Please Me" and "With The Beatles" topped the Record Retailer charts for a total of 51 weeks.

The Beatles first recording session in 1964 did not take place at Abbey Road. Instead, the group and George Martin found themselves at EMI's Pathé Marconi Studios in Paris, France. The January 29 session was held during the Beatles three-week stay in the City of Lights, where the group played 19 days of concerts at the Olympia Theatre. At the request of EMI's West German branch, Electrola, the group recorded German lyric versions of "I Want To Hold Your Hand" and "She Loves You" for release on Germany's Odeon label. After knocking out "Komm, Gib Mir Deine Hand" and "Sie Liebt Dich," the band began recording what would be their next single, "Can't Buy Me Love."

Upon returning from their first U.S. visit, the boys were back at Abbey Road recording songs for their first film, *A Hard Day's Night*. All remaining 1964 sessions, as well as all 1965 and 1966 sessions, took place there. During these sessions, the Beatles recorded five albums, including two of their finest, *Rubber Soul* and *Revolver*. They also recorded three stand-alone singles, "I Feel Fine," "We Can Work It Out" c/w "Day Tripper" and "Paperback Writer."

Except for the February 9, 1967, session for "Fixing A Hole" held at Regent Sound Studio, all of *Sgt. Pepper's Lonely Hearts Club Band* was recorded at Abbey Road. The songs for the Beatles next two projects, the TV film *Magical Mystery Tour* and the feature-length cartoon *Yellow Submarine*, were primarily recorded at Abbey Road, but there were some exceptions. "Baby, You're A Rich Man" was recorded and mixed at Olympic Sound Studios on May 11. Later that month, the Beatles were at De Lane Lea Music Recording Studios for a May 25-26 session during which they recorded "It's All Too Much." The group returned to the studio on June 1 and 2 for largely non-productive evenings of jamming, although they did add four trumpets and a bass clarinet to "It's All Too Much." (The song was mixed there on October 12.) On June 14, the group started work on "All You Need Is Love" at Olympic. The first version of "Your Mother Should Know" was recorded at Chappell Recording Studios on August 22-23.

The Beatles spent significant time in September, October and November 1967 at Abbey Road finishing up the songs for *Magical Mystery Tour* and recording their next single, "Hello Goodbye," and an elaborate Fan Club Christmas disc titled "Christmas Time (Is Here Again)."

On January 12, 1968, George Harrison recorded the musical backing to his composition "The Inner Light" with local Indian musicians at EMI Recording Studio in Bombay (now known as Mumbai). The session took place towards the end of George's trip to India to record music for the soundtrack to the movie *Wonderwall*. The Beatles added their vocals to "The Inner Light" during February sessions at Abbey Road in which they also recorded "Lady Madonna," "Across The Universe" and "Hey Bulldog."

After studying transcendental meditation with the Maharishi in Rishikesh, India, the Beatles were back at Abbey Road on May 30. During the next five months, the group recorded 34 tracks, 30 of which would end up on a double album titled *The Beatles*, more commonly known as *The White Album*. Two more, "Hey Jude" and "Revolution," were issued as the Beatles first single on Apple Records. All of the May 30- July 30 sessions were held at Abbey Road. On July 31 and August 1, the Beatles went to Trident Studios to take advantage of the studio's eight-track recorder to record "Hey Jude." (George and Paul were familiar with the Trident, having produced tracks there with Jackie Lomax and Mary Hopkin.) The group returned to Trident for three days starting on August 28 to record "Dear Prudence."

Up to this point, nearly all of the Beatles sessions were produced by George Martin. But for the month of September, Martin went on vacation and left his assistant, Chris Thomas, in charge. Thomas' first assignment was the recording of "While My Guitar Gently Weeps" on Abbey Road's newly-installed 3M eight-track. When Martin returned, the first five days of October were spent at Trident recording "Honey Pie," "Savoy Truffle" and "Martha My Dear." The remaining sessions for *The White Album* were held in the familiar surroundings of Abbey Road. During the five months of recording, the group took full advantage of Abbey Road's three studios, with some days having simultaneous sessions in different studios. Not counting the two German-language recordings, all but eight of the 180 tracks released from 1962- 1968 were recorded at Abbey Road.

After recording more than 95% of their songs at Abbey Road, the Beatles became nomads during the first half of 1969. On January 2, the group gathered at Twickenham Film Studios to rehearse songs for a planned television show, concert and new album. The cavernous and cold film soundstage was in sharp contrast to intimate environment of Abbey Road. The new location was not the only change. Paul recruited producer/engineer Glyn Johns to serve as balance engineer. While George Martin attended some of the Twickenham sessions, Johns was present throughout the entire proceedings, sometimes serving as unofficial producer. Although the rehearsals gave birth to classics such as "Get Back," "Don't Let Me Down" and "Two Of Us," the atmosphere was at times tense and full of bad vibes. By January 10, Harrison had enough and quit the group. Four days later, the Twickenham sessions came to an end.

The Beatles, at full strength again with Harrison's return and augmented by Billy Preston on keyboards, next recorded from January 21-31 at their Apple headquarters on Savile Row. With the exception of a rooftop concert held on the afternoon of January 30, these sessions took place in the building's basement, with two four-track consoles borrowed from EMI to pair with their fledgling studio's eight-track recorder. Martin attended most of the Apple sessions. Johns was there full time, serving as engineer (and unofficial producer when Martin was not there).

After taking off three weeks, the Beatles returned to Trident Studios on February 22 with Billy Preston in tow. George Martin served as producer, with Glyn Johns back as engineer. When the Beatles resumed recording in mid-April, they were at Abbey Road for eight sessions running through May 2. Martin was producer for the April 14 and 16 sessions before his assistant, Chris Thomas, took over. The next stop on the Beatles magical mystery tour of London recording studios was Glyn Johns' favorite, Olympic Sound Studios. The group held two long sessions there on May 5 and 6 with Martin as producer and Johns serving as engineer.

After this erratic start to the year, the group decided it was time to get back to where they once belonged. That July, the Beatles returned to Abbey Road, where seven years earlier they had their first recording session with EMI and producer George Martin. During the next few months, the Beatles and Martin recaptured the magic and camaraderie that, at times, was missing during the January sessions. They had found their way back home.

Twickenham Film Studios, January 1969

# From Tucson, Arizona to Abbey Road:
# An American Perspective of the Beatles in 1969

During the second half of April 1969, Americans first heard that Jo Jo had left his home in Tucson, Arizona for some California grass. A month later, the Beatles "Get Back" single featuring Jo Jo and sweet Loretta Martin was topping the charts. The May 24, 1969, issue of Billboard had the song at number one, where it would remain for five weeks during its 12-week run on the charts.

To get to the top of The Hot 100 in its third week, the Beatles single passed a pair of recordings of songs from the American Tribal-Love-Rock Musical *Hair*, "Aquarius/Let The Sunshine In" by the Fifth Dimension and "Hair" by the Cowsills. That week, "Aquarius" was at number two and "Hair" at four, with "Love (Can Make You Happy)" by Mercy at three. The top five was rounded out by the Edwin Hawkins Singers' "Oh Happy Day," which would serve as inspiration for George Harrison's "My Sweet Lord." (Although Harrison's recording of "My Sweet Lord" seems far-removed from the gospel tune, the Harrison-produced arrangement of his composition by Billy Preston, which was recorded first, has an R&B/gospel groove and backing vocals by the Edwin Hawkins Singers.) Other top twenty hits included: "It's Your Thing" by the Isley Brothers (#6), whose recordings of "Twist And Shout" and "Shout" were early concert favorites of the Beatles; Donovan's "Atlantis" (#7), whose anthem-style ending was reminiscent of "Hey Jude;" Simon and Garfunkel's "The Boxer" (#8); the Ventures' "Hawaii Five-O" (#11); Mary Hopkin's "Goodbye" (#14), written and produced by Paul McCartney; "Time Is Tight" by Booker T. & the MGs (#15); Elvis Presley's "In The Ghetto" (#17); the Who's "Pinball Wizard" (#19); and "Bad Moon Rising" by Creedence Clearwater Revival (#20).

The "Get Back" single performed equally well on the other American charts, with Cash Box matching Billboard's showing of five weeks at number one and 12 weeks on the charts. Record World was similar, with four weeks at one and 11 weeks on the charts. The flip side, "Don't Let Me Down," also charted, with a peak of 35 in Billboard, 33 in Record World and 57 in Cash Box. The disc was certified gold (one million units) by the RIAA on May 19, 1969.

The Beatles had started 1969 with their double album *The Beatles* at the top of the Billboard Top LP's chart, where it would remain for all but one week through March 1. That week, the Beatles *Yellow Submarine* was at number two, giving the group the top two albums for the first time since 1964 when they did it for 20 weeks. Although the Beatles "Hey Jude" single would remain in the Billboard Hot 100 through January 18, the band had not released a new single since August 1968. That drought continued for more than a quarter of 1969.

Americans who were wondering what the Beatles were up to during the first part of 1969 got their first answers in TV Guide. The magazine's April 19-25 issue contained a two-page spread featuring one group and four individual photos of the band in action. The brief article, titled "Four cats on a London roof," informed readers of a TV documentary detailing the making of a new Beatles album. It stated that the filming was done to "let the world—all over which the Beatles hope to sell the documentary in a few months—know just how the Beatles go about their work." Readers also learned that the album was recorded in a studio in London's elegant Savile Row and that neighbors had called the bobbies (police) to quell the noise. We later learned that the concert was held on the roof of Apple headquarters.

Shortly after the magazine was mailed to households and distributed to stores, radio stations began playing the Beatles new single, "Get Back" and "Don't Let Me Down." The former song got the most spins, with its pure rock 'n' roll sound, propelled by Ringo's galloping drums, blasting out of radios throughout the land. Paul's energetic vocal and nifty guitar work by John and George added to the excitement. The flip side, "Don't Let Me Down," was more of a soulful blues number with John on lead vocal.

The image of the Beatles on the rooftop shown in TV Guide sprang to life about two weeks after its debut on the evening of Wednesday, April 30, when film of the band performing "Get Back" and "Don't Let Me Down" was shown on the Glen Campbell Goodtime Hour. The "Get Back" clip featured the Beatles performing the song during their London rooftop concert with Paul on lead vocals and John playing the song's rockabilly-styled guitar solo. When the song was over, the camera panned to the crowd forming in the streets below.

**6:30** **3** **8** COLOR NEWS
—Chet Huntley, David Brinkley

**6** COLOR NEWS—Frank Reynolds

**12** ON GUARD—Instruction
Topic: "Airport Operations." Chief James Moore is the instructor.

**17** TWILIGHT ZONE—Drama
"One for the Angels." Informed by Death that he is scheduled to die at midnight, pitchman Lew Bookman hopes he can now do what has always eluded him—make the pitch of a lifetime. Lew: Ed Wynn. Death: Murray Hamilton.

**20** LOST IN SPACE—Adventure
The Robinsons construct a small two-man, vehicle to fly back to earth. Smith: Jonathan Harris. Will: Billy Mumy. John: Guy Williams. Maureen: June Lockhart. (60 min.)

**48** PERRY MASON—Mystery
"The Frantic Flyer." Carol Taylor doesn't believe that her late husband stole money from his wealthy father. Carol: Rebecca Welles. Howard Walters: Simon Oakland. Janice Atkins: Patricia Barry.

stops at New York City's Central Park, San Francisco's Golden Gate Bridge, Georgia's Andersonville National Cemetery and Hawaii's Pearl Harbor.

**10** COLOR NEWS—Walter Cronkite

**12** HIGH SCHOOL OF THE AIR

**17** JOAN RIVERS
COLOR Topic: pearls. TV personality Ed McMahon is a guest.

**7:30** **3** **8** VIRGINIAN—Western
COLOR Burgess Meredith in "The Orchard." An old cattleman, trying to rebuild a ranch, is caught in a clash between his sons. One wants to farm the land; the other prefers gambling and rustling Shiloh cattle. Virginian: James Drury. Grainger: John McIntire. Holly: Jeanette Nolan. (Rerun; 90 min.)

**Guest Cast**

| | |
|---|---|
| Tim Bradbury | Burgess Meredith |
| Walt Bradbury | Brandon De Wilde |
| Chick Mead | William Windom |
| Mike Bradbury | Ben Murphy |
| Faith Bradbury | Tyre Daly |
| Gummery | Lew Brown |

**6** HERE COME THE BRIDES

**Guest Cast**

| | |
|---|---|
| Ox | Don Pedro Colley |
| Charlie | Gary Dub'n |
| Corky | Robert Biheller |
| Sam | Buck Kartallan |

**10** **15** **21** **43** GLEN CAMPBELL
COLOR On film: the Beatles perform "Get Back," "Don't Let Me Down." Studio guests: Liza Minelli, the Righteous Brothers, country singer Waylon Jennings and Glen's parents, who join him in song. In a rerun segment, Pat Paulsen stars in a parody of an artsy European film. Earl Brown singers, George LaFave dancers; Marty Paich orchestra. (60 min.)

**Highlights**

| | |
|---|---|
| "La Breakdown" | Liza |
| "My Babe" | Righteous Brothers |
| "Elusive Butterfly," "If This Is Love," "Born Free" | Glen |
| "Delia's Gone" | Waylon |
| "Alimony," "Good Old Texas Home," "Soldiers, Joy" | Glen, Parents |

**12** NET SPECIAL REPORT
SPECIAL COLOR Dr. Lee A. DuBridge,

President Nixon's special advisor on science and technology, is interviewed. Formerly president of the California Institute of Technology, Dr. DuBridge returns to the campus to reflect on his radiation research during World War II, and ways in which the Nixon Administration may strengthen the national research effort. CIT scientist Albert Hibbs hosts.
Repeated May 3 at 7 P.M.

**17** OF LANDS AND SEAS
COLOR The various outdoor attractions of British Columbia are described by C.P. Lyons. Films show the oyster fishermen on the inland waterway; the nesting rocks of the sea birds in the Gulf Islands; the old gold-rush town of Barkerville; and the wildlife in the Cascade Mountains. Col. John D. Craig is the host. (60 min.)

**20** HONEYMOONERS—Comedy
Ralph appears in an amateur theatrical production. Ralph: Jackie Gleason. Norton: Art Carney. Alice: Audrey Meadows. Trixie: Joyce Randolph.

# Four cats on a London roof

A TV documentary will detail the making of the Beatles' new record album

The cats on the roof are, of course, the Beatles. And what they're up to up there is a recording session, the entire proceedings of which were, coincidentally, filmed for a television documentary.

In the panel of pictures at top are, from left to right: Ringo Starr, George Harrison, a hirsute Paul McCartney and John Lennon. In the bottom photo, the Beatles en masse in a *furor poeticus*.

The reason for making an album is obvious. The reason for filming the session is to let the world—all over which the Beatles hope to sell the documentary in a few months—know just how the Beatles go about their work. At least part of the world, however, was less than enchanted with the opportunity. Their neighbors (the recording studio just happens to be in London's elegant Savile Row) dispatched bobbies to quell the noise. Even bobbies couldn't do that.

The "Don't Let Me Down" promo film provided additional information about the TV documentary and the recording of the songs. At the beginning, the group is indoors in what appears to be a dimly lit location. John is shown singing lead, with Paul and George providing backing vocals mainly on the chorus. John's scraggly beard indicates that this part of the film was shot before the rooftop footage. At the beginning of the bridge, as John sings "I'm in love for the first time," there is a closeup of Yoko's face, showing that she was present during the sessions. The film then switches to a rooftop performance of the song. During this sequence, a black musician (who we later learned was Billy Preston) is shown playing electric piano. The film then moves back indoors during the last chorus. As the song comes to an end, the camera pulls back, revealing what appears to be a film studio backdrop with scaffolded lighting.

While the "Hey Jude" and "Revolution" videos had been shown on the Smothers Brothers Comedy Hour, by the time the "Get Back" single was released, CBS had canceled the show. This led to country singer/guitarist Glen Campbell getting promotional films of the Beatles for his own show. Campbell provided a wonderful tongue-in-cheek introduction to the "Get Back" film, pretending that he was presenting an unknown act discovered by comedian Pat Paulsen: "Well we like to give new talent a break here on the show, and Pat brought a brand new group back from London, and uh, he asked me if I'd give them a break, and I said, 'well sure Pat, we'd be very grateful to have them on the show.' So we're gonna present them right now on the Goodtime Hour. Uh, what's the name of that group, Pat? Oh yeah, ladies and gentlemen, directly from England, the Beatles."

Although the single's official release date is listed as May 5, 1969, the disc was most likely available for purchase on Friday, April 25. Thus, many Americans had already bought the single prior to the promo films being broadcast on television. For those who hadn't, that broadcast and saturation radio air play sealed the deal. The record was the Beatles first stereo single. The labels to the disc credited the recordings to "THE BEATLES with Billy Preston." Back then, there was no Internet, so many purchasers had no way of knowing who Billy Preston was even though he appeared in the "Don't Let Me Down" promo film. That summer, Beatles fans finally got to see a photo of Preston on the picture sleeve to his single "That's The Way God Planned It," which was produced by George Harrison.

APPLE
1808

Apple Records
# BILLY PRESTON

## That's the way
## God planned it
### What about you?

The headline for Apple's ad for the Beatles first single of 1969, which ran in the April 26 issues of Billboard and Cash Box, was "The Beatles as nature intended." It stated that the new record was "as live as can be, in this electronic age" and bragged "There's no electronic watchamacallit." "Get Back" was described as a "pure spring-time rock number." Paul stated that the group "made it up out of thin air" in the studio and that the song was "recorded at Apple Studios and made into a song to rollercoast by." John took credit for the song's "fab live guitar solo." As for the flip side, John was quoted as saying "don't let me down about 'Don't let me down.'"

All three of the music trade magazines ran mini-reviews of the single in their April 26 issues. Cash Box picked up on the lack of electronics stressed in the single's ad, noting that the disc "eliminates electronic gadgetry for the simple appeal that marked early efforts by the Beatles, but with the sophistication they have gained." In describing the A-side, the magazine found the group "Rocking with a blues-ier feel than ever before" and noted that "'Get Back' could mark the team's entrance on a new phase of development." Cash Box warned not to overlook the ballad B-side, observing that "'Don't Let Me Down' sounds more like the group with a blues/country touch." Billboard told readers to "Save two places at the top of the charts for these two." "Get Back" was described as a "driving rhythm with a strong blues feel and good lyric line," while the flip side was called "an easy-funky number with powerful emotion-packed vocal work." Record World commented that "The Beatles indulge in some country rock on 'Get Back'...which echoes some of the cuter sides on their last album."

While Record World's classification of "Get Back" as "country rock" seems a stretch, the magazine's reference to the group's previous album was more on the mark. That collection introduced us to Prudence, Desmond, Molly, Bungalow Bill, Rocky Raccoon, Sexy Sadie and others. "Get Back" gave us Jo Jo and Loretta. The ambiguity of the second verse was both naughty and edgy: "Sweet Loretta Martin thought she was a woman, but she was another man/All the girls around her said she's got it coming, but she gets it while she can." In the song's coda, even Loretta's mummy came across as sexy "wearing her high-heel shoes and her low-neck sweater." And for Americans, the song's references to Tucson, Arizona and California made the story line even more compelling.

# The Beatles as nature intended.

"Get Back" is the Beatles new single. It's the first Beatles record which is as live as can be, in this electronic age.

There's no electronic watchamacallit.

"Get Back" is a pure spring-time rock number.

On the other side there's an equally live number called "Don't let me down".

Paul's got this to say about Get Back… "we were sitting in the studio and we made it up out of thin air…we started to write words there and then…
when we finished it, we recorded it at Apple Studios and made it into a song to roller-coast by".

P.S. John adds, It's John playing the fab live guitar solo.

And now John on Don't let me down. John says don't let me down about "Don't let me down".

In "Get Back" and "Don't let me down", you'll find the Beatles, as nature intended.

**Get Back / Don't let me down (Apple 2490)**

**Apple Records**

As spring rolled on, the Beatles surprised program directors and fans by rush-releasing another single. During the week ending May 24, 1969, all three trade magazines had "Get Back" at number one for the first time. That week, Capitol sent advance copies of a new Beatles single, "The Ballad Of John And Yoko," to several radio stations. As proper Apple labels had not yet been printed, the initial promo copies of the disc had white labels with song titles, the group's name, running times and, in some cases, the record's catalog number hand-written in blue ink. Some West Coast stations added "Air Date 5-23-69 9:PM L.A. Time" to the A-side label to indicate the earliest time the new Beatles song could be played. At least one program director took action to ensure his station would not play "The Ballad Of John And Yoko" at all by writing "No No Bad Lyric" on the label.

The troublesome lyrics were in the song's chorus: "Christ you know it ain't easy, you know how hard it can be/the way things are going, they're gonna crucify me." And this was being sung by the same John Lennon that had caused a furor in America three years earlier when the teen magazine Datebook quoted him saying "We're more popular than Jesus." By the time the single went on sale (officially June 4, but more likely on May 30), the battle lines were drawn. The June 7 Billboard reported that the Beatles had released a controversial single that "mentions Christ in a manner considered blasphemous by some critics." The article stated that the song had been banned by a flock of radio stations. In New York, WMCA and WABC refused to play the disc. WABC's program director said he banned the record "because I'd be talking to more monsignors in two minutes than I've talked to all year." WNEW-FM added the song to its playlist. In Chicago, ABC-owned WLS refused to play the record, while WCFL placed the song in heavy rotation. The same issue of Billboard reviewed the single, erroneously naming it *The Battle Of John And Yoko*." Billboard correctly predicted that regardless of the controversy over the song, it would follow in the footsteps of "Get Back" from a sales standpoint. Record World stated that the Beatles would "stir controversy and business" and found the song "compelling." Cash Box observed that the usual race to air a new Beatles record had not greeted the song, but fans were nevertheless seeking the single, making it an in-store hit despite its difficulties. Musically the song was described as "an exciting old-Elvis flavored track with other 50's touches." The song peaked at eight in Billboard, ten in Cash Box and seven in Record World. The disc was certified gold by the RIAA on June 16, 1969.

GET BACK STEREO
(Lennon-McCartney)
Maclen Music, Inc. BMI-3:11
2490
(S45-X46843)
Recorded in England
THE BEATLES
with Billy Preston

DON'T LET ME DOWN STEREO
(Lennon-McCartney)
Maclen Music, Inc. BMI-3:34
2490
(S45-X46844)
Recorded in England
THE BEATLES
with Billy Preston
MFD. BY CAPITOL RECORDS, INC., A SUBSIDIARY OF CAPITOL INDUSTRIES, INC., U.S.A. • T.M. Capitol MARCA REG. • U.S. PAT. NO. 2,631,859

THE BALLAD OF JOHN AND YOKO STEREO
(John Lennon-Paul McCartney)
Maclen Music, Inc. BMI-2:58
2531
(S45-X46865)
THE BEATLES
Recorded in England

OLD BROWN SHOE STEREO
(George Harrison)
Harrisongs Music, Inc. BMI-3:17
2531
(S45-X46866)
Recorded in England
THE BEATLES
MFD. BY CAPITOL RECORDS, INC., A SUBSIDIARY OF CAPITOL INDUSTRIES, INC., U.S.A. • T.M. Capitol MARCA REG. • U.S. PAT. NO. 2,631,859

In cities where "The Ballad Of John And Yoko" was not banned, it performed well on the charts. The song topped the charts in Lincoln, Nebraska (KLMS) and Cleveland, Ohio (WIXY), and most likely did so in other cities based on its ranking on the annual 1969 charts in cities such as Toledo, Ohio (WTTO; #2) and Davenport, Iowa (KSTT; #3). The song also made the 1969 top ten list in Indianapolis, Indiana (WNAP; #6), Hartford, Connecticut (WDRC; #7) and Salt Lake City, Utah (KCPX; #7). And no, the record wasn't banned in Boston as WMEX listed the song at #25 in its Top 100 Songs of 1969 chart. Other cities playing and charting the song included Los Angeles (KRLA), Cincinnati (WSAI), Portland, Maine (WLOB), Worcester, Massachusetts (WORC, WAAB), Orlando, Florida (WLOF), San Bernardino, California (KMEN, KFXM), Allentown, Pennsylvania (WAEB), Flint, Michigan (WTAC) and St. Joseph, Michigan (WSJM).

Even in cities where radio refused to play the song, word got out and Beatles fans purchased the disc. Back in the day, teens and college students regularly went to record stores, so even if they hadn't heard the song on the radio, they would see the single prominently displayed, forbidden fruit ready for the tasting. And, unlike the previous Beatles Apple singles, "The Ballad Of John And Yoko" came in a picture sleeve featuring a different color photo of the Beatles and Yoko Ono on each side (see pages 128 and 129). The front side picture had John and Yoko sitting among knee-high stone figurines, with Paul, Ringo and George standing behind them. The somber facial expressions made us wonder if Paul, George and Ringo resented having Yoko included in the group photo. The picture on the "Old Brown Shoe" side of the sleeve had a more relaxed atmosphere than the picture on the "Ballad" side. An old brown shoe was wedged between the branches of a flowered bush, indicating that the pictures were taken specifically to promote the new single. We later learned that the photos were taken by Paul's new wife, Linda Eastman, in the garden of Paul's Cavendish Avenue home in London's St. John's Wood neighborhood. Apple's trade ad for the single ran in the June 14, 1969 issues of Billboard and Cash Box and featured the "Ballad" photo from the picture sleeve.

The next month brought yet another single featuring a John Lennon vocal, "Give Peace A Chance" by the Plastic Ono Band. We learned from the label that the catchy sing-along for peace was recorded in Room 1742, Hotel La Reine Elizabeth in Montreal, Canada. The song peaked at 14 in Billboard, 11 in Cash Box and 10 in Record World.

# The Beatles

## Ballad of John and Yoko

1809

# GIVE PEACE A CHANCE / Remember love

**PLASTIC ONO BAND**  Apple

During the second week of September 1969, a number of American radio stations began playing songs from an unauthorized tape of a new Beatles album, *Abbey Road*. While Capitol had sanctioned radio air play of *The White Album* a week ahead of its release, the company was furious with this pre-release play as it had only mastered the album a few days earlier. Rather than preparing for an orderly roll out in early to mid-October, Capitol had to begin immediate production of the new Beatles LP and move its release date up to October 1. With initial demand for the album at 1,500,000 units, Capitol ordered its factories to work overtime, running triple shifts in hopes of getting the album into stores by its new release date. The company also had to deal with angry program directors from stations who did not have access to the *Abbey Road* tape, particularly those in markets where a competing station was already playing the album. To level the playing field, Capitol pressed 4,000 copies of the disc even though the album covers had yet to be manufactured. It then sent these records to stations in generic white cardboard jackets, along with a letter from its Vice President of Promotion, Charles Nuccio, who requested that stations delay air play to coincide with the availability of the LP in record stores. Capitol hoped to complete shipments by Friday, October 3.

In some markets, *Abbey Road* wasn't the only source of previously unheard Beatles music. On September 20, WKBW-AM in Buffalo, New York played songs from a tape dubbed from a March 2 acetate of performances from the January 1969 sessions held in the basement of Apple's Savile Row headquarters. Two days later, Boston's WBCN broadcast songs sourced from a March 28 acetate, erroneously describing it as the *Get Back* LP. Also on September 22, the promotional film for "The Ballad Of John And Yoko" finally aired in America on the debut of the ABC-TV show The Music Scene, albeit with "Christ" being silenced. The October 4 Billboard reported that one of the highlights of the new show was a special film segment of the Beatles performance of "You Know It Ain't Easy." Apparently the writer of the article was unaware of the single's previous release and the controversy surrounding it.

Tapes of the "*Get Back*" tracks were circulated among other American radio stations, leading to the songs being played in several cities across the country. This unauthorized air play was quickly met with cease and desist letters from Capitol and/or Northern Songs. By the end of September, stations were once again focused on *Abbey Road*.

Executive and General Offices

Capitol Records Inc.

The Capitol Tower, Hollywood, California 90028, Telephone (213) HO 2-6252, Cable Address: Caprecords, Hollywood

16 September, 1969

Dear Program Director,

Please find enclosed the new Beatle album "Abbey Road".

We know the past week has been very frustrating to you and your station due to the unauthorized tapes distributed around the country.  We sincerely hope that this disc will allow you to be competitive in your market.

It was not our intention, at this early date, to release the album for radio station airplay, but the unauthorized tape release has forced us to send this L.P. to 4,000 stations.

The scheduled release date of Abbey Road is October 1st and I can only ask that you delay airplay to co-incide with the availability of the album in the local record stores.  We should complete shipments by October 3 .  I know you don't want to displace available 45 records and/or albums with product that is not available for sale. In the past, this has caused undue hardships at your station's switchboard as well as in the local record stores.

I certainly hope that this request will be honored by each and every station.

Very warmest regards,

Charles Nuccio
Vice President Promotion

Although *Abbey Road* cost a dollar more than previous releases ($6.98 list), fans were not deterred. And while many had heard some of the album's songs on the radio before buying and playing the album, those who had not listened to the record in its entirety on an FM station were in for a treat laced with a few surprises. The album opens with "Come Together," a funky-sounding tune with a swamp rock feel sung primarily by John. Its lyrics are full of word-play in-jokes, starting with "old flat top" (a nod to Chuck Berry's "You Can't Catch Me") and moving on to the Beatles: George ("one holy roller" with "hair down to his knees"); John ("He bag production, he got walrus gumboot, he got Ono sideboard"); and Paul ("Got to be good looking 'cause he's so hard to see"). The message of its chorus, "Come together, right now, over me," fits comfortably with John's "Give Peace A Chance" released a few months earlier by the Plastic Ono Band. "Something" is a beautiful love song written and sung by George. Its verses move elegantly, leading into a bridge similar in feel to the ending chorus of Billy Preston's "That's The Way God Planned It" followed by Harrison's exquisite guitar solo. Fans who had purchased James Taylor's debut album on Apple noticed that the song's opening line, "Something in the way she moves," came from the title of one of Taylor's songs.

"Maxwell's Silver Hammer" is another bit of vaudeville from Paul. Its upbeat lighthearted sound softens its black humor storyline of a mass murderer armed with a silver hammer. "Oh! Darling" is a return to basic rock 'n' roll and doo-wop, with Paul singing in his gritty "I'm Down"/"Long Tall Sally" voice. "Octopus's Garden" is another undersea fantasy sung by Ringo, but unlike "Yellow Submarine," it was written by the drummer. Side One closes with John's "I Want You (She's So Heavy)," which starts as a slow blistering blues and ends with a recurring riff embellished by a swishing Moog sound effect. The song's hypnotic second half conjures up images of waves crashing on a rocky shoreline. And just when you think it will go on forever, the song, along with the side, comes to an abrupt end.

Side Two opens with George's upbeat "Here Comes The Sun," which features bright-sounding acoustic guitars, effective backing vocals and a restrained George Martin score. This is followed by the dreamy three-part harmonies of "Because," with its sparse instrumental backing consisting primarily of harpsichord and bass. The remainder of the side is dominated by an eight-song medley opening with Paul's "You Never Give Me Your Money," whose caustic message gives way to nostalgia and hope ("one sweet dream came true today"). This leads to a nursery rhyme ending ("One, two, three, four, five, six, seven/All good children go to heaven") embellished with the sound of tubular bells, birds and chirping crickets that crossfades into the next track. John's "Sun King" returns to the "Here comes the sun" theme of the side's opening track and the dreamy quality of "Because," declaring that everybody's laughing and happy before moving to an ending string of non-sequiturs. The next two songs are about oddball characters, "Mean Mr. Mustard" and "Polythene Pam." While both of these songs, written and sung by John, come across as unfinished, they fit seamlessly into the medley. Paul returns with quirky characters of his own in "She Came In Through The Bathroom Window." The medley's next two tracks feature Paul on lead vocals and piano. The lullaby "Golden Slumbers" brings a return to nostalgia ("Once there was a way to get back home"), while "Carry That Weight" returns to the theme of dissatisfaction from "You Never Give Me Your Money," which is reprised with different lyrics. The medley ends with "The End," featuring a brief Ringo drum solo and dueling guitars before giving way to piano and the closing couplet: "And in the end, the love you take is equal to the love you make." And just when you think the album is over, Paul's little ditty about Her Majesty appears after a dozen or so seconds of silence.

All three trade magazines published mini-reviews in their issues dated October 11, 1969. Billboard made *Abbey Road* one of its Pop Spotlight listings, opening with the obvious: "Chalk up another No. 1 LP chart item for the Beatles!" The magazine described the material as "potent and commercial with the spotlight on the new single driving ballad, 'Something' and the funky swinger, 'Come Together.'" It also mentioned "Maxwell's Silver Hammer" and "Mean Mr. Mustard" as clever and typical Beatles material. Cash Box described the album as "a witty and charming set of sixteen tunes, all of which are bright and presented with the usual Beatle flair for invention and innovation." The magazine observed that *Abbey Road* was more basic and less dependent on orchestration, thus displaying the group's talent on its instruments. It singled out "Maxwell's Silver Hammer," "She Came In Through The Bathroom Window" and Ringo's "Octopus's Garden" as "especially outstanding" and predicted that the album would soon be number one. Record World stated that the Beatles "may have produced their finest to date" with *Abbey Road*, observing that "the musical evidence in support is heavy."

As expected, *Abbey Road* topped all three charts for several weeks. The album entered the Billboard Top LP's chart at number 178 on October 25, 1969. The following week it jumped up to number four behind *Green River* by Creedence Clearwater Revival, *Johnny Cash At San Quentin* and the Rolling Stones' *Through The Past Darkly (Big Hits Vol. 2)*. It reached the top in its third week on November 1 and remained number one for eight straight weeks before trading places with *Led Zeppelin II* a couple of times. All told, *Abbey Road* spent 129 weeks on the charts, including 11 weeks at number one, seven at number two and a total of 27 in the top ten. In addition, the album topped Billboard's 4-Track, 8-Track and Cassette charts (simultaneously with the LP chart on December 6, 1969).

On October 6, 1969, a week after the album's release, Capitol issued a single with George Harrison's "Something" on the A-side and John Lennon's "Come Together" as the flip side. This was reportedly done at the request of Apple manager Allen Klein, who believed in George's talent and wanted to enhance his reputation as a songwriter. "Something" was clearly a worthy choice, being called one of the greatest love songs of the past 50 years by Frank Sinatra, who, unfortunately for George, erroneously credited the song to Lennon and McCartney!

Although "Something" was officially designated as the A-side, both songs received extensive airplay. At first, disc jockeys went with Apple's recommendation, with George's "Something" getting more spins. But soon "Come Together" took over top billing as listeners began showing a preference for the B-side. Both songs entered the Billboard Hot 100 on October 18, with "Something" debuting at number 20 and "Come Together" at 23. The following week "Something" was at 11 and "Come Together" at 13. The November 1 chart showed "Something" still at 11 with "Come Together" pulling ahead at ten. The next week "Something" crept into the top ten at number nine while "Come Together" jumped up to the third spot. The November 15 chart listed "Come Together" at two and "Something" at three. The following week "Something" remained at three while "Come Together" fell to seven. Effective November 29, Billboard began reporting singles as a sole entry rather than listing each side of a double-sided hit separately. The Beatles single benefited from this new policy with "Come Together"/"Something" topping the Hot 100 that week, moving past the Fifth Dimension's "Wedding Bell Blues." In all, the *Abbey Road*-spawned single spent 16 weeks on the charts, including nine in the top ten.

Cash Box reported each song separately, with "Something" debuting at number 36 and "Come Together" at 39 on October 18. By its third week, "Something" moved up to the second spot, where it remained for two weeks as "Come Together" gained momentum at 16 and 8. The crossover came on November 15, with "Come Together" at two and "Something" at three. The following week, both songs moved up a notch, giving the Beatles the top two spots on the chart. "Come Together" charted for 14 weeks, including three at number one and seven in the top ten, while "Something" charted for 13 weeks, including three at number two and six in the top ten. Record World initially charted the single as "Something" when it made its debut at number 63 on October 11, 1969, and in its second week at 43. The disc was next listed as "Something"/"Come Together" as it moved up the charts to numbers 14 and four, and when it held the top spot for the weeks of November 8 and 15. When the single dropped to number two behind "Wedding Bell Blues," the listing was flipped to "Come Together"/"Something" for the remainder of its run, which included a return to the top spot for two more weeks on November 29 and December 6. All told, the single charted for 15 weeks, including four weeks at number one and nine in the top ten. As expected, the single quickly went gold, selling 1.6 million copies by mid-November. The RIAA certified sales of over 2 million units.

One of the first American reviews of *Abbey Road* appeared in Time magazine's issue dated October 3, 1969. It began with John talking about the sessions that produced the album. "We were more together than we had been for a long time. It's lucky when you get all four feeling funky at the same time." This quote surprised most American Beatles fans, who were unaware of the tensions within the group during 1968 and early 1969. We also learned that the album was named *Abbey Road* in honor of the group's favorite London studios. Time described the album as "Melodic, inventive, crammed with musical delights" and the group's best since *Sgt. Pepper*. But rather than stretching the ear and challenging the mind and imagination like *Sgt. Pepper*, the new LP marked a return to the modest style of *Rubber Soul* and *Revolver*, having a "cheerful coherence—each song's mood fits comfortably with every other—and a sense of wholeness clearly contrived as a revel in musical pleasure."

Time magazine was impressed with the unpretentious way the disc combined a variety of styles such as old-line rock 'n' roll ("Oh! Darling"), low blues ("I Want You"), high camp ("Maxwell's Silver Hammer") and folk ("Here Comes The Sun"). Although listeners would find an occasional swash of electronic sound, most of the instrumental textures were free of overdubbing. Time praised John's guitar playing on "I Want You (She's So Heavy)," which was described as a "cunning combination of two songs with a chilling, mean blues throb," and Paul and Ringo's "cohesive yet flexible rhythm" on "Mean Mr. Mustard" and "Polythene Pam."

The magazine found the Side Two medley "intriguing" and "a kind of odyssey from innocence to experience." "Because" was a "childlike vista of the world, intoned by the group in their best breathy choirboy manner." The medley contained "loneliness and frustration," but ended with "a final note of acceptance of life's burdens." That, however, was followed by Paul's "brief snoot-cocking ditty" ("Her Majesty") to "avoid too much of an amen quality."

Time observed that George's "Something" was getting the most air play on U.S. radio stations. The magazine believed that the time Harrison was spending with Bob Dylan had "helped him achieve a new confidence in his own musical personality" and reported that the other Beatles thought that "Something" was the album's best song.

Newsweek did not review *Abbey Road*, but rather made reference to the album in an article in its October 20 issue about the tangled web of the Beatles financial empire in the wake of the 1967 death of their manager, Brian Epstein. After printing the opening verse of "You Never Give Me Your Money," the article quotes Ringo as saying, "Usually our songs aren't about anything, but this one, well, we really are in the office all the time as businessmen and nobody wants it." In discussing the group's relationship with Apple, John said "All our money comes into this little building and it never gets out." The article pointed out that the Beatles weren't exactly begging, with Apple providing tax protection and footing all the personal bills of the members of the group. Although they were struggling to regain control of their own finances, their earning power was greater than ever, as evidenced by the sales of *Abbey Road*.

John viewed *Abbey Road* as a good album, but nothing special, calling it a pleasant but unadventurous collection of basically low-voltage numbers. He noted that six of its songs were spin-offs from another LP expected later in the year. Newsweek observed that the group had "moved closer to its original sound, rarely drawing on large orchestrated backgrounds," with songs that were "straightforward, seldom mixing styles for collage effect." Ringo saw the album bringing the group together musically, saying that for him, "it's more important that we play good together than have a lot of violins play good together." Newsweek found that togetherness was a sometimes thing for the Beatles, with each following their own interests: Ringo's film career; Paul's songwriting; John's life with Yoko and involvement with the peace movement; and George's work as a record producer. While the Beatles were trying to free themselves from "the horrors of the bureaucratic life" they always satirized, Ringo remained optimistic, saying "We're practically in a position to know our position." [Or, as he said five years earlier, "It's been a hard day's night."]

Ellen Sander praised the Beatles and *Abbey Road* in the October 25 Saturday Review. Her opening paragraph set the stage: "Whenever a new Beatles album is released it's generally a critical and social as well as musical event. Rock fans spend an entire week listening to the blessed product, radio stations play it incessantly, teachers bring it to class for discussion and retailers scramble for stock. Musicians listen and compare; opinions, analysis, hypotheses, and suspicions fly; much is written; much is discussed; and whatever else happens, Beatles lovers on all cultural levels are intensely involved with the new album for a week or so. The world is more fun for a little while...."

As for the disc itself, Sander calls *Abbey Road* a wonderful album full of "sublimely executed, elegantly composed Beatles music." For those who had misgivings about the group's prior LP, her opening thoughts provided comfort. "Shimmering brilliance and unbounded creative energy grace every moment of *Abbey Road*. It is alternately bright, silly, warm, funny, childlike, funky, and glib, seamlessly bound into a perfectly molded entity born fresh into the day. All the insecure raggedness of the plain white album is gone and *Abbey Road* emerges a glowing tour de force."

Sander then turns to the songs, describing "Come Together" as a "fresh, salty rock 'n' roll stompalong...peppered with spicy Lennon one-liners." "Something" is a tender love song and one of the most beautiful written by George. She characterizes "Maxwell's Silver Hammer" as a "jolly ditty of mischief and manslaughter, full of musical imagination and lyrical buffoonery." In a rare mistake on her part, Sander attributes "Oh! Darling" to John, an error made by a few other reviewers, but nails her description of the song: "a blistering rock 'n' roll wailing wall" with "steamroller guitar assaults" and a roaring, gasping vocal. Ringo's "Octopus's Garden" is "full of sweet silliness, cartoon images, and pretty guitar figures." It is "pure enchantment...carried off with straight-faced, childish delight." "I Want You (She's So Heavy)" is a hard rock song that "builds into an ear-splitting maximum-volume chord crescendo" and ends "so dramatically that you don't know what hit you." Sander calls the first side "spectacular" and praises its effective programming, which places songs of different character next to one another in a complementary way.

While viewing Side One as a study in contrasts, Sander sees the second side as "the ultimate in tonal blending and rhythmic balance." She calls it the "sun side, suffused with mellowed warmth, woven together with motifs, bridging, reprises, surprises...." The opening track, "Here Comes The Sun," serves as "an awakening, an exaltation of the dawn." "You Never Give Me Your Money" is a song of "estrangement, business, and art." "Sun King" returns to the tonality and theme of "Here Comes The Sun," before moving into five interwoven mini-songs that exert the identity of each in a gentle but firm way. The upbeat pace is then broken by an overflowing lullaby, "Golden Slumbers," that leads into "Carry That Weight," with its reprise of "You Never Give Me Your Money." Following Ringo's brief drum solo, the music returns, leading to the concluding couplet on the love you make. Sander describes the side's final surprise as a "bit of McCartney sass about Her Majesty [that] ends the album with an afterthought."

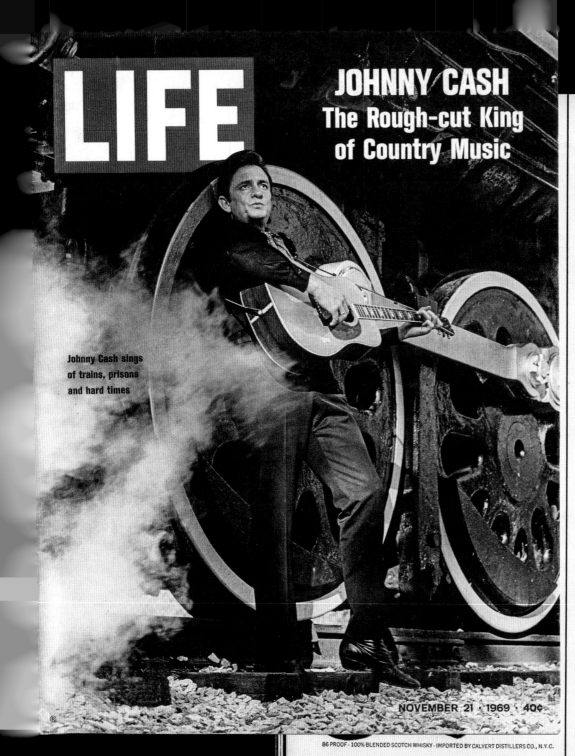

# LIFE

## JOHNNY CASH
## The Rough-cut King of Country Music

Johnny Cash sings
of trains, prisons
and hard times

NOVEMBER 21 · 1969 · 40¢

22

---

### Beatles: Nostalgia, Irony

THE BEATLES' "ABBEY ROAD"

Mr. and Mrs. Lennon: "He got Ono sideboard"

**P**op music today is being transformed by the esthetic of pop art. That sounds like tautology but it is the formula for a revolution. No longer does the pop musician go round and round in the same adolescent groove until he dies of superannuation. No longer does the pop genius go mad from imprisonment of imagination or betray his integrity by dragging his piano onto the stage of Carnegie Hall to make with the Grieg concerto in ragtime.

Now, thanks to the freaky contortions of contemporary sensibility, a commercial musician can grow and develop as an artist without abandoning the simple popular music that established his fame and earned him his millions. Slipping over their eyes the subtly distorting lenses of irony and nostalgia and taking ever more sophisticated sightings of their original tunes and times, groups like the Beatles are now filling the airways with sly pop facsimiles such as John Lennon's *Come Together* from the recent *Abbey Road.*

Heard out of the corner of your mind while driving the car, *Come Together* is just a catchy bit of jungle music with a mean whisk of vocal hiss, a hypnotic beat and the Lennon voice chanting on one note through a speaking tube. Endless repetition brings out the words like lemon juice on invisible writing, bit by bit. Lennon's singing about "Old Flat Top" (there's a '50s word for you!), some great old cat who has grooved right down to the present with his "ju-ju eyeball," hair down to his knees and heavy mystic words of Rosko philosophy: "One and one and one is three!" The song hits you as a good-natured put-on of the whole funky, boogie, bluesy soul bag—pop music's big black sacred cow. You love the line "[He] got to be good-looking 'cos he's so hard to see." Then in the third verse, the put-on switches suddenly from the soulman to the song's audience and to Lennon himself; for what are those cryptic lines—"He bag production/he got walrus gumboot/he got Ono sideboard"—if not John's private jokes with his Oriental missus (their film company is called Bag Productions) and his well-known public sass, here making millions strain to catch the meaning of nonsense?

Just as a mocking fantasia on the idea of being super-hip, the song is great, but there is more—not least the refrain, "Come together," an obvious pun with a tricky hook—"Coming Together" is a hexagram of the *I Ching,* the rock world's favorite oracle. How's them apples, Elvis?

*Abbey Road* is not one of the Beatles' great albums but it contains lots of good things: *Oh! Darling,* a ritually perfect parody of a classic R&B ballad by Paul McCartney; *Something,* a sentimental tune by George Harrison with a plangently rising guitar phrase off the 1939 shortwave from London; and *Octopus Garden,* a little ditty by Ringo Starr that reminds me of *The Icecaps Are Melting* by that other ugly duckling, Tiny Tim. The album's B side is devoted almost entirely to a medley of Lennon and McCartney tunes. This cornucopia of melodies and countermelodies, of brief snatches of song and bits of heavily orchestrated padding seems symbolic of the Beatles' latest phase, which might be described as the round-the-clock production of disposable music effects. Some of the phrases are lovely, some of the segues stirring, but what sustains the production is a strong updraft of show-biz inflation that fills the mind with fleeting half-glimpses of '40s movie musicals, of Betty Grable, Alice Faye, thousands of marching soldiers—hold it! The Beatles were babies when those stars burst forth!

*Mr. Goldman is a critic who frequently reviews popular music for LIFE.*

**by Albert Goldman**

Sander calls the balance and feeling of the songs on *Abbey Road* "a brilliant example of the Beatles' perspective on their own work, the variety and ultimately the synthesis of the sounds they make," ranging from "cricket noises to a Moog synthesizer to everything in between." She finds new discoveries in every song with each listening. Sander ends her review by stating that *Abbey Road* is one Beatles album of which she will never tire.

The November 21, 1969, Life magazine contains a review of the album by Albert Goldman, who would later write biographies on Elvis Presley and John Lennon that were infamous for their negative portrayals. While Sander opened her piece with a brilliant summation on the effects of a new Beatles album, Goldman starts with his view of pop music with words beyond the vocabulary of most young fans of pop music that was in sharp contrast to the down-home approach of the man in black featured on the magazine's cover, Johnny Cash. "Pop music today is being transformed by the aesthetic of pop art. That sounds like tautology but it is the formula for a revolution. No longer does the pop musician go round and round in the same adolescent groove until he dies of superannuation...." Goldman observes that a "commercial musician can grow and develop as an artist without abandoning the simple popular music that established his fame and made him millions." This sets up his first mention of *Abbey Road*, commenting that by using "subtly distorting lenses of irony and nostalgia," groups like the Beatles produce "pop facsimiles" like John Lennon's "Come Together." He writes extensively on the song, calling it a "good-natured put-on of the whole funky, boogie, bluesy soul bag." He sees the *I Ching* as the source of its title, ending with: "How's them apples, Elvis?"

Goldman states that *Abbey Road* is not one of the Beatles great albums, but admits it has some good things: "Oh! Darling" ("a ritually perfect parody of a classic R&B ballad"); "Something" (a sentimental tune with a "plangently rising guitar phrase off the 1939 shortwave from London"); and "Octopus's Garden," which reminds him of Tiny Tim's "The Icecaps Are Melting." He calls the Side Two medley a "cornucopia of melodies and counter melodies, of brief snatches of songs" and describes the Beatles latest phase as the "round-the-clock production of disposable musical effects." He finds some of the phrases lovely, but is most impressed with what he sees as a "strong updraft of show-biz inflation that fills the mind with '40s movie musicals, of Betty Grable, Alice Faye, thousands of marching soldiers." Goldman ends his review by pointing out "The Beatles were babies when those stars burst forth!"

By mid-November 1969, Rolling Stone had just celebrated its second anniversary. Its circulation had increased well beyond its San Francisco home, with satellite offices in New York and London. The magazine was now available in many record stores throughout the country. For Beatles fans, the November 15 issue was too much to resist. There they were, on the cover of the Rolling Stone: Ringo, George and John sporting beards, standing with a clean-shaven Paul. The text was also attention grabbing: "Inside Apple Corpse" (an obvious pun on the Beatles company, Apple Corps, Ltd., but was Apple dead?); "Stones in L.A." (Beatles fans also dug the Rolling Stones); and "Paul is Not Dead" (well that's a relief!). Inside, fans were treated to a treasure trove of information on the group. The lead article, titled "The Beatles: 'You Never Give Me Your Money,'" startled readers by telling them that the Beatles Apple Corps was about to collapse and the group was squabbling. While the opening paragraphs contained quotes already familiar to those who had read Newsweek's recent article on the Beatles business ventures, the remainder provided great detail on the hiring of Allen Klein and its aftermath. There was also a four-page article by former Apple employee Francie Schwartz. Although it was penned by Paul's ex-girlfriend, it was not a gossipy tell-all. While there were some personal stories, it had tons of information on the inner workings of Apple, its managers and its musicians.

The Random Notes section told of: a new Mary Hopkin single produced by Paul ("Que Sera Sera"); the closing of The Star Club in Hamburg, Germany, where the Beatles refined their musical chops; and three new Apple singles, "Cold Turkey" by the Plastic Ono Band, "Give Peace A Chance" by Hot Chocolate and "Golden Slumbers/Carry That Weight" by White Trash. There were also quotes from John and Ringo on their new *Abbey Road* LP, which had previously appeared in Newsweek. *Abbey Road* was called "the fastest-selling Beatles LP of all time," with sales of over two million copies in its first two weeks of release. The article on Paul's supposed death assured us it was BS.

As expected, *Abbey Road* was reviewed in the magazine's Records section. But, surprisingly, there were two separate and opposing reviews! The first, by John Mendelsohn, raved about the new LP. But the second, by Ed Ward, mocked and panned everything about it, from the cover to the music, which was dismissed as garbage. We would later learn that Ward wrote his review first, and Rolling Stone wisely commissioned Mendelsohn to provide an alternate point of view. (In 2009, Ward admitted he was wrong: "I was just a 20-year kid who was very full of himself.")

A&M

INSIDE
APPLE
CORPSE

# Rolling Stone

ACME  November 15, 1969  No. 46  UK: 2/6 35 Cents

STONES IN L.A.

PAUL
IS
NOT
DEAD

CAMERA PRESS-PIX

Mendelsohn sets the stage with his opening salvo: "Simply, side two does more for me than the whole of *Sgt. Pepper*, and I'll trade you *The Beatles* and *Magical Mystery Tour* and a Keith Moon drumstick for side one." He then praises the first four songs. "Come Together" opens things in grand fashion with Lennon near the peak of his form. The song is "twisted, freely-associative, punful lyrically, pinched and somehow a little smug vocally" and is "breathtakingly recorded" as is the entire LP. "Something" is praised for George's vocal and "dead catchy guitar line," excellent drums, perfectly subdued strings and nice melody. "Maxwell's Silver Hammer" is described as a "jaunty vaudevillian/music-hallish celebration wherein Paul, in a rare naughty mood, celebrates the joys of being able to bash in the heads of anyone threatening to bring you down," performed "perfectly with the coyest imaginable choir-boy innocence." On "Oh! Darling," Paul "delivers an induplicably [sic] strong, throat-ripping vocal of sufficient power to knock out even those who would otherwise have complained about yet another Beatles tribute to the golden groovies' era." Mendelsohn further praises the song's "'ouch!'-yelling" guitar and wonderful harmonies.

With the album's second side, the Beatles demonstrate that they can "unify seemingly countless musical fragments and lyrical doodlings into a wonderful suite," providing "potent testimony that no, they've far from lost it, and no, they haven't stopped trying." Here, Mendelsohn seems to be responding to Ed Ward's previously written review, which would appear immediately following. In the side's opening tracks, Mendelsohn finds moods of "perky childlike wonder" and innocence, with beautiful and intricate harmonies. The pensive opening mood of "You Never Give Me Your Money" gives way to boogie-woogie piano and happy thought with "Oh, that magic feeling" leading into chirping crickets, a child's nursery rhyme and John's dreamy "Sun King." Then it's off to a meeting with two human oddities (Mean Mr. Mustard and Polythene Pam), Paul's "She Came In Through The Bathroom Window" (a "surreal afternoon telly programme") and the melancholy "Golden Slumbers," only to awake to "Carry That Weight," described as a "rollicking little commentary of life's labours" with its reprise of "You Never Give Me Your Money," which Mendelsohn calls the album's "most addicting melody and unforgettable words." The ending couplet on love is called the "perfect epitaph for our visit to the world of Beatle daydreams." As for Paul's claim that he's gonna make Her Majesty his, Mendelsohn hesitates to say anything's impossible for Paul after listening to *Abbey Road* a thousand times, with the other Beatles not far behind. To his mind, the Beatles are "equalable, but still unsurpassed."

Mendelsohn's praise is followed by Ed Ward's panning of the Beatles and *Abbey Road*. Ward opens his review by mocking the album cover: "Eeeeeeeeeeeeck, it's the Beatles. Look. Look. They're crossing Abbey Road in London." He then takes a jab at the cover's construction and higher list price: "A nice yellowish colored picture on one of these nice new instant fall-apart covers. Sixteen new Beatles songs for just under seven bucks." After asking "What's it like?," he responds "Well, I don't much like it," and goes on to admit that he hasn't liked any of the group's albums since *Revolver*, finding them forgettable. While being as close to perfect as one can come (engineering masterpieces with a melodic gift and occasionally excellent lyrics), Ward laments "the albums just don't seem very vital." He feels that the orchestration and Moog "disembodies and artificializes their sound," resulting in music that is "complicated instead of complex." Ward prefers the Rolling Stones. As for *Abbey Road*, Ward retorts, "Of course, the Beatles are still the Beatles, but it does tend a rather tenuous line between boredom, Beatledom and bubblegum."

"Come Together" is one of the few tracks spared of Ward's wrath, described as "superb" and "very catchy, very funny, and quite mad." He finds "Something" to be "vile," with an "easy-listening melody, vapid lyrics and a gigantic string section oozing like saccharine mashed potatoes all over the place." "Maxwell's Silver Hammer" hits him as a *Sgt. Pepper* leftover, a "nice bouncy catchy little song" that is "cute and pretty well done, but not particularly memorable." "Oh! Darling" is "embarrassingly bad," a "cross between a doo-wop and Elvis' 'If I Can Dream.'" Ward surprisingly likes "Octopus's Garden," finding it "charming, catchy and cute, and definitely Ringo's best to date."

Ward calls Side Two a disaster. While he finds "Here Comes The Sun" pleasant, he rips just about everything else. "Because" is a "nothing song." "You Never Give Me Your Money" has "so many sections that it never gets anywhere." "Sun King" degenerates into Muzak and is "probably the worst thing the Beatles have done since they changed drummers." While Ward likes the melody of "Golden Slumbers" and calls "Carry That Weight" infectious, he finds the rest of the medley hard to listen to. He finds it ironic that the group failed to follow the advice of its "Get Back" single and get back to its roots. Ward wonders if the Beatles alternative to getting back is "producing more garbage on this order," priced "outrageously so that fewer people would buy it." He feels the Beatles have "been shucking us," adding "Surely they have enough talent and intelligence to do better than this. Or do they? Tune in next time."

The New York Times also ran a pair of *Abbey Road* reviews. The first, by Mike Jahn, was published on October 4, 1969. Jahn's introduction described the appearance of a new Beatles album as a "time of festivity among the rock audience," during which "Record sellers are bothered for weeks before the release; articles appear in the music press speculating on what will be the latest word from the throne, and for weeks after, the underground and music press is filled with articles examining the new work on every possible basis from astrology to zen."

Jahn writes that *Abbey Road* is not much of a shocker and is rather dull when compared to the group's previous two albums. It doesn't have the luster or "spectacular fireworks" of those recordings. For him, that is a good thing. The new LP is missing what Jahn sees as the frivolity and excess of "ostrich-plume frills" of *The White Album* and the "attempted profundity" of *Sgt. Pepper*. Hidden in the "comparative sobriety of *Abbey Road* is the feeling of surefootedness that the Beatles have needed in the last few years." Jahn calls the album a "sincere, simple and powerful collection of songs," with its music falling "somewhere between the country-influenced, firm footing of *Rubber Soul* and the rolling, low-swinging 'Revolution No. 1.'" The album mixes sweet melodic songs with "earthy rock songs built on a heavy blues or boogie foundation."

"Octopus's Garden" and "Maxwell's Silver Hammer" are described as light sing-alongs similar in style to "Yellow Submarine" and "When I'm Sixty-Four." "Oh! Darling" is 1950's rock 'n' roll similar to Elvis' "One Night." Other tracks are "quiet, harmonious and generally pleasant," with the Beatles occasionally breaking the calm with a blues progression or hard rock. While the "pretty and perfected vocal harmony" of "Because" could please "the most ardent antirock tastes," Jahn laments that such songs "evoke visions of an album titled 'The Beatles Play Montovani.'"

Jahn finds that "Through all the prettiness and relatively noncontroversial nature of this album, the Beatles maintain enough grit and vigor to keep their creation rocking." And while the subjects of the songs are often mundane (love, looking at nature and feeling lonely), there is "enough lyrical ambiguity in these songs to keep the underground and music press writers interpreting for months." Jahn concludes by assuring us that "The Beatles wouldn't desert their greatest fans."

Nic Cohn's review appeared the following day in the October 5 New York Times under the headline "The Beatles: For 15 Minutes, Tremendous." Cohn opens with words of praise for the Side Two medley, calling it the most impressive music the Beatles have made since *Rubber Soul*. Although he is not impressed by the individual numbers ("pretty average stuff" with some melody lines that have been used elsewhere and some lyrics that are "quite painful"), Cohn calls the medley a terrific tour de force for three reasons. First, it is brilliantly produced, with the entire medley perfectly paced. (Cohn comments that "the Beatles know as much about recording as anyone outside of Phil Spector." A half-year later, the Beatles would bring in Spector to sweeten their rough tracks recorded during the *Get Back* sessions.) Second, it is full of genuine surprises: "before you get a chance to be bored by anything, something new is happening and, by the end, there's a real sense of speed, they're almost flying." Third is the "sheer range of melodic invention." Cohn writes that "no one else in rock could have achieved the same result...there are maybe 15 tunes in as many minutes — all of them instantly hummable, all of them potential hits."

But while Cohn raves about the melodies, he finds the words to be a great drawback. He misses earlier times, when Lennon-McCartney lyrics were a great attraction and sounded real, strong and evocative, as in "She was just 17, you know what I mean." Now he finds the lyrics are "only marshmallow" and "limpwristed, pompous and fake," but nonetheless finds that "Lyrics and all, the *Abbey Road* medley remains a triumph."

As for the rest of the album, he finds it an "unmitigated disaster," with the remaining tracks "all write-offs." Cohn leaves no doubt as to how he feels: "The badness ranges from the mere gentle tedium to cringing embarrassment." Ringo's ditty ["Octopus's Garden"] is "purest Mickey Mouse." "I Want You (She's So Heavy)" is an "endless slow blues" that is "horribly out of tune." George Harrison's two songs are dismissed as "mediocrity incarnate." Cohn labels two songs, "Come Together" and "Oh! Darling," as "interesting failures." He calls "Come Together" a "slowed-down reworking of Chuck Berry's 'You Can't Catch Me,'" which is "intriguing only as a sign of just how low Lennon can sink these days." As for "Oh! Darling," Cohn mistakenly credits the vocals to John and criticizes him for trying too hard: "Lennon flounders in an orgy of gulps, howls and retches, flung together at random, and the whole point is lost." He laments that this kind of overkill ruined *The White Album* and ruins two-thirds of *Abbey Road*.

Towards the end of his review, Cohn harkens back to the medley, praising it for its lack of overkill: "It gets back toward the kind of ease and style that the Beatles had five years ago." A year earlier, Cohn characterized *The White Album* as "boring almost beyond belief." Here, his prejudice against the rock music of the day is exposed in his final words. "As it stands, *Abbey Road* isn't tremendous. Still, it has 15 fine minutes and, by rock standards, that's a lot."

Although Cohn found only "15 minutes of fame" on *Abbey Road*, most Beatles fans fell instantly in love with the entire long-player, making it the Beatles fastest selling album. But with critics sharply divided, fans wondered how the Beatles would do at the 12th annual Grammy awards for recordings issued in 1969.

None of the Beatles singles from 1969 were nominated for Song of the Year or Record of the Year. While no one expected any honors for "The Ballad Of John And Yoko," it was somewhat surprising that neither "Get Back" nor "Something" was even considered. After all, "Something" was "their type of song." Record of the Year went to "Aquarius/Let The Sunshine In" by the Fifth Dimension, while Song of the Year went to songwriter Joe South for "Games People Play." As for Album of the Year, *Abbey Road* was nominated, but lost out to Blood, Sweat And Tears for their self-titled LP *Blood, Sweat And Tears*. The other nominees were *Crosby, Stills And Nash*, *Johnny Cash At San Quentin* and *The Age Of Aquarius* by the Fifth Dimension. *Abbey Road*'s iconic crosswalk cover was not even nominated for Best Album Cover. Does anyone today remember the winning cover of *America The Beautiful* by Gary McFarland? Didn't think so. At least *Abbey Road* was not entirely shut out with Geoff Emerick and Philip McDonald winning the Grammy for Best Engineered Recording—Non-Classical for their work as engineers on the LP. For Emerick, it was his third Grammy, having previously won for *Revolver* and *Sgt. Pepper's Lonely Hearts Club Band*.

Listening to the album today, it's hard to believe *Abbey Road* received negative reviews from prestigious newspapers and magazines and was virtually ignored by the Grammys. The opening tracks on Side One rank with the best the band ever recorded. Side Two, with George's "Here Comes The Sun," the beautiful harmonies on "Because" and the long medley, is an incredible showcase of the band's talents. Although Beatles fans did not know it at the time, *Abbey Road* was to be the final album recorded by the group. It was a fitting end to a remarkable recording career.

BLOOD, SWEAT & TEARS

THE AGE OF
AQUARIUS
THE 5TH DIMENSION
AQUARIUS / LET THE SUNSHINE IN
WORKIN' ON A GROOVY THING • THOSE WERE THE DAYS
SUNSHINE OF YOUR LOVE • LET IT BE ME
AND MORE

CROSBY, STILLS & NASH

JOHNNY CASH AT SAN QUENTIN

A Boy Named Sue
Wanted Man
I Walk the Line
Wreck of the Old 97
San Quentin
Darling Companion
Starkville City Jail
Folsom Prison Blues
Peace in the Valley

# From Twickenham to Abbey Road:
# A British Perspective of the Beatles in 1969

Unlike their cousins from across the Pond, British Beatles fans had numerous newsstand options to contemporaneously follow the happenings of their heroes. There were four weekly music magazines that went on sale every Friday: New Musical Express ("NME"); Disc and Music Echo ("Disc"); Record Mirror; and Melody Maker. There was also a weekly music industry trade magazine, Record Research. And for those who wanted to read exclusively about the Beatles, there was the The Beatles Book, which was published monthly with the assistance of the Beatles Fan Club.

The January 4, 1969, issue of Disc was sure to catch the attention of Beatles fans. It featured a color picture of John Lennon and the intriguing banner headline: "Beatles plan five new LPs—one 'live!'" While four of the discs were to be issued by Capitol Records in a special collection of previously released recordings for the American market, the other LP sounded much more interesting. According to Apple press officer Derek Taylor, "It will be their first-ever LIVE album. All the songs will be new and fresh. There'll be no hangover numbers from a year ago or anything like that." That same week Melody Maker provided additional details from Taylor: "The group started writing and rehearsing a number of songs this weekend. There is no shortage of material. Paul has eight or nine songs finished, John has a few, and George also has some material." The plan was for the group to do a run-through, a rehearsal and then the live show to be taped for future television broadcast. The concert had been set for January 18, but most likely would take place later. The Beatles would perform 12 to 14 songs for the album. The January 11 Disc disclosed that the Beatles were at Twickenham studios rehearsing for their TV concert.

A week later the January 18 Melody Maker reported that a documentary of the Beatles at work was being shot at Twickenham Studios. That week NME announced that the Beatles had called off their "'Live Album' TV." The following week the magazine reported that the Beatles were still rehearsing new songs for their next album, but plans for the TV concert were fading away. Instead, there would be a TV documentary of the group's rehearsals.

# DISC
## and MUSIC ECHO 1s

JANUARY 4, 1969                    USA 20c

# Beatles plan five new LPs — one 'live!'

BEATLES are to record their first - ever LIVE album. And a special package of FOUR separate LPs — each one the individual choice of John, Paul, George and Ringo —is also planned.

Beatles were meeting at their London Apple headquarters this week to choose and consider brand new Lennon - McCartney numbers for the LP, which will be recorded at the same time as they tele-record their live TV spectacular.

Says their press officer Derek Taylor. "It will be their first-ever LIVE album. All the songs will be new and fresh. There'll be no hangover numbers from a year ago or anything like that."

They will probably record the new tracks AND the TV show around January 15 or 18. But a suitable venue for the show had still to be found.

The "Beatles' Choice" album — although this isn't necessarily the title—is the idea of America's Capitol label.

✳

John, Paul, George and Ringo will each be invited to choose their favourite Beatles songs, and they will be released in a special four-LP package.

A d d e d Taylor: "This multi-album will be done mainly for America. But, like everything, there is a strong possibility it will come out in Britain also."

No definite choice of tracks has been made yet, but favourites like "Yesterday," "Michelle," "Hard Day's Night" and "I Want To Hold Your Hand" are expected to be included.

This week their current chart-topping "double" album was approaching the four - million world sales mark. But the "Hey Jude" single—at nearly six million sales—still has a long way to go to catch "I Want To Hold Your Hand" at 11 million.

● Pictured left: John as he appears in the Rolling Stones' TV spectacular, "Rock - n - Roll Circus."

● J o h n as Father Christmas and Yoko as Mother Christmas — see page 2.

The February 8 Disc speculated that the Beatles next single might be "Get Back," one of the songs recorded in the Apple basement studio. The article quoted Billy Preston, an American pianist, describing the session: "The track was called 'Get Back' and I played solo piano on it. They said then that it was good enough to become their next single."

Beatles road manager Mal Evans gave a detailed account of the January Beatles sessions at Twickenham and Apple in the March issue (No. 68) of The Beatles Book. He mentioned that Billy Preston had been a "Fifth Beatle" during most of the recent sessions and was signed to Apple on January 31. Among the songs mentioned by Evans was "Maxwell's Silver Hammer," which was almost recorded during the sessions for the group's previous LP, *The Beatles*. The Fan Club Newsletter disclosed that one of Ringo's new numbers "takes him back into 'Yellow Submarine' territory—all about an octopus' garden at the bottom of the sea." The issue contained several pictures from the sessions, including ten black and white photos, a color center-spread and color pictures on the front and back cover.

After reading about the Beatles 1969 sessions for three months, fans finally got their first taste of the group's latest efforts over Easter weekend. The April 5 Melody Maker, on newsstands by Good Friday, reported that "Get Back" would be the next Beatles single and would feature Billy Preston on keyboards. No decision had been made on the B-side. Although the article talked of a possible June release, fans received a pleasant surprise on Easter Sunday when disc jockeys John Peel and Alan Freeman played "Get Back" on their BBC Radio 1 shows.

The May issue (No. 70) of The Beatles Book provided the following explanation from Apple for the hasty decision to air "Get Back" and schedule it for rush-release as a single paired with "Don't Let Me Down" on April 12: "The fellows decided they wanted to have a Spring single so they pulled out two titles which had been intended for the next album. Organist Billy Preston is featured on these recordings for the first time with the Beatles. Otherwise both tracks are instrumentally like the group's earliest recordings—in other words, they are the only instrumentalists who play on them." The magazine reported that the Beatles ran an advertisement for the single in the April 15 Daily Mirror newspaper at a cost of £2,000. The ad was also published in British music magazines such as NME and in the American music trade magazines Billboard and Cash Box (see page 13).

# The Beatles Book MONTHLY BOOK

**MARCH No. 68 2/6**

# BEATLE NEWS

## SURPRISE EASTER SINGLE

switchboards at the Beatles' Fan Club and Apple offices were
fan calls immediately after Easter weekend following the
y period radio plays of the new single.

vance warning the two Beatles tracks—Paul's *Get Back* and
Let Me Down*—were rushed to Radio 1 deejays in time
r broadcasts. Apple instantly set an April 12 rush-release
ngle although in most areas first copies reached record
five and seven days later.

of the hasty decision from Apple: "The fellows decided
have a Spring single so they pulled out two titles which
ed for the next album. Organist Billy Preston is featured
ings for the first time with the Beatles. Otherwise both
umentally like the group's earliest recordings—in other
the only instrumentalists who play on them."

## ' BEDTIME LP

th their wedding" is the only comment Apple people
an LP album recorded by John and Yoko during their
ymoon "lie-in". As with the couple's previous re-
derstand the Amsterdam LP "made entirely in bed!"
ost unusual sounds rather than conventional singing

e LP, John and Yoko made another new film while
sterdam, the content matter being cloaked in secrecy!

## TRONIC WATCHAMACALLIT

k a quarter-page advertisement at a cost of £2,000
on Tuesday, April 15, to announce the release of
t Back*. The advertisement was headed "The Beatles
" and *Get Back* was described as "It's the first Beatles'
live as can be in this electronic age".

opy was equally tongue in cheek. "*Get Back* is the
It's the first Beatles record which is as live as can be,
e. There's no electronic "watchamacallit". *Get Back*
e rock number. On the other side there's an equally
*Don't Let Me Down*. Paul's got this to say about *Get
sitting in the studio and we made it up out of thin
write words there and then . . . when we finished it,
pple Studios and made it into a song to roller-coast
: It's John playing the fab live guitar solo. And now
e Down*. John says don't let me down about *Don't
*Back* and *Don't Let Me Down*, you'll find the Beatles,

o. Ltd., Lancing, Sussex
wson & Co. Ltd., 136-142 New Kent Road, London, S.E.1. Telephone: ROD 5480.

## New Album Delays

Latest information from the
Apple Records HQ suggests a
late summer release date for the
Beatles' next album although at
one stage the group aimed to have
this first 1969 LP ready in time for
April or May issue. The 68 hours
of special filming have been
edited into two special shows
which will be shown on TV to
coincide with the LP release.

Further new LP recording sessions are taking place at the
moment, but it is unlikely that
these will provide enough fresh
tracks to finish the album programme before the end of May.
After that a cover will have to be
designed and prepared.

Reasons for the delay? In part
the cause has been the Beatles' individual involvement in other recording work — George with a
series of massive Billy Preston
sessions, for instance — and in
part the fact that two of the completed tracks have been released
as the Beatles' new single. One of
these — John's *Don't Let Me
Down* — was recorded several
months ago and is one of the
numbers he sang on the roof of
the Apple buildings as part of the
filming project to produce a
Beatles' TV documentary.

## Not Final Version

The version of *Get Back* that
was played by DJs John Peel and
Alan Freeman on Sunday, April 6,
was not the actual final record that
was released a week later.

The boys decided that it needed more work done on it so they
went back into the studio on
Monday, April 7, and re-mixed
the tapes.

29

Although Apple had hoped to release the single on April 11, the disc did not appear in stores until the following week. Record Retailer reviewed the single in its April 16 issue, pointing out that there were "mutterings of disappointment in this obvious chart topper" on grounds that it was not progressive enough. "Get Back" was straight rock 'n' roll with a powerful Paul vocal. The song was "more subtle than one would think after only one play." "Don't Let Me Down" was noted for John's "rough throated mood." The music weeklies reviewed the single in their April 19 issues. NME observed that the Beatles were "getting back to their 1964-5 approach" with unadulterated rock 'n' roll, more polished, but still dependent on the beat. "Nothing adventurous or experimental...just honest-to-goodness pop-rock." The flip was called powerful blues. Record Mirror sought the opinions of six of its writers. All wrote of the rock 'n' roll revival, with three liking "Get Back," finding it Chuck Berry influenced. Rex Gomes thought the single could be a double A-side and even preferred "Don't Let Me Down," praising John's soulful performance. The others expressed differing degrees of disappointment, with Lon Goddard asking if the disc was supposed to be a double B-side. Penny Valentine in Disc called the single "brilliant," saying it would sell on its raw and unsophisticated sound. Disc jockey John Peel described "Get Back" in Melody Maker as a very simple song with a Chuck Berry guitar riff. He said his reaction to a new Beatles song was always the same—first disappointment, then after a few plays, awe.

"Get Back" debuted at number one in the April 23 Record Retailer, displacing "The Israelites" by Desmond Dekkar. For the next two weeks, the song held off Mary Hopkin's "Goodbye." After six weeks at the top, "Get Back" dropped to number two behind "Dizzy" by Tommy Roe. The magazine charted "Get Back" for 16 weeks. "Get Back" was number one for five weeks in NME (11 weeks charted) and Melody Maker (12 weeks charted). It was awarded a silver disc by Disc on May 3, 1969, for sales of over 250,000. Sales would soon reach 500,000. Top Of The Pops aired the "Get Back" promo clip in black and white on April 24 and May 8, 15 and 22.

Readers of the April 26 NME learned that a new Beatles single might be released almost immediately, even though "Get Back" had only been out two weeks. The NME Scoop stated that "The Ballad Of John And Yoko" was recorded at an impromptu session the week before and featured only John (guitar) and Paul (drums and piano). The next week NME reported that John indicated its release would be delayed so as not to interfere with sales of "Get Back."

(7XCE.21296)

**R 5777**

Northern
Songs

℗ 1969

Mfd. in U.K.

Sold in U.K. subject to
resale price conditions
see price lists

An E.M.I.
Recording

45 r.p.m.

**GET BACK**

(Lennon—McCartney)

**THE BEATLES**
with Billy Preston

(7XCE.21297)

**R 5777**

Northern
Songs

℗ 1969

Mfd. in U.K.

Sold in U.K. subject to
resale price conditions
see price lists

An E.M.I.
Recording

45 r.p.m.

**DON'T LET ME DOWN**

(Lennon—McCartney)

**THE BEATLES**

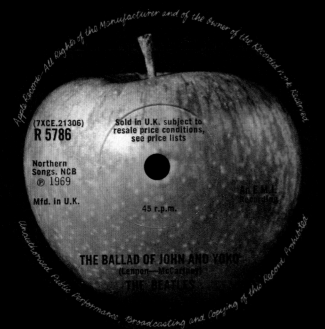

(7XCE.21306)

**R 5786**

Northern
Songs. NCB

℗ 1969

Mfd. in U.K.

Sold in U.K. subject to
resale price conditions,
see price lists

An E.M.I.
Recording

45 r.p.m.

**THE BALLAD OF JOHN AND YOKO**

(Lennon—McCartney)

**THE BEATLES**

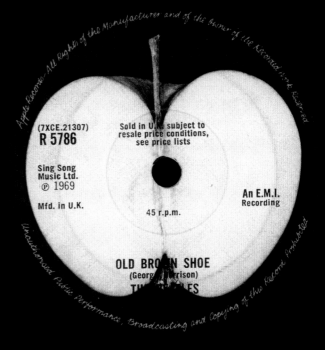

(7XCE.21307)

**R 5786**

Sing Song
Music Ltd.

℗ 1969

Mfd. in U.K.

Sold in U.K. subject to
resale price conditions,
see price lists

An E.M.I.
Recording

45 r.p.m.

**OLD BROWN SHOE**

(George Harrison)

**THE BEATLES**

Apparently John and Apple decided that six weeks between release dates was enough, so "The Ballad Of John And Yoko" was issued on May 30 while "Get Back" was still number one. The reviews were mixed. Peter Jones, writing in the May 31 Record Mirror, described the single as having a country-style backing and recognized its instant commercial appeal, predicting it would be a massive seller. Jones called it "yet another retrogression for the Beatles" and commented that "After 'Get Back' we thought they might have followed up with something more adventurous." The flip side, "Old Brown Shoe," was dismissed with: "faster tempo, but nothing new about this side either." That same week in Disc, Penny Valentine crucified the song, calling John out for being self-indulgent and complaining about being martyred along with Yoko. The song was called sub-standard and uninspired, with lyrics that were far from imaginative or brilliant and a sound that was empty and dated. It should not have been the next Beatles single.

NME saw it differently, titling its review "Rock and Cry with John's Ballad." The reviewer called it "One of the most emotionally moving songs ever to come from the pen of Lennon and McCartney," stating that "the lyric very nearly brought a tear to my cynical eye" with "the only thing that stopped the flood was the driving, raw earthy rock to which the words are set." The song's lyrics told the "poignant and true story of people's attitude to John and Yoko and their marriage and honeymoon." The driving rock backing relieved the tension and made the song a "stomper and a great one to dance to." He presumed that the song had to be released at this time due to its topical lyric, but could not help but wonder if "Get Back" still topping the charts would detract from the new single's sales.

Fortunately for the Beatles, the "Get Back" effect was minimal. "The Ballad Of John And Yoko" entered the Record Retailer chart on June 4. By the next week, June 11, it was number one, followed by "Dizzy," the Edwin Hawkins Singers' "Oh Happy Day," Fleetwood Mac's "Man Of The World" and "Get Back." After three weeks at the top, "The Ballad Of John And Yoko" dropped to three behind Thunderclap Newman's "Something In The Air" (which would be featured in the film *The Magic Christian*) and "In The Ghetto" by Elvis Presley. It would chart for 14 weeks. Melody Maker reported the single at number one for three weeks and NME for two weeks. The song topped the charts in Canada, Mexico, Denmark, Norway, Holland, Belgium, Austria and Spain and reached number two in Switzerland and Malaysia, three in Germany and New Zealand and four in Argentina. It was also a top-ten hit in Israel.

The May 3 NME had a wide-ranging interview with John by Alan Smith. After complaining about the time-consuming "Monopoly and financial business with Northern Songs," John talked about his songwriting in a manner that implied he was still writing with Paul. He later explained: "you can't say Paul and I are writing separately these days. We do both. When it comes to needing 500 songs for Friday, you gotta get together." He described their current writing as straightforward and nothing weird, mentioning "Get Back" as an example. His next remarks provided insight into why the Beatles current records sounded so different from their 1967 psychedelic recordings. In contrast to those sessions, John was no longer interested in the production of the group's records. "For me, the satisfaction of writing a song is in the performance of it. The production is a bit of a bore.... All I want to do is get my guitar out and sing songs." John admitted that he fancied giving some live shows, but couldn't give any plans as the group was not even in agreement. And there was too much going on to realistically consider going on tour.

Lennon's next remarks were about "the next Great Beatle Event," the next LP, which he expected to be out in eight weeks. He stated that most of the tracks would be like "Get Back" and that they had done about 12 tracks, adding that some needed to be remixed. Of particular interest was John's early talk of what would become the *Abbey Road* medley: "Paul and I are working on a kind of song montage that we might do as one piece on one side." He also stated that the group had two weeks to finish the LP, so they were really working at it. To him, all the songs sounded normal, but could be unusual to others. "There's no 'Revolution No. 9' there—but there's a few heavy sounds." John didn't want to pin the Beatles down to a particular scene. "We're just on whatever's going now. Just rockin' along."

John described the Beatles next single, "The Ballad Of John And Yoko," which was not out at the time: "it's like an old-time ballad...the story of us going along getting married, going to Paris, going to Amsterdam, all that. It's 'Johnny B. Paperback Writer!'" As for why the record was recorded entirely by him and Paul, John explained that George was abroad and Ringo was on the film (*The Magic Christian*). He mentioned the Mary Hopkin records were "pure Paul" and that he was going to make a pop record with Yoko. John also told of Yoko's contribution to a new song of his, "Because." "Yoko was playing some classical bit, and I said 'play that backwards,' and we had a tune." As for the rush release of "Get Back," everyone kept calling it a single, so "we suddenly said: 'O.K. That's it. Get it out tomorrow.'"

The release of the next Beatles album, however, was an entirely different matter. It was becoming increasingly clear that the LP would not be coming out anytime soon. The May 10 Disc reported that the album had run into troubles and its release had been pushed back from June to late summer as finishing touches on the songs were taking longer than expected. Disc explained that part of the problem was that most of the album had been recorded live in the studio, as it happened, with bits of dialog interspersed between songs. The album played continuously, like *Sgt. Pepper*. Apple's Mavis Smith explained: "At the moment all the recordings are unedited and the plan originally was to release the LP like this. But they may decide to make some changes."

The June 1969 issue (No. 71) of The Beatles Book stated that Apple's Tony Bramwell was hopeful the next album would be released in mid-July, but cautioned that no release date could be confirmed "until all four Beatles have expressed full satisfaction with the re-mixed tapes." The next month the magazine reported that the album might be released in late August. There was also a "chance that several additional tracks would be added to the finished production." John and Ringo were waiting for the return of Paul and George before deciding whether to add the newer numbers or hold them as surplus for a later album. Apple managing director Neil Aspinall confirmed that the new album was tentatively titled *The Beatles; Get Back*. The June 14 Melody Maker contained similar information, stating that the new album was probably going to be named *Get Back* and that it was set for July release.

As June came to a close, the ongoing saga of the next Beatles LP took an unexpected twist. The June 28 NME reported that the Beatles were "expected to begin work next week [July 1] on completing the second of the two albums they now have awaiting release." The magazine speculated that the second album might be issued first. The other album [then named *Get Back*] was related to their TV documentary and was to be released by the end of the year. That same issue, John talked about "this other half album we're into." He speculated that it would please the critics as the group had gotten tired of "just strumming along forever" and "got a bit into production again." Lennon said it would be "really something" and advised armchair people to "Shut-up and listen." He reminded readers that "there can be just as much complexity in one note as there can be in any symphony or *Sergeant Pepper*." The July 19 NME confirmed its previous forecast and predicted an August or September release for the non-soundtrack LP.

# DISC

## and MUSIC ECHO 1s

MAY 10, 1969      EVERY THURSDAY

# Is this man sick?

'PINBALL WIZARD' STORM: BACK PAGE

BEATLES' next LP—the one made during rehearsals, recording and filming of the TV documentary about their Apple activities—has run into trouble.

A last-minute hitch means that release has been switched from next month to late summer. And the reason, according to Apple, is that the group is running behind schedule.

Last week John Lennon revealed that he and Paul McCartney were writing non-stop to meet a deadline. But now it seems that although the songs are finished final touches will take longer than expected.

Part of the problem is that most of the album has been recorded as it happened—"live" in the studio, interspersed with ad-lib comments and other sounds—and runs continuously, without breaks, similar to "Sgt. Pepper."

"At the moment all the recordings are unedited and the plan originally was to release the LP like this," explained Apple's Mavis Smith. "But they may

# Beatles' album delayed

decide to make some new changes."

Meanwhile, the group's single "Get Back" remains at number one in the chart, with total United Kingdom and American sales soaring to two million.

Next week, Ringo Starr flies to New York for a week's final filming of "The Magic Christian," on location.

And this week, John Lennon bought for £150,000 a seven-bedroom Georgian mansion with 72 acres of land at Tittenhurst Park, near Ascot.

The purchase comes soon after John's claim that he was "down to his last £50,000." But, says Apple, this remark was made "for a joke!"

The Lennons move into their new home in August. Their neighbours will be Queen's dress-maker, Norman Hartnell, and Leapy Lee.

● The exclusive new colour picture (above) of the Beatles was taken aboard a boat on the Thames at Twickenham.

## IS CARNABY STREET SWINGING OR HAS KINGS ROAD TAKEN OVER? SEE PAGE 13

The August 30 NME reported that a new 16-track album by the Beatles would be released on September 12. Its title, *Abbey Road*, was inspired by the address of EMI's London studio. Derek Taylor called the album "very compact and very real." That week Record Mirror informed readers that the Beatles new *Abbey Road* LP would be issued by the end of September and would replace the *Get Back* LP, which was now expected out by the end of the year. According to Paul, one side of the album featured a medley of songs that "Goes on long enough to have a bath by." Taylor said that the album, which the group worked on for eight weeks, marked a return to the style of *Rubber Soul*.

The September 1969 issue (No. 74) of The Beatles Book was full of information on *Abbey Road* in its Beatle News page. The LP's cover was a color photo of the Beatles taken on the zebra crossing in Abbey Road near EMI Studios on the morning of August 8. One side featured a medley of songs lasting 17 minutes, along with two other numbers. The other side had six songs. The magazine reported that the Beatles had assembled "the old team back again" at EMI's Abbey Road studios, with George Martin once again in the recording manager's chair and Geoff Emerick in the sound balancing seat. George Harrison bought a Moog Synthesizer and had it shipped to the studio for the album sessions. Pictures of the group working on the Moog were featured both inside the magazine and on its cover.

Tony Barrow, under his pen name Frederick James, contributed a detailed article on the album's recording sessions. Barrow admitted that no one could blame fans for being confused by the 1969 recording policy of the Beatles: the rush release of two singles in close proximity, along with the Plastic Ono Band's "Give Peace A Chance," but no new album due to the postponement of the *Get Back* LP. Now *Abbey Road* was set for September. According to Barrow, the group had been recording songs for the new album since July, when the *Get Back* album was postponed. During that month, the group recorded six new numbers and revisited six tracks recorded earlier. "Maxwell's Silver Hammer" is a "jolly up-tempo presentation" despite its theme of murder. George's "Something" is a great slow track that "just flows along." Paul's "Oh! Darling" is an exceptionally strong song, "a real tear-jerker of a ballad." "Come Together" is "bluesy but up-tempo" with very freaky lyrics, typical John. Barrow explained that although a lot of the earlier recording during the year was done in the basement to Apple's Savile Row HQ, the July and August sessions were held at Abbey Road because the group was waiting for the proper fitting of its new Apple Studio.

# The Beatles MONTHLY BOOK

SEPTEMBER No. **74**

2'6

TLE NEWS BEATLE NE

## NEW ALBUM OUT THIS MONTH

The Beatles have definitely decided to release their first LP this year during the first half of September. It will be titled *Abbey Road* and will have a coloured photograph of the Beatles the cover taken on the zebra crossing in Abbey Road, near EMI's St. John's Wood studios, Ian Hamilton.

One side will have a continuous series of numbers performed one after the other lasting 17 minutes as a main track together with two other numbers. The other side will be made of six songs.

### 'GET BACK' LP IN DECEMBER

he Beatles are planning usual large-scale album se for the end of the which will be centred on *Get Back* album. A full has been written by Cosh and loads of graphs have been taken e book by Ethan Russell Mal Evans. Sounds like rfect Christmas present Beatle people.

### HE TONY PROBLEM

tied himself up in a very situation recently when people who were work- him were all called

y Fawcett was his another Anthony was eur, and he also had a hony with a Canadian und who was helping various ways. It must very confusing for

### THE OLD TEAM AGAIN

During the recent sessions at EMI's Abbey Road studios for the September LP, George Martin has once again been in the recording manager's chair and red-headed Geoffrey Emerick in the sound balancing seat. It could be described as very much the old team back again.

The crowd outside the studios has varied from just a few to 200 to 300, the average has been around the 100 mark, and Mal Evans reports that although a large percentage have been visitors—particularly American, German and French—he still recognises a few faces which he first saw more than five years ago.

### UNRECOGNISED

On the 8th August, the Beatles assembled in Abbey Road at the unusually early hour of 10 o'clock in the morning for the photo session for the cover of their *Abbey Road* LP.

After they had finished being photographed, they decided it was much too early to start recording, so Ringo went shopping, Paul took John back to his home for a cup of tea, and George and Mal went to visit the Regent's Park Zoo. They spent several hours wandering around the cages and animal houses and afterwards walked around Regent's Park.

The extraordinary thing was that during the whole morning absolutely no one recognised George Harrison. Perhaps there are so many similar haircuts in London these days that no one spares a second glance for anyone with long locks.

### MOOG

Many leading pop personalities have recently acquired Moog Synthesizers. What is a Moog Synthesizer? Well, the experts describe it as a piece of electronic equipment which can imitate and vary the sounds of almost any known instruments.

George bought one and has been playing about with it for several weeks now. He also had it shipped into the St. John's Wood studios for the recent LP sessions so could be that *Abbey Road* will be full of new sounds, unlike the *Get Back* album which, of course, is traditional Beatles.

*Mal Evans pictured in the recording studio* Road LP. Haven't their beards grown?
BELOW: *Ringo and George working on the Moog.*

The first opportunity for British fans to hear tracks from *Abbey Road* took place on September 19. But it was not on BBC radio, but rather on BBC2 television on Late Night Line-Up, broadcast on Fridays from 10:55 - 11:30 PM. The entire show was devoted to the new album, with all but "Oh! Darling," "I Want You" and "She Came In Through The Bathroom Window" being played. Although no tape of the broadcast exists, viewers have memories of a spinning Apple album on a turntable and the images accompanying some of the songs: "Come Together" (footage from the then-unreleased "A Day In The Life" video); "Maxwell's Silver Hammer" (a cartoon of the Beatles dressed as a barbershop quartet, see page 135); "Something" (a dancing girl); and "Because" (Apollo 11 moon footage).

The first detailed review of *Abbey Road* was published in the September 20 NME, which went on sale the day before. After putting down a young lady who complained to Radio One that record reviewers and disc jockeys were driveling fools who praised every Beatles record in mindless adulation, the reviewer moved to the album itself: "it's beautiful blistering music...it's something of *Revolver*...it's something all its own...it exceeds the double album and parts of it touch the heights of *Sgt. Pepper*." The album is packed with originality of composition and honest pop music. "Come Together" is a "rumbling, rolling piece...with a raspy Lennon vocal," one of the funkiest tracks ever recorded by the band. "Something" is a lovely song with a "floating, aching melody," one of the best George has ever written. "Maxwell's Silver Hammer" is a catchy tune with an "instantly-remembered story." Paul's "Oh! Darling" brought back memories of the Platters, Little Richard and 1958. "Octopus's Garden" was compared favorably to "Yellow Submarine" and called the best song written by Ringo. "I Want You (She's So Heavy)" is "deep-down-south blues... with a sensual emphasis" and a long instrumental ending as hypnotic as the second part of "Hey Jude."

The chiming guitar and warmth of "Here Comes The Sun" brought "Images of sunshine to remove the chill from a winter's day." "Because" has smooth close harmonies, but was found to be a little tedious. "You Never Give Me Your Money" starts quiet before getting harder and thumpier. "Carry That Weight" has a "solid mass of voices...like a well-disciplined well-rehearsed pub chorus" that leads into refined woodwinds and solid guitar. "The End" has a fusion of music and a "beautiful piece of precision drumming by Ringo." The review concluded by calling the album "almost always brilliant, and only occasionally fair."

The following week, Lon Goddard reviewed *Abbey Road* in the September 27 Record Mirror. He opened his review with: "YES, IT GETS more amazing every minute, folks. Those four likeable Liverpool lads have turned into two bearded wonders, an actor and the barefoot boy." Goddard thought that *Abbey Road* was every bit as good as their last three albums. His favorite song on the album was "Here Comes The Sun," with its western style harmony (shades of Beach Boys or Vanity Fare), nice guitar picking and excellent melody. "Come Together" is called excellent and a "subtle combination of bass, vocal hiss and piano." "Something" is a beautiful love song with George's "simple but effective guitar style." "Maxwell's Silver Hammer" is a return to 1920 that mixes a bouncy happy beat with the story of the murderous Maxwell Edison. Paul screams out "Oh! Darling" with "hideous pleading in his voice." "Octopus's Garden" is an extension of "Yellow Submarine" with Ringo's "boyhood sensitivity" lead vocal. "I Want You (She's So Heavy)" is a heavy blues with Lennon engaging in a type of scat singing that suddenly "bangs into electric picking, loud percussion and weighty bass" leading to a surprise ending. "Because" is symphonic with its Beach Boys harmonies and an opening reminiscent of "Lucy In The Sky With Diamonds." Although "You Never Give Me Your Money" starts softly, it becomes frantic with Paul's heavy rock voice and George's guitar. John's three songs in the medley are full of rapidly changing styles with influences of Buddy Holly, Delaney and Bonnie and others. Goddard talks of the confusing lyrics of "She Came In Through The Bathroom Window" and calls the medley's ending couplet the "phrase of all phrases." As for "Her Majesty," he views it as a "loving poke at Liz [Queen Elizabeth]."

Melody Maker ran Chris Welch's review in its September 27 issue. Welch observes that we no longer worry about what the Beatles are doing musically: "Now we can just sit back, relax and enjoy Beatle offerings and appreciate them on their own level." He calls *Abbey Road* a "natural born gas, entirely free of pretension, deep meanings or symbolism." Welch praises Paul and John for writing some good tunes, as well as their improved instrumental interpretations of their work. Although he notes that George's guitar playing is becoming Clapton-influenced, he fails to even mention that Harrison wrote two of the album's songs. He mistakenly states that Paul plays drums on several of the tracks, describing his approach as "surprisingly funky." He only mentions two of the album's songs, "Carry That Weight" and "I Want You," which "show the Beatles in extremely heavy mood." While Welch finds that the production is simple compared to past intricate efforts, it is "still extremely sophisticated and inventive."

Disc gave *Abbey Road* its top rating of four stars in its September 27 issue. Readers were assured that "They haven't let us down yet, and this record proves they're still the most inventive force around." "Come Together" was called "beautifully understated," while "Here Comes The Sun" was described as "pretty." The review also mentioned the frivolity of Ringo's "Octopus's Garden." The album was an enchanting collection of excellent songs. And while it broke little new ground and was not a "milestone" album, it was "Just superb. That's enough." Record Retailer stated that the album "spells sales in the biggest way" and that "While *Sgt. Pepper* remains the group's greatest achievement, *Abbey Road* is an admirable release in all senses" and an improvement over the last double album.

*Abbey Road* was officially released in the U.K. on Friday, September 26, 1969, with advance sales of about 190,000 units. It was the first U.K. Beatles album pressed only in stereo. The album made its debut in the Record Retailer LP chart at number one on October 4, 1969, replacing Blind Faith's self-titled album. It held down the top spot for ten straight weeks before dropping to number two behind the Rolling Stones' *Let It Bleed* on December 20. It returned to the top the following week, and remained there for six weeks before dropping to number three behind *Led Zeppelin II* and the *Motown Chartbusters Vol. 3* compilation. *Abbey Road* charted for 81 weeks from 1969 through 1973, including 16 weeks at number one and 22 weeks in the top five. The album also debuted in the Melody Maker October 4 chart at number one and remained there for 19 straight weeks. It charted for 35 weeks, including 23 in the top five and 30 in the top ten. NME charted the album at number one for 18 weeks.

Derek Jewell of The Sunday Times described the album as "refreshingly terse and unpretentious." While he did not care for the band's "cod-1920s jokes" ("Maxwell's Silver Hammer") or "Ringo's obligatory nursery arias" ("Octopus's Garden"), overall he was satisfied, noting that *Abbey Road* "touches higher peaks than did their last album." [That comment would have been even more appropriate had the album been named *Everest*, as previously planned.] On the other hand, Suzanne Harris, writing in the September 27 Daily Mirror, had little positive to say in her brief mention of the album's release. "SORRY, but there's only a rare glimpse of magic of the Beatles in their new album 'Abbey Road.' It is saved by two superb George Harrison tracks and Ringo's infectious 'Octopus's Garden.' Shame if we ever come to ask what happened to Lennon and McCartney."

Tony Palmer, who had praised *The White Album*, thought that the Beatles were caught in a trap in his review of *Abbey Road*, which ran in The Observer on September 28, 1969. Palmer accused the group of being lazy—that they had self-consciously chosen to be just like everyone else. To him, the group's simplicity on *Abbey Road* was "not the simplicity which genius in full flight attains." He finds it a paradox that they claim to be just a rock 'n' roll band, while they have "reshaped and revitalized the tradition from which they sprang whilst...asking us to believe that their only interest is getting back to their roots."

Palmer believed that the Beatles "confused and ill-directed roles as businessmen" made some believe they had "sold out to the hipsters from whom, with their wealth and power, the Beatles struggled to escape." While it appeared that they had "turned their backs on sophisticated music," there was "endless beauty and energy" on their double LP that "kept the Yellow Submarine afloat." Then they got fed up as there were "endless problems in Appleland," with each Beatle seeking his own identity. They then "ached to get back to where they thought they belonged— Liverpool, touring, rock and rolling all the way back to the cradle." After going down "too many unexplored paths of musical invention," they were caught and saw musical simplicity as their only escape.

While acknowledging that *Abbey Road* had "infinite delights" with tenderness, wit, elegance and melody flowing from the Beatles, Palmer was generally unimpressed. To him, the Side Two medley "sounds like a load of unfinished songs dumped together to clean the cupboard." While Ringo's drumming was skillful and easy, the excitement and bite was missing. While Paul's sentimentality was touching, it was no longer moving. George had "lost the ability to translate cleverness into fire." Only John escaped his criticism. Lennon was battling on: "His songs urge and cry and despise and fight. In 'Come Together' and 'I Want You (She's So Heavy),' he sounds as if he's almost bullying the others to keep going because all is not lost." Palmer thinks that the band's prolific output may be the problem. While other groups are always getting themselves together, "the Beatles have already been and gone." They have "shunned making allies with symphony penguins" and know they are alone, but have no reason to be afraid. Palmer finds it curious that the cover shows the Beatles crossing Abbey Road "back-to-front," implying it represents the group's current course: "Why are the Beatles walking backwards we ask ourselves?"

Geoffrey Cannon also believed that the Beatles were going backwards in his review of the album in an article titled "Abbey Road backtrack" published in The Guardian on October 8, 1969. Cannon's opening paragraph is an oversimplification of the Beatles activities since the release of their prior album. He states that they have been involved in personal activities and occasionally gotten together at their recording studios in Abbey Road. This ignores the *Get Back* rehearsals and sessions of January and the group's nomadic existence until July when they got back to Abbey Road. He then informs us that the Beatles have done it again, that they have a new album. For him, "That's the trouble: they've done it again." He views *Abbey Road* as an album full of "all their old tricks and gifts."

Cannon then runs through the perceived old tricks. "Maxwell's Silver Hammer" shows "John Lennon's magic funny schoolboy cruelty" (although the song was actually sung and written by Paul). "Oh! Darling" is their "suave celebration track," with bits of the Rolling Stones' "If You Need Me" and "You Can Make It If You Try" (both actually covers of American blues songs) and Buddy Holly. "I Want You (She's So Heavy)" uses Alan Price's arrangement of the Animals' recording of "House Of The Rising Sun." "Golden Slumbers" is Paul's mandatory "sad-happy number," while "Because" is John's mandatory "sad-happy number." "You Never Give Me Your Money" provides an enigma in its lyrics ("nowhere to go" could be "know where to go"). Ringo's "Octopus's Garden" is a variation of "Yellow Submarine." As for surprises, Side 1 stops dead and Side 2 has a little bit you miss unless you let the record keep playing, which Cannon describes as "for Prince Anne to play to her mother."

Cannon writes that the Beatles music has an unrivaled "special dense texture" and that even their slightest tracks have "an ambiguity and complexity, which...turns the music into an object rather than tune." And while old rockers like Carl Perkins and Jerry Lee Lewis "contented themselves with a driving line," their music had "energy and purpose" which Cannon finds lacking in *Abbey Road*. He acknowledges that the album is "clever and deft," touches new ideas and "contains talent comparable with any other Beatles album," but still finds it "a slight matter," believing that "the Beatles have lost the desire to touch us." Cannon's concluding shot tells us: "You will enjoy *Abbey Road*. But it won't move you."

Five weeks after the album's release, EMI and Apple issued "Something" and "Come Together" as a U.K. single on October 31. Although planned only for North America, the single's success in America led to its broader release. Record Retailer gave "Something" a favorable review, impressed by "some splendid moments on guitar and a gentility that is carried through perfectly in terms of musicianship." "Come Together" was called a "Great flip." NME described George's first solo showcase on an A-side as a "real quality hunk of pop" with a "wistful feel that's heightened by the inherent plaintive timber in George's voice—plus the strident lead guitar which exudes a mean and moody quality." Record Mirror's Peter Jones called out "Something" as "one of the most satisfying things among lots of satisfaction" on *Abbey Road*. He praised George's excellent vocal and splendid guitar playing. "Come Together" showed John and Paul in great form. Jones predicted it would be a massive seller and probably a top three single even though so many had bought the album. In Disc, Penny Valentine found it bewildering that the Beatles would, for the first time, release a song from an album that had been out for many weeks, even if it was a pretty song.

Reported as a two-sided disc, "Something"/"Come Together" entered the Record Retailer singles chart on November 9 at number 15. Two weeks later the record peaked at number four behind "Sugar Sugar" by the Archies, "(Call Me) Number One" by the Tremeloes and "Oh Well" by Fleetwood Mac. It charted for 12 weeks, including four in the top ten. The disc also peaked at number four in Melody Maker, while NME reported the record at five. The single sold in excess of 200,000 copies, but did not reach the 250,000 mark required for a silver disc award. The record's relatively poor performance had nothing to do with the quality of the songs, but rather was due to the significant number of Beatles fans who had no reason to buy the disc because they had already purchased the *Abbey Road* album.

Some of the later reviews of *Abbey Road* made reference to prior bad press. Writing in the November 13 BBC publication The Listener, Tim Souster believed that negative reviews in The Observer and The Guardian gave some the impression that the Beatles were "finished *years* ago." Acknowledging that the Beatles did not need him or anybody else to defend them as people, he stated that his concern was the music. Souster called *Abbey Road* the Beatles finest album ever, finding it "more rich, complex, stylish and wide-ranging than *Sgt. Pepper*."

Souster noted the "consistently high standard of production and performance," but it was the medley that drew his greatest praise: an "important advance" where "ideas fall over each other in riotous profusion" and "transitions are beautifully managed." The album's stylistic allusions to the current pop scene gave it the "character of a sympathetic but often gently mocking musical survey." The group's humor allows them to "remain Beatles to the core."

Barry Miles reviewed *Abbey Road* in the November 1969 issue of Oz. He admitted that his initial reaction was not favorable. Miles believed that the Beatles isolation had affected their work: "that they lacked new experience and stimulus and consequently had few new musical or lyrical ideas." But then he realized that the more you play the album, the better it gets. Miles observed that the cover perfectly represented the album, with the Beatles, after a brief flirtation elsewhere, happily back at EMI Studios on Abbey Road with George Martin and Geoff Emerick on board. As for the album itself, it was "good British Rock," with the Beatles reaching undreamt-of highs with few lows, with even the lows being good. It was even an album you could dance to.

Miles found "Come Together" to be simple and good, while "Something" showed George's maturation as a song writer. "Maxwell's Silver Hammer" was complex, with Paul perfectly blending American Rock with British brass band music. Ringo's "Octopus's Garden" had brass band and country influences with high harmony backing vocals. He found those tracks to be absolutely perfect. Miles also had praise for the two heavy tracks on Side One, "Oh! Darling" and "I Want You (She's So Heavy)." The Beatles could do it better than everyone else, with the latter song being heavier than most heavy blues, but with subtle and delicate passages.

Miles describes Side Two as "an exercise in harmony, colour and texture...very complex in tone and mood change." He finds the words to be, for the most part, meaningless, but that doesn't matter as "the language of music and musical images are what counts." Miles see the Beatles "evolving a whole new musical language again...progressing to a new simplicity (lyrically) but a new complexity (musically) and between them creating a new high in British pop." He finds "You Never Give Me Your Money" to be more complex in its editing than anything on *Sgt. Pepper*. Miles was happy to see that the Beatles have again passed the Rolling Stones and the Who.

William Mann's review of *Abbey Road* did not appear until the December 5 issue of The Times (of London). By then, negative sentiments had been expressed about the album in The Daily Mirror, The Observer and The Guardian. Mann advised readers that if adverse reviews had discouraged the purchase of the new LP, one should not delay any longer. The album "teems with musical invention," with Side Two being "altogether remarkable and very exciting." Mann dismisses complaints that the stereo recording is gimmicky to those who want records to sound like live performances. He finds the effect of the panning guitar in "Here Comes The Sun" as being agreeable and adding a "non-visual drama to the music." The stereo manipulation in the song, like the horns in "Maxwell's Silver Hammer" and the distorted voice in "Oh! Darling," is "used for musical purpose, not just to sound ravey."

"Come Together" and "Something" are nice, but just minor pleasures in context of the album. "Maxwell's Silver Hammer" (a neo-vaudeville comedy song about a murderer) and "Octopus's Garden" (son of "Yellow Submarine") delight the "teenybopper in all of us." "I Want You (She's So Heavy)" is an exciting track, with its second half "built on a haunting ground bass" that takes over a grand build-up (like "Hey Jude") that grows and gets louder until the song, along with the first side, ends with the cutting of the tape.

Although Mann praises Side One of the LP, it is not as marvelous as the second side. He describes "Here Comes The Sun" as torrid and the most powerful song ever written by Harrison. Mann finds the "mind-blowing close harmony" of "Because" reminiscent of "This Boy," but with more subtle harmonies. Its musical backing has "an asymmetrical three plus five rhythmic pulse." "You Never Give Me Your Money" is a wistful romantic song with a honky-tonk-style second half. He states that the following rock 'n' roll songs "seem to find their tunes in developments of the same initial mood and musical invention." Although called a medley, Mann views its effect as more dramatic and structural, tied further together with a reference to the ground bass of "She's So Heavy." Although "Golden Slumbers" is a companion piece to "Good Night," it is a straight rock ballad. "Carry That Weight" has a heavy rock beat and a reprise of "You Never Give Me Your Money," whose return Mann equates to the satisfaction of finding "a ten-bob note you've been missing for a week." Mann's only complaint is that the album's lyrics are not included with the record.

# The Beatles Get Back to Abbey Lane: The Beatles in Canada in 1969

## by Piers Hemmingsen

Pierre Elliott Trudeau became the 15th Prime Minister of Canada on April 28, 1968. He was the youngest to assume the role to that point, and his ascent to power in early 1968 was accompanied by a phenomenon called "Trudeaumania." The mania that surrounded his election as the replacement for the outgoing Liberal Prime Minister Lester Pearson reminded many of what the Beatles had brought to Canada at the end of 1963 and the beginning of 1964. Young people in 1968, including myself, were enamored with the image of our hip new Prime Minister. Twenty months later, he would meet and be photographed with Beatle John & Yoko.

By early 1969, less than one year into the new Liberal government, there was a general feeling in Canada that things were, in fact, more liberal. Young people, in particular, were happy with someone who was "young thinking" and who, as the former Minister of Justice, had campaigned on a "just society." The new P.M. was single, good looking and a very eligible bachelor. In short, Trudeau blew away decades of stuffiness attached to his high office. He very much appeared to be a man for the 1960s. Unlike his predecessor, he was fluently bilingual in both French and English, and many felt that would help ease the long-standing separatist tensions that existed in his home province of Quebec.

Canada did not officially participate in the Vietnam War and was viewed as a destination for young Americans who wanted to avoid the draft. Many "draft dodgers" found their way to Toronto, which had a support network of anti-war activists. Over the long weekend of Easter 1969, a rally was held in Toronto, where thousands marched upon the provincial government office at Queen's Park as a protest against Canada's assistance to the U.S. effort in Vietnam.

While many in the establishment worried over hippie-driven "anti-war" protests, the new Liberal government was under the leadership of a former justice minister who had campaigned on a "just society." Pierre Trudeau had not fought in World War II and it was perceived that he would be averse to getting involved in the Vietnam conflict. The election of a young and dashing Prime Minister in the wake of Canada's Centennial celebrations ushered in a new and positive era for Canada. The new liberalized environment in Canada would be the most fertile place in the Western World to host John & Yoko's BED-IN FOR PEACE, LIVE PEACE and WAR IS OVER campaigns in 1969.

As 1969 began, *The White Album* was still selling like hotcakes. A staggering 200,000 double album sets were pressed and sold in Canada during the first 6 months of its release. The album entered the RPM Top 50 Album chart at number 11 on December 9, 1968, and charted continuously through June 23, 1969. The film *Magical Mystery Tour* was finally given screenings in Canada. There were special showings in Montreal, Toronto and Ottawa between early January and late February. At the same time, the newer *Yellow Submarine* animated film was being shown in many theatres across Canada. The *Yellow Submarine* LP was issued on or about January 13, 1969. George Harrison appeared in a short interview with the Canadian Broadcasting Corporation ("CBC") program The Way It Is at the end of January. The Canadian press continued to monitor the activities of the Beatles throughout February and March.

The Beatles first single of 1969, "Get Back"/"Don't Let Me Down," was issued in the U.K. on Friday, April 11, 1969. Toronto's mighty CHUM 1050 AM aired the new disc just two days later on April 13. The single was officially released in Canadia on April 21, 1969. "Get Back" entered the RPM Music Weekly 100 Singles chart a week later on April 28 at number 74. The next two weeks it moved to 40 and 17 before spending its first of five straight weeks at number one on May 19. CHUM charted both sides of the disc together, with "Get Back"/"Don't Let Me Down" topping the charts for five weeks from May 14 to June 14. Radio station CKOC in Hamilton, Ontario listed the single at number one in its May 7 and 14 charts as "Get Back/Don't *Bring* Me Down." Perhaps the person compiling the listing had the Animals on his mind when he typed in the B-side! CFOX Montreal charted both sides of the single at number four for the week ending May 30, 1969. CKXL in Calgary, Alberta listed "Get Back" at number seven on its May 17 survey.

# chum 30

| This week | Title | Artist | Dist. | Last week |
|---|---|---|---|---|
| 1 | Get Back / Don't Let Me Down | Beatles | Capitol | 1 |
| 2 | Hair | Cowsills | Quality | 3 |
| 3 | Love (Can Make You Happy) | Mercy | | |
| 4 | Goodbye | Mary Hopkin | | |
| 5 | Hawaii Five O | Ventures | | |
| 6 | The Boxer | Simon & Garfunkel | | |
| 7 | More Today Than Yesterday | Spiral Staircase | | |
| 8 | Gitarzan | Ray Stevens | | |
| 9 | Bad Moon Rising | Creedence Clear | | |
| 10 | Oh Happy Day | Edwin Hawkin | | |
| 11 | In The Ghetto | Elvis Presley | | |
| 12 | Nothing But Heartaches | Flirtations | | |
| 13 | Too Busy Thinkin' | Marvin Gaye | | |
| 14 | Heather Honey | Tommy Roe | | |
| 15 | Happy Heart | Andy Williams | | |
| 16 | The River Is Wide | Grassroots | | |
| 17 | Chokin' Kind | Joe Simon | | |
| 18 | Morning Girl | Neon Philharmo | | |
| 19 | Grazing In The Grass | Friends Of Distin | | |
| 20 | Where's The Playground Susie | Glen Campbell | | |
| 21 | Atlantis | Donovan | | |
| 22 | Honey Love | Martha & Vandellas | | |
| 23 | Sweet Cherry Wine | Tommy James | | |
| 24 | Medicine Man | Buchanan Brothers | Comp | 30 |
| 25 | Theme From Romeo And Juliet | Henry Mancini | RCA | — |
| 26 | It's Your Thing | Isley Brothers | | 13 |
| 27 | Day Is Done | Peter Paul & Mary | | |
| 28 | I've Been Hurt | Bill Deal | | |
| 29 | Truck Stop | Jerry Smith | | |
| 30 | Everyday With You Girl | Classics IV | | |

## chum chargers

| | |
|---|---|
| No Matter What Sign You Are | Supremes |
| Too Experienced | Eddie Lovette |
| Baby I Love You | Andy Kim |

## chum

| | |
|---|---|
| Blood Sw | Blood Sweat & Tears |
| The First | The First Editi |
| My Way | |

Following the success of John & Yoko's first "Bed-In for Peace" at the Amsterdam Hilton, the couple opted to try a second Bed-In in the Bahamas. After their arrival there, they quickly changed their minds and decided to relocate their efforts to a cooler climate. John was barred from entering the United States at this time, so Canada was chosen as the next best location. It was close to the U.S. and its powerful mass media. John, Yoko, Yoko's daughter Kyoko, manager Derek Taylor and a 2-man film crew flew from the Bahamas to Toronto on Sunday, May 25.

With the Beatles "Get Back" single sitting at number one all across Canada, John Lennon was "Getting Back" to Toronto. Lennon and his new bride Yoko checked into the King Edward Hotel, where he had previously stayed with his fellow Beatles for the group's 1964, 1965 and 1966 concerts in Toronto. Canada's national media jumped on the story. Following a Toronto press conference at the King Edward Hotel and a lengthy immigration meeting the next day, John decided to hold the second Bed-In for Peace at Montreal's Queen Elizabeth Hotel. Lennon's party flew to Montreal on May 26. Suite 1742 at the Queen Elizabeth Hotel would be their home for the next seven days.

During their bed-in, John & Yoko conducted hundreds of interviews of varying lengths. The CBC saw this as a million-dollar opportunity to create a TV documentary around the event. Its program would later air on June 8, 1969, on the show The Way It Is. Tommy Smothers, Timothy Leary, Al Capp, Dick Gregory, Petula Clark and others made their way to the bedside of the famous couple. When John decided to record his new composition "Give Peace A Chance" during the bed-in, Capitol of Canada's Pierre Dubord (Quebec A&R) arranged for Montreal sound engineer André Perry to set up recording equipment in the hotel suite. On Saturday evening, May 31, John, backed by himself and Tommy Smothers on acoustic guitars, sang lead with the room full of extras clapping and singing the "All we are saying is give peace a chance" choruses. Members of the Hari Krishna Temple of Canada provided drums and percussion, while others pounded on the room's mahogany dining table. Canadian peace activist Rabbi Abraham Feinberg sang along, having earlier suggested to John to add the words "bishops and rabbis" to the song's lyrics. After everyone left, Perry recorded John on acoustic guitar, playing in the same finger-picking style used on "Julia," backing Yoko on her composition, "Remember Love." The songs were later issued as the first single by the Plastic Ono Band in July 1969. Perry received a credit on the label, along with Room 1742.

John & Yoko's bed-in came to an end on June 3. The couple attended a late afternoon Peace conference at the University of Ottawa in Canada's capital city. Afterwards, they attempted to meet with Prime Minister Pierre Trudeau at his official residence at 24 Sussex Avenue, but he was not available. They took an overnight train from Ottawa back to Toronto and, in typical honeymoon fashion, drove to Niagara Falls the next day.

The day before their bed-in ended, Capitol of Canada rush-released Apple's new Beatles single, "The Ballad of John And Yoko," on June 2. The couple's presence in Canada made the unexpected release even more exciting. The single's controversial lyrics caused some stations to refuse to play the disc, including Toronto's CHUM-AM; however, sister station CHUM-FM played the song upon its release without censorship from station owner Allan Waters. "The Ballad Of John And Yoko" entered the RPM Weekly charts at number 44 on June 16, while "Get Back" was still number one. The single peaked at number seven on July 7 and 14. Montreal's CFOX debuted the new Beatles 45 at number 13 in its June 6 survey, which featured pictures of CFOX DJs Roger Scott and Charles P. at John & Yoko's bedside at the Queen Elizabeth Hotel. CFOX billed itself as "THE EXCLUSIVE BEATLE LIE-IN STATION!" The single would top the CFOX chart on July 4. Billboard reported "The Ballad Of John And Yoko" as the number one single in Canada on its special survey in the magazine's July 19 and 26 issues.

Less than three months after their Canadian bed-in, John & Yoko returned to Canada on a spur-of-the-moment decision. On September 12, John received a phone call from the promoter of the Toronto Rock 'n' Roll Festival, John Brower, asking if he would be willing to fly to Toronto the next day to introduce some of the performers. When told of the Festival's lineup of Chuck Berry, Little Richard, Gene Vincent, Jerry Lee Lewis and Bo Diddley, Lennon was so impressed that he shocked the promoter by conditioning his appearance on being able to play. The promoter, of course, agreed. John put together a new version of the Plastic Ono Band, with Eric Clapton on guitar, Klaus Voormann on bass and Alan White on drums. After a brief rehearsal in the back of the plane heading to Toronto, John led the group through three old rockers ("Blue Suede Shoes," "Money" and "Dizzy Miss Lizzie"), "Yer Blues," a new Lennon song ("Cold Turkey") and "Give Peace A Chance." Yoko did two of her compositions, including "John, John (Let's Hope For Peace)." The performance was released on the LP *Plastic Ono Band—Live Peace In Toronto 1969*.

STEREO

THE BALLAD OF JOHN AND YOKO
(John Lennon–Paul McCartney)

THE BEATLES
Maclen Music, Inc.
BMI–2:58
2531
(S45-X46865)
Recorded in England

**FRIDAY – JULY 4th – 1969**

| | | | | |
|---|---|---|---|---|
| 1 | 1 | THE BALLAD OF JOHN AND YOKO | THE BEATLES | APPLE 2531 |
| 2 | 2 | Israelites | Desmond Dekker | UNI 11529 |
| 4 | 3 | Spinning Wheel | Blood, Sweat and Tears | Columbia 44871 |
| 8 | 4 | Good Morning Starshine | Oliver | Jubilee 5659 |
| 5 | 5 | My Pledge of Love | Joe Jeffrey Group | Wand 11200 |
| 6 | 6 | My Cherie Amour | Stevie Wonder | Tamla 54180 |
| 7 | 7 | When I Die | Motherlode | Revolver 002 |
| 12 | 8 | Color Him Father | The Winstons | Metromedia 117 |
| 9 | 9 | Hands of the Clock | Life | Polydor 540.009 |
| 10 | 10 | Let Me | Paul Revere | Columbia 44854 |
| 11 | 11 | One | Three Dog Night | Dunhill 4192 |
| 3 | 12 | It's Never Too Late | Steppenwolf | Dunhill 4192 |
| 21 | 13 | Good Old Rock and Roll | Cat Mother and All Night News Boys | Polydor 541.046 |
| ** | 14 | In the Year 2525 | Zager and Evans | RCA Victor 0174 |
| 23 | 15 | Windmills of Your Mind | Dusty Springfield | Philips 2623 |
| 22 | 16 | What Does it Take(To Win Your Love) | Jr. Walker and the All Stars | Soul 35062 |
| 15 | 17 | Quentin's Theme | Charles Randolph Greane Sounde | Ranwood 840 |
| 18 | 18 | Tomorrow Tomorrow | The Bee Gees | Atco 6682 |
| 19 | 19 | The Prophecy of Daniel and John the Devine | The Cowsills | MGM 14063 |
| 17 | 20 | See | The Rascals | Atlantic 2634 |
| 27 | 21 | Welcome me Love | Brooklyn Bridge | Buddah 95 |
| 13 | 22 | Love Theme from Romeo and Juliet | Henry Mancini | RCA Victor 0107 |
| ** | 23 | Crystal Blue Persuasion | Tommy James & The Shondells | Rouleyye 7050 |
| ** | 24 | Ruby, Don't Take Your Love to Town | Kenny Rodgers & First Edition | Reprise 0829 |
| 25 | 25 | I Want You | Brian Redmond and Soundbox | Regency 983 |
| 28 | 26 | Moody Woman | Jerry Butler | Mercury 72929 |
| 28 | 27 | The Girl I'll Never Know | Frankie Valli | Philips 40622 |
| ** | 28 | Can I Sing a Rainbow/Love is Blue | The Dells | Cadet 5641 |
| 30 | 29 | Theme from A Summer Place | The Ventures | Liberty 56115 |
| ** | 30 | Early Morning | The Collectors | WT/New Syndrome 6037 |

CFOX – PICK ALBUM

10 To 23    Feliciano    RCA LSP 4185

OLD BROWN SHOE
(George Harrison)
Recorded In England

THE BEATLES
Harrisongs Music, Inc.
BMI–3:17

STEREO

2531
(S45-X46866)

MFD. BY APPLE RECORDS, INC.

**FRIDAY – JUNE 6th – 1969**

| | | | | |
|---|---|---|---|---|
| 5 | 1 | LOVE THEME FROM ROMEO & JULIET–HENRY MANCINI | | RCA VICTOR 0131 |
| 1 | 2 | Love (Can Make You Happy) | Mercy | Columbia 2875 |
| 3 | 3 | Bad Moon Rising | Creedence Clearwater Revival | Fantasy 622 |
| 2 | 4 | Baby I Love You | Andy Kim | Steed 716 |
| 5 | 5 | No No No No | Danish Lost and Found | Barry 3503 |
| 7 | 6 | Grazin' In the Grass | Friends of Distinction | RCA Victor 0131 |
| 4 | 7 | Oh Happy Day | Edwin Hawkins Singers | Pavillion 20001 |
| 4 | 8 | Get Back/Don't Let Me Down | The Beatles | Apple 2490 |
| 20 | 9 | Proud Mary | Solomon Burke | Bell 783 |
| 15 | 10 | What is a Man | Four Tops | Motown 1147 |
| 6 | 11 | Gitarzan | Ray Stevens | Monument 1131 |
| 14 | 12 | Ban Jap | Byron Lee | Jad 1038 |
| ** | 13 | THE BALLAD OF JOHN AND YOKO | THE BEATLES | APPLE 2531 |
| 27 | 14 | In the Ghetto | Elvis Presley | RCA Victor 9741 |
| 11 | 15 | Harley Hurt Drive | Jose Feliciano | RCA Victor 9739 |
| 13 | 16 | Nothing But a Heartache | The Flirtations | Deram 85038 |
| 29 | 17 | It's Never Too Late | Steppenwolf | Dunhill 4192 |
| 18 | 18 | Hands of the Clock | Life | Polydor 540.009 |
| 19 | 19 | When I Die | Motherlode | Revolver 002 |
| 26 | 20 | Happy Heart | Andy Williams | Columbia 44818 |
| 21 | 21 | I Threw it all Away | Bob Dylan | Columbia 44826 |
| 22 | 22 | My Cherie Amour | Stevie Wonder | Tamla 54180 |
| 23 | 23 | Where's the Playground Susie | Glen Campbell | Capitol 2492 |
| 28 | 24 | Manhattan Spiritual | Sandy Nelson | Imperial 66375 |
| 25 | 25 | The April Fools | Dionne Warwick | Scepter 12249 |
| ** | 26 | ISRAELITES | DESMOND DECKER & THE ACES | UNI 55129 |
| 30 | 27 | Let Me | Paul Revere | Columbia 44854 |
| ** | 28 | MY PLEDGE OF LOVE | JOE JEFFREY GROUP | WAND 11200 |
| ** | 29 | GOOD MORNING STARSHINE | OLIVER | JUBILEE 5659 |
| | 30 | WHILE YOU'RE OUT LOOKING FOR SUGAR | THE HONEY CONE | HOT WAX 6901 |

CFOX – PICK ALBUM

THE AGE OF AQUARIUS    THE FIFTH DIMENSION    SOUL CITY SCS 92005

CFOX, MONTREAL; THE EXCLUSIVE BEATLE LIE-IN STATION!!!!! &

CHARLES R    JOHN & YOKO    JOHN & YOKO    ROGER SCOTT

That fall, the Beatles *Abbey Road* album was officially released on Wednesday, October 1, although it was in some shops the Friday before. That is when my next door neighbor, Linda Thomson, bought the LP in Ottawa. No doubt she had pestered the record shop for days in advance. She paid $6.98 for the new LP, which I thought was a fortune. The album's name seemed very odd to me as I did not know that Abbey Road was the location of the studio where they recorded their songs.

As much as I loved the Beatles, I could not afford to buy the album upon its release. This unfortunate reality led to a now-humorous story of my first attempt to hear *Abbey Road* in the comfort of my home. On a very cold Sunday afternoon, my friend Gilles Dupont and I went to see the film *Easy Rider*. We had to take a couple of buses to get there and to "get back." On the way home, it was too cold for us to wait for a bus, so we decided to walk. Along the way, Gilles ducked into a Shell gas station, apparently to warm up. A few minutes later he emerged with a smile on his face. After we walked a little further, he mischievously handed me a small package. It was a new 8-track tape of *Abbey Road*. He told me that the gas station had a carousel of tapes for sale and he picked that one from the rack. He knew I liked the Beatles and that I could play tapes. When I finally got home and warmed up, I took the new Beatles tape cartridge up to my room. Although I did not own an 8-track player, I had a Craig reel-to-reel tape player and recorder I had been given the previous Christmas.

My tape player was the same model as the one shown at the beginning of the Mission Impossible TV series, so I took on the role of the show's electronic and mechanical genius, Barney Collier, and tried to figure out how to play my new *Abbey Road* 8-track on my reel-to-reel machine. While I should have been doing my homework, I carefully and painstakingly sliced the tape and un-spooled it from the white 8-track shell and wound it onto a take-up reel. After I finally figured out how to mount my creation, I moved the T-bar into the play position and waited to be entertained by the Beatles new album. What I heard shocked me. I was hearing a mix of four different songs all at the same time! "Octopus's Garden" wailed away while a cacophony of other Beatles sounds burst through simultaneously: "I Want You (She's So Heavy)," "Maxwell's Silver Hammer" and "Sun King." My attempt to overcome this new technology was truly a mission impossible.

The new Beatles album was given the usual quick "thumb-nail" review in the October 4, 1969, edition of RPM Weekly, which incorrectly listed the title of the album as "ABBEY ROAD NORTH." In all likelihood, the reviewer pulled this off the album's back cover, which shows the London road sign with the lettering "ABBEY ROAD N." The review simply read: "Hot, hot, hot. Contains current outing 'Something., Should be big seller." No kidding! *Abbey Road* debuted in the magazine's Top 50 Albums chart a week later at number 48. It reached the top on November 1, 1969, its first of 12 weeks in the number one slot.

The Ottawa Journal featured a write-up of the album in its October 10 edition. The reviewer, David Farrell, turned in his article to the newspaper prior to the album's release, making it a strange piece. Farrell had also heard tracks from the *Get Back* sessions and showed favoritism to the yet-to-be-released back-to-basics LP. Oddly, Farrell thought the title of the newly released album was *Abbey Lane*. One has to wonder if he was confusing the LP with the Beatles single "Penny Road." After stating that *Revolver* had led to *Sgt. Pepper*, he viewed *Abbey Lane* as a parallel to *Revolver* since its followup would be *Get Back*, which he viewed as a more complete album overall. Although *Abbey Lane* was no lyrical masterpiece, the LP showed the Beatles as musicians and "takes the curtains down and let's all in."

As Farrell had not seen the album's cover at the time he wrote his review, he commented that its content was a carefully kept secret. One rumor was that it would feature a photo taken at Woodstock.

Farrell viewed the album as a "fine piece of work." He stated that it contained ten tracks, including two with multiple songs, meaning he counted the medley as two separate selections. He enjoyed Ringo's overall fine job, gusty voice and heavy drumming on "Octopus's Garden," along with George's lead guitar, which made the song hard not to enjoy. He found "Oh! Darling" similar to Elvis' "Heartbreak Hotel." He thought that "Sun King" integrated part of the Rolling Stones' "Heart Of Stone" (although the song is really based on "Albatros" by Fleetwood Mac) and found "Pollyethelyne [sic] Pam" to be quite amusing. He found it hard to sum up the album as the Beatles always surprise the listener. Farrell assured readers that the *Get Back* LP was worth waiting for, but "In the meantime, *Abbey Lane* is an album worth enjoying."

As in the U.S., the album's opening two tracks were issued as a single shortly after the album's release; however, in Canada, a small number of discs were initially pressed with labels showing "Come Together" as the full apple A-side and "Something" as the sliced apple B-side. Despite the confusion, Canadian stations played "Something" as the A-side, with CHUM charting the song at number one for two weeks starting on November 8. RPM Weekly charted "Something" at number one for 4 weeks.

In December, Polydor Records reissued a collection of tracks recorded by the Beatles in Hamburg, Germany, mostly with Tony Sheridan on lead vocals. The album was titled *Very Together* and featured a cover with four candles, one snuffed out symbolizing the recently rumored death of Paul McCartney. It was completely tasteless.

On December 16, 1969, John & Yoko flew BOAC to Toronto disguised as Mr. and Mrs. Chambers. The couple were the guests of Ronnie Hawkins and his wife, Wanda, at their farm in Streetsville, Ontario, northwest of Toronto. Between December 16 and 23, John & Yoko attended press conferences in Toronto (Ontario Science Centre) and Montreal (Chateau Champlain Hotel) to announce support for John Brower's PEACE Festival, met with Marshall McLuhan at the University of Toronto, appeared with Rabbi Abraham Feinberg on the CBC Television program Weekend to talk about their plans for peace in 1970 and witnessed the roll-out of the WAR IS OVER posters and billboards in Toronto.

But what had been arranged secretively beforehand was the closed-door, face-to-face meeting that would take place with Canada's Prime Minister Pierre Trudeau two days before Christmas. The meeting was held at Trudeau's office in the main block of the Parliament Building in Ottawa and lasted for almost 50 minutes. The subject was peace. Photos were taken as John & Yoko emerged from their meeting with Canada's Prime Minister (see page 59). John & Yoko told the CBC that if all the leaders in the world were like Pierre Trudeau, there would be world peace.

Things would change in 1970, but John & Yoko had waged a peace campaign in Canada that would influence young Canadians and stay with them for many years.

the beatles
very together

STEREO

COME
TO-
GETHER
(Lennon-
McCartney)

THE
BEATLES
Maclen Music
Inc. BMI-2:16

2654
(S45-X46991)
Prod. By
George
Martin

SOMETHING
(George Harrison)
Recorded in England

THE BEATLES
Harrisongs Music Inc.
BMI-2:59
Prod. By George Martin

2654
(S45-X46992)

STEREO

MFD. BY APPLE RECORDS, INC.

# He Couldn't "Let It Be"
# John Lennon in 1969

### by Jude Southerland Kessler
### Author, *The John Lennon Series*

In 1968-69, John Lennon was being re-engineered: transformed from a rock 'n' roller into a performance artist; from a Northern man—a male chauvinist—into a spokesman for women's rights; from a dominant husband into an equal partner. But despite the myriad changes (or perhaps *because* of them), John returned to age-old themes for his singles and for his songs recorded during the *Get Back/Let It Be* sessions. He returned to lifelong mantras and sang them with a shorthand urgency that swept all embellishments away.

In "Don't Let Me Down," therefore, John dove headlong into the most familiar theme of his career: his terror of abandonment. In a blunt, rat-a-tat Morse code, he repeated the theme of his favorite early-Beatles cover songs such as Arthur Alexander's "Anna" or Burt Bacharach's "Baby, It's You." John returned to the cornerstone of "If I Fell," "Not A Second Time" and "I'll Cry Instead." Having been abandoned by his parents—for very complicated reasons—when he was only five years old, John had always lived a life of mistrust, anxiety and loneliness that left him reluctant to trust or to love, lest that love destroy him.

In his late teens and early adult years, John began to protect himself by preemptively taking the defensive. He began to brutalize strangers before they could brutalize him. Never again did he want to feel the pain he'd experienced when his father disappeared...when his mother left him to be reared by an aunt and uncle, while only a mile away, she was happy with another family of her own...or when, his mother (closely reconnected to him during his teen years) was cruelly snatched away from him again by death.

In 1969, struggling in his new relationship with Yoko—who, it seemed, expected much more of John than he felt he was able to give—he finds himself living moment-to-apprehensive-moment, terrified that, like his parents, Yoko will walk away. He's afraid he will "lose that girl." (After all, truth be told, John believed himself "a loser" and a "Nowhere Man.") Best, he thought, to lay his fears on the line and tell Yoko exactly where he stood. In "Don't Let Me Down," John does exactly that.

In a guttural, primitive and impassioned appeal, he begs Yoko to be faithful to him. It is a plea rising out of a percussive heartbeat supplied by Paul's bass and Ringo's drums, but straight from the actual heart of John's primal fear. In fact, during one rehearsal, John asks Ringo to smash the cymbals just prior to John's vocal entry to give him "the courage to come screaming in." Pre-Janov scream therapy, this is John Lennon reaching into his most sequestered anxieties and then releasing them straight onto tape.

Billy Preston's work on the organ provides the tearful soul sound that John opts to shout rather than sing. And note-for-harmonic-note, Paul stands beside his mate, never truly understanding the obsession with Yoko Ono, but, nevertheless, supplying the camaraderie John needs to "sing his heart."

It is only in the bridge of "Don't Let Me Down" that John settles into melody, a melody that woos and quietly proclaims his love. But then, once again, poignancy is swept aside as John throws himself into the next verse—a verse laden with need, with great longing. John is, of course, dwelling in the same emotional maelstrom that Julia had always created for her boy. But this time, he refuses to settle for second-best (for a life with Aunt Mimi and Uncle George a mile away from the woman he loved). This time, he fights for what he needs: he implores, *beseeches* Yoko to love him. "Don't Let Me Down" is a song that is almost too personal and painful to overhear.

Far less personal and much catchier is the humorous tale of John and Yoko's wedding. "The Ballad Of John And Yoko" is a witty, bouncy ballad that recounts the objections that the famous couple encountered when they tried to marry (in one locale after another, with the press looking on, sadly wagging their heads at the "two gurus in drag").

But the ballad is so much more than a jaunty, tongue-in-cheek travelogue. It's a proud proclamation that "Lennon is alive and well and up to no good!" Full of sardonic sneers—even brashly conjuring a reference to his controversial 1966 "bigger than Jesus" statement by singing, "Christ, you know it ain't easy...they're gonna crucify me!"—the newly-married Lennon puffs himself up, thumps his chest, and says, "Come at me! I'll have at all takers!" John brazenly takes a swing at British government officials who refuse to let the couple wed here, there and almost everywhere. They have to go to Gibraltar near Spain. He taunts the press who have said all manner of rude things about Yoko, only to hypocritically welcome the couple home with the line, "We wish you success. It's good to have the both of you back!" And he even challenges the fans who refuse to accept his recent marriage. "The Ballad Of John And Yoko" is a bold declaration of independence...or more accurately, a declaration of co-dependence. All John needs, he tells us, is love...a.k.a. Yoko.

Recording the song with only Paul (on drums, bass and vocals), we find the Nerk Twins years later, in all their mature glory. Paul's harmony resurrects the old, familiar sound the world has come to love. Brian Epstein's boys are back! Only the names, years, partners and stage have changed. The charisma remains.

Completed in eleven takes (prefiguring "Instant Karma" both in its *"Think!"* lyric and in the swift immediacy of its recording), "The Ballad Of John And Yoko" draws John and Paul together again, despite their very public disagreements and battles. It gives fans one more opportunity to hear them "the way they was before they was." While loudly proclaiming his new future and his new partner in "The Ballad Of John And Yoko," Lennon works alongside the partner of his past and rekindles the Beatle magic that he sees slipping away into history.

Completely different, but just as magical, is John's first Plastic Ono Band single, "Give Peace A Chance"—the product of Lennon 2.0, John the Peace activist, John the Performance Artist. A pacifistic jingle of the highest caliber, John does what he does so well: he creates a melodic slogan which swiftly burrows into the listener's psyche. He fashions an incurable ear-worm.

While John's wedding in Gibraltar might have been private, Yoko and John's honeymoon at the Amsterdam Hilton was anything but that! And two months later, when the "Bed-in for Peace" concept is repeated in Montreal, this song is shaped. Recorded live against a backdrop of friends (Derek Taylor, Murray the K), celebrities (Allen Ginsberg, Petula Clark, Dick Gregory, Timothy Leary, Tommy Smothers, etc.), skeptical journalists and members of the Hare Krishna faithful, John and Yoko encourage the gathered group to sing along. Smothers plays acoustic guitar. Tambourines are scattered through the crowd. And voices—both trained and untrained—take part.

Thus, the Montreal Bed-In accomplishes what the Amsterdam event did not; it sires a powerful song that grows and gains strength and strides out into the world to speak vehemently against Vietnam and war in general. On November 15, 1969, this anthem is performed at the Vietnam Moratorium in Washington, D.C. with thousands raising their voices in protest singing "All we are saying is Give Peace a Chance." Quickly, it came of age.

Although generously credited to "Lennon-McCartney" (perhaps payback for Paul's participation in "The Ballad Of John And Yoko"), this singularly Lennon track—a product of the Plastic Ono Band, not the Beatles—functions as a "first night" for John's solo career. It thrusts him into the fray, full-bore. The proper days of the suited, bow-at-the-waist Beatle are gone. Here is John Lennon of the 1970s artfully directing his first "musical happening" with a success that none of Yoko's solo events had yet achieved. But as a couple they reveal themselves to be a mighty force for change. Their simple yet powerful message: "Give Peace a Chance." All heads pivot to take notice.

John would, of course, follow this peace anthem with "Power To The People," "John Sinclair," "Luck Of The Irish," "Sunday Bloody Sunday," "Woman Is The Nigger Of The World," "Instant Karma" and so many other powerful, effective political songs, but "Give Peace A Chance" (recorded on four microphones on a four-track tape machine by André Perry) was the debut anthem that established John's new-found role in the world. In room 1742 of Montreal's *La Hotel Reine Elizabeth*, the "Lead Beatle" dramatically abdicated the throne. In his stead, large and in charge, stood John Ono Lennon, the radical voice of the 1970s. And thus, for all intents and purposes, ended the Sixties.

# DISC
## and MUSIC ECHO 1s

AUGUST 16, 1969     EVERY THURSDAY

# Elvis in action!
## 2 fantastic pages of pictures inside

# The Beatle you most want to meet

JOHN LENNON is Britain's most popular Beatle. His extrovert antics with Yoko Ono in the cause of promoting world peace have made him a figure of respect rather than ridicule.

This is the fascinating major fact to emerge from POP—Disc's Pop Opinion Poll on the Beatles which is the most important nationwide opinion poll ever organised by a pop paper and the first and only searching inquiry into what young people really think about the Beatles.

From 10 questions put to readers by Disc, it emerges that the young people of Britain are still solidly behind everything the Beatles attempt—and overwhelmingly in support of the much-abused John Lennon.

We asked whether you thought John and Yoko's behaviour had been eccentric. Half of you felt it was! But you then qualified that by confirming your belief that, even if it seemed eccentric, it was still sincere—and that fact mattered most.

We then wanted to know whether their "antics" had done anything to affect your opinion of the Beatles. And here we really discovered just how much John has endeared himself to the younger generation of Britain. More than 70 per cent said their opinion was unaltered.

The final massive vote of confidence for John came in answer to the further question: Which Beatle would you most like to meet, and why? Disc did a straightforward popularity poll a couple of years ago when Paul McCartney emerged as overwhelming winner. But the mood has changed.

And the Beatles collectively? They are still No. 1 in the world, they have never made a big mistake, they have used their fame and power intelligently, they have passed their peak of popularity, but their best is yet to come.

● The Beatles—Your Verdict: pages 4 and 5.

# 1969: Carry That Weight

## by Al Sussman

1968 was a year that, to say the least, was an emotional challenge for most people who lived through it. Perhaps that's why 1969 isn't looked on as nearly as traumatic an experience, although at times it wasn't a whole lot better. We still had to carry that weight. The year was the second bloodiest of the U.S.'s involvement in the war in Vietnam and there were some very dark passages, including the Zodiac Killer, the Tate-LaBianca murders, Chappaquiddick and Altamont. But there were also stories like the Stonewall riots that continued the parade of changes for which the '60s are best remembered. And, most of all, there were the events that were uplifting at a time when we really needed our spirits lifted such as the moon landing, Woodstock and the Cinderella stories of the Super Bowl-winning New York Jets and the Miracle Mets. And one other miracle—a final triumph by the greatest of all bands.

The journey to that final triumph for the Beatles began on January 2 with the beginning of filmed rehearsals at London's Twickenham Film Studios. After flirting with the idea of a few live concerts in London in the weeks after the release of *The White Album*, the group instead opted for a TV special that would chronicle the creation of a new back-to-basics album. Unfortunately, the rehearsals placed the increasingly-nocturnal Beatles in a cold film studio in the morning and resulted in often uninspired and out-of-tune playing, as well as frayed nerves, particularly on the part of George Harrison, who walked out of the sessions on January 10 and refused to return until the project was moved to the Beatles new Apple Studios in the basement of Apple's headquarters at 3 Savile Row. The new round of sessions, under much more positive conditions, began on January 21 and were improved even more the following afternoon with the arrival of Billy Preston, who Harrison had invited to play keyboards with the band. Just over a week later, the filming climaxed with the Beatles performing a set of their new songs during lunchtime on a cold January day on the Apple building's rooftop. It turned out to be the last time the Beatles would ever perform in public. The saga of the album created in those January sessions, as well as the TV special that would morph into the feature film *Let It Be*, would have a long and winding road that would extend into the next year.

# Newsweek

OCTOBER 20, 1969 50c

## Which Way Out?

THE WAR: Nixon's Big Test

*Secretary of Defense*
Melvin R. Laird

The first of the miracles of 1969 took place at the Orange Bowl in Miami on January 12. It was the third NFL/AFL pro football championship game, which became officially known as the Super Bowl with that game. The NFL champion Baltimore Colts were a huge 18-point betting favorite over the AFL champion New York Jets. Despite this, the Jets' shaggy-haired ladies' man quarterback, Joe Namath, had guaranteed a Jets' victory. In Super Bowl III, he made good on his boast, piloting the Jets to a 16-7 win despite not throwing a touchdown pass and depending on the Jets' running game, field goal kicker Jim Turner and three interceptions by the Jets' defense. The Jets' victory gave the nine-year-old AFL instant credibility and made the merger of the two leagues in 1970 a viable option.

The day after the Jets' Super Bowl victory, Elvis Presley walked into American Sound Studios for his first session in Memphis since leaving Sun Records at the end of 1955. Elvis was coming off his triumphant December 1968 comeback TV special and brought his renewed enthusiasm into the sessions. He produced enough material for two albums and several singles, including what would be the final pop No. 1 hit of his lifetime, "Suspicious Minds."

That same week, the debut album by a group whose popularity in the '70s would rival that of Elvis and the Beatles was released. Led Zeppelin was a band that had formed out of the ashes of the Yardbirds and continued the British blues/rock tradition, but with a harder edge provided by guitarist Jimmy Page, bassist John Paul Jones and drummer John Bonham, with wailing, blues-shouting vocals from singer Robert Plant. The group's eponymous first album included tracks like "Communication Breakdown" and "Good Times Bad Times" that would become staples of FM rock radio for decades to come and serve as appetizers for Led Zeppelin's more fully-realized work in the early '70s.

On January 28, the worst U.S. oil spill to that point in time began at the Dos Cuadras Offshore Oil Field near Santa Barbara, California. Within the next ten days, 100,000 barrels of crude oil spilled onto the Santa Barbara County beaches, killing much of the marine life there. This was not the first mass oil spill and it wouldn't be the last, but the public outrage would serve as one of the building blocks for the modern environmental movement in the U.S. Among the initiatives that sprang from the aftermath of the spill was the organization by Sen. Gaylord Nelson of Wisconsin and Rep. Pete McCloskey of California of the effort that resulted in the first Earth Day on April 20, 1970.

**LED ZEPPELIN**

Authentic arrangements! • The complete album featuring
COMMUNICATION BREAKDOWN • GOOD TIMES BAD TIMES
plus photos, biographies and tips to players by
JIMMY PAGE, JOHN PAUL JONES, JOHN BONHAM and ROBERT PLANT
EXTRA: special guitar arrangement of BLACK MOUNTAIN SIDE

PLAY-ALONG
WITH THE RECORD

VOCAL
PIANO
GUITAR
ORGAN
BASS

# ROLLING STONE.

ACME          No. 37  JULY 12, 1969  UK: 2/6  35 CENTS

**ELVIS
IN
HOLLYWOOD**

**TOWNSHEND
ON TOMMY**

**BEATLES
NEW LP**

Sports Illustrated

JANUARY 20, 1969    50 CENTS

**SUPER HERO
SUPER JOE**

On February 3, with Apple hemorrhaging money, a contentious business meeting was held with all four Beatles, New York lawyer and Paul McCartney's soon-to-be brother-in-law John Eastman, and the notorious music business shark Allen Klein. Klein was appointed the group's new business manager at this meeting over McCartney's objections, though the law firm run by Eastman and his father Lee would be appointed Apple's general counsel the next day.

That contentious meeting and its aftermath could serve as a metaphor for the worldwide turmoil that was still dominating the headlines. With nearly 550,000 U.S. troops in Vietnam and "peace" talks in Paris going nowhere, there were protests in the streets of Washington for Richard Nixon's inauguration as president, even though Nixon had promised a "secret plan" to extricate the U.S. from the quagmire. In what started like a repeat of the April 1968 student disturbances at Columbia University, a group of 30 student rebels took over Harvard's University Hall at noon on April 9. But this time the university administration took immediate action. At its request, city and state police cleared the building at 3:00 AM and, using billy clubs and mace, arrested over 100 demonstrators. This show of force precipitated a week-long student strike at Harvard. Later that month, in an echo of the mass demonstrations in the streets of Paris a year earlier, French President Charles de Gaulle resigned following a constitutional referendum on a series of reforms that were supported by de Gaulle but were rejected by some 53% of the French voting public.

A pleasant alternative to all this turmoil was following the momentum of the U.S. manned space program as it hurtled toward fulfilling President Kennedy's call in 1961 for landing an American on the moon before the end of the decade. The flight of Apollo 8 in December 1968 had been the first manned flight to go into lunar orbit. In March, Apollo 9, with a crew of Jim McDivitt, David Scott and Rusty Schweickart, was the first flight of the complete Apollo spacecraft that was slated to make the mission to the moon, including the first in-space test of the lunar excursion module (LEM) that would land two astronauts on the moon. The crew successfully separated the LEM from the command module (CM) and then re-docked it and also successfully tested the crew transfer from the CM to the LEM. Two months later, Gene Cernan, Tom Stafford and John Young took Apollo 10 for a dress rehearsal of the moon mission that Apollo 11 would attempt in July, including going into lunar orbit with Cernan and Stafford taking the LEM down to within eight and a half miles of the lunar surface and back up to the CM. The stage was set.

Newsweek

FRANCE AFTER DE GAULLE

MAY 12, 1969    50c

Newsweek

MARCH 10, 1969    50c

STUDENT
REBELS

How To Tame
The Turmoil?

LIFE

The
daring
contraption
called
LEM

UNITED STATES

A double exposure
superimposes
the lunar module
on the
Apollo 9 launch

MARCH 14 · 1969 · 40¢

Cand
Pomp

For the Beatles, the transition to spring of '69 seemed to take them in several different directions. On February 12, McCartney was appointed sole director of a new production company, Adagrose Ltd., which would be renamed M.P.L. (McCartney Productions, Ltd.). The company would handle his post-Beatles professional work. On March 1, Paul produced Mary Hopkin's second Apple single, his composition "Goodbye." During this time, Ringo was involved with the filming of his second solo film role, with friend Peter Sellers, in the film adaptation of Terry Southern's *The Magic Christian*. And, on March 2, Lennon made the first solo concert appearance by a Beatle at Cambridge University's Lady Mitchell Hall, providing guitar feedback as accompaniment for Yoko Ono's "vocalizations."

On March 12, as George and Pattie Harrison were being busted for pot by the same corrupt cop who had busted John & Yoko the previous November, McCartney and Linda Eastman were married at Marylebone Register Office (the same place where George and Pattie and Ringo and Maureen Starkey had gotten married). Eight days later, John & Yoko flew from Paris to Gibraltar and were married at the British Consulate there before quickly flying back to Paris. Next, the honeymooners drove from Paris to the Amsterdam Hilton, where they launched their peace campaign with a week-long "bed-in for peace." John would chronicle all this in a new song, "The Ballad Of John And Yoko," which he and McCartney would record in an old-fashioned Beatles session (with George Martin and Geoff Emerick on board, but without Ringo and George) at EMI's Studio Three on April 14.

Shortly after this session, the first Beatles single of 1969 was released, first in England and then in America in late April. It paired Paul's "Get Back" with John's "Don't Let Me Down." While the music signaled all was well, the Beatles were dealing with business hassles on multiple fronts. On February 24, Triumph Investment gained control of NEMS Enterprises (former Beatles manager Brian Epstein's company), and on May 5, Lew Grade's ATV gained control of Northern Songs Ltd., publisher of virtually the entire Lennon-McCartney songwriting catalog. Dick James, who had overseen Northern Songs, sold the company out from under Lennon and McCartney. Three days later, Lennon, Harrison and Starr signed a contract making Klein, in effect, the Beatles new manager. The next day, Klein's company, ABKCO, was appointed business manager of most of the Beatles companies. McCartney refused to sign any such contract and remained bitterly opposed to Klein's involvement with Apple and the Beatles business affairs.

That same day, May 9, an experimental/avant-garde subsidiary of Apple Records, Zapple, was launched with the release of an album by Harrison of Moog synthesizer experiments, *Electronic Sound*, and John & Yoko's second album, *Unfinished Music No. 2: Life With The Lions*, which included the recording of the Cambridge "event."

Meanwhile, "Get Back" quickly topped the charts, spending five weeks at number one in the U.S. Surprisingly, while "Get Back" was still at the top, Apple rush-released "The Ballad Of John And Yoko" as a new Beatles single. The new record, though, had a much more difficult time on the American charts than "Get Back," largely because many radio stations refused to play it because of the "Christ you know it ain't easy/You know how hard it can be" refrain. "The Ballad Of John And Yoko" took five weeks to struggle into the Top Ten, peaking at an un-Beatles-like number eight.

In May, American news magazines reported on the Beatles business woes. The May 12 Newsweek told of the group's financial issues and the hiring of Allen Klein in an article titled "A Worm in the Apple." Time's article, "Britain: The Beatles Besieged," ran in its May 30 issue. Time observed that a "multimillion-million dollar business cannot be run on fun and flowers." It discussed the takeover of Northern Songs, how the battle with Triumph Investment led to EMI freezing $3,000,000 in royalties, the failures of Apple's retail and film operations and the hiring of Klein. John was ecstatic about Klein: "The point of Klein is for me not to be a businessman—to take it off me back so I don't have to worry about the details." Time estimated that each Beatles was worth between five and nine million dollars.

Also in May, the Lennons tried to enter the U.S. to stage a bed-in, but their November 1968 pot bust was an obstacle. They ended up journeying from the Bahamas to Toronto to Montreal, where they encamped in Room 1742 of the Queen Elizabeth Hotel. They spent much of this bed-in doing print and radio interviews and having an acrimonious visit from Lil' Abner cartoonist and arch-conservative Al Capp. On Sunday night, June 1, the second anniversary of the release of *Sgt. Pepper*, John & Yoko led a group of visitors that included Tommy Smothers, Petula Clark and Timothy Leary in the recording of a song that would become an anthem of the peace movement that fall, "Give Peace A Chance." The song would become a U.S. Top 15 single and reach number two in the U.K. in late September.

In the late sixties, homosexuality was still illegal in much of the United States. In an era when the NYPD was rife with corruption, the police often allowed bars to have gay clientele and/or serve liquor without a license in exchange for payments. Generally, if there was going to be a raid at a gay bar, the cops would call ahead so the raid would be mostly for show, although some patrons might be arrested. Early in the morning of June 28, though, a phalanx of plainclothes and uniformed cops invaded the Stonewall Inn, a popular gay bar on Christopher Street in Greenwich Village. Stonewall had no liquor license, so it operated much like a Prohibition-era speakeasy, with police receiving regular payoffs. The 200 patrons in the bar were lined up, with some being released. While police waited for patrol wagons to arrive, a crowd formed outside the bar, including some who had been inside at the time of the bust. Tensions escalated when patrons and employees were put into the arriving paddy wagons. After a lesbian was roughed up by cops, the crowd turned on the police and tried to overturn police vehicles. As the situation deteriorated, several police officers and some detainees barricaded themselves inside the Stonewall and escaped only after attempts were made to set the bar on fire. The confrontations between the crowd and police continued for three hours and spread down Christopher Street to Seventh Avenue. A second night of rioting by gays, drag queens, street hustlers and radicals sympathetic to the plight of gays was followed over the next several days by sporadic demonstrations along Christopher Street, particularly after accounts of the first two nights of violence were described in the Village Voice with what were perceived as anti-gay references. Demonstrators threatened to burn down the newspaper's offices. In the wake of the Stonewall riots, moderate gay rights groups were sidelined by more militant groups. Stonewall became a symbol of the gay rights movement that gained real traction in the '70s.

As all this was happening in New York, a new round of Beatles recording sessions began on July 1. There had been intermittent sessions, in different studios, since the "Get Back" sessions wrapped up in January, but this round was going to be done under what one might call "traditional circumstances"—in EMI Studios Two and Three on pretty much a regular schedule, and with George Martin and (much of the time) Geoff Emerick in the booth. On the first day of the sessions, John and Yoko were involved in an auto accident in Scotland and both were briefly hospitalized. When the Lennons joined the sessions on July 9, a bed was rolled in to accommodate the injured and pregnant Yoko.

Despite all the external forces and internal bickering that were tearing the Beatles apart, over the course of the next several weeks they were somehow able to block all of that out and devote themselves to the creation of a new album. Whether the group was looking at this project as the last Beatles group effort for at least some time is open to debate. But for what turned out to be one last time, they were putting on a united front as they worked on individual tracks and parts of what came to be known as the "huge medley" on side two of an album that would be named after the street which housed the studios where they changed the course of pop music history, Abbey Road.

On July 16, George, Paul and Ringo added overdubs on two of the finest songs Harrison ever contributed to a Beatles album, "Something" and "Here Comes The Sun." As the session was getting underway, Project Apollo, named after the Greek God of the Sun, roared again, with Apollo 11 lifting off from Kennedy Space Center in Florida for its journey to the moon. With its crew of Neil Armstrong, Buzz Aldrin and Michael Collins, the mission proceeded without a hitch and the command module Columbia went into lunar orbit on Saturday, July 19. The next day, Armstrong and Aldrin moved into the LEM, named Eagle, and began their descent to the lunar surface some five hours later. The descent turned out to be less than automatic, with computer problems that led to a program alert that could have aborted the landing and the LEM overshooting the planned landing spot in the Sea of Tranquility by several miles to a boulder and crater-strewn area. Armstrong had to take near-manual control of Eagle and guide it to a smoother landing spot before the LEM's descent stage fuel supply ran out. They landed with about 25 seconds of fuel at 4:17 PM EDT on Sunday, July 20, 1969. The first words (by Aldrin) were "Contact light. OK, engine stop." After acknowledgment by NASA, Armstrong announced, "Houston, Tranquility Base here. The Eagle has landed."

Some six and a half hours later, Armstrong opened Eagle's hatch door and climbed down a nine-rung ladder to the lunar surface, saying as he stepped off the ladder, "That's one small step for [a] man, one giant leap for mankind." A large percentage of mankind watched the ghostly image of a man on the surface of another planet for the first time, soon joined by Aldrin. The pair were more business-like than subsequent moonwalkers, using their time on the surface of the moon to collect samples of rocks and soil, take photos, erect an American flag, take a call from President Nixon and read a plaque commemorating man's arrival on the moon ("We came in peace for all mankind").

After returning to Eagle and spending man's first night on the moon, Armstrong and Aldrin prepared for man's first takeoff from the lunar surface. Some 21½ hours after landing on the moon, Eagle had a virtually flawless liftoff and ascent to re-dock with Columbia, which had been orbiting the moon all through Eagle's journey to the lunar surface with Collins piloting the command module solo. The trip back to earth took about three days and Columbia splashed down in the Pacific on the morning of July 24. Man's first trip to the moon was complete and the goal set by President Kennedy eight years earlier had been met with months to spare.

On the evening of July 18, as the Apollo 11 spacecraft was 2½ days into its mission, President Kennedy's youngest brother, Senator Ted Kennedy, was hosting a party on Chappaquiddick Island in Edgartown, Massachusetts, for a group of young women who had served on the staff of brother Robert Kennedy's presidential campaign until his assassination just over a year earlier. Late in the evening, Kennedy left the party with one of the women, 28-year-old Mary Jo Kopechne, ostensibly to give her a ride to the Edgartown ferry. On route, Kennedy made a wrong turn and shortly thereafter his car went off the Dike Bridge and plunged into the water. Kennedy escaped the submerged vehicle and allegedly tried to free Kopechne. Failing that, he left the scene and didn't report the accident for ten hours, by which time the car and the drowned body of Kopechne were found. Kennedy ended up pleading guilty to leaving the scene of an accident and was given a suspended two-month jail sentence. But the myriad of questions left unanswered regarding the circumstances of the accident and Kennedy's behavior cast a shadow over his chances of running for president, though he did make an unsuccessful try at challenging President Jimmy Carter for the 1980 Democratic nomination.

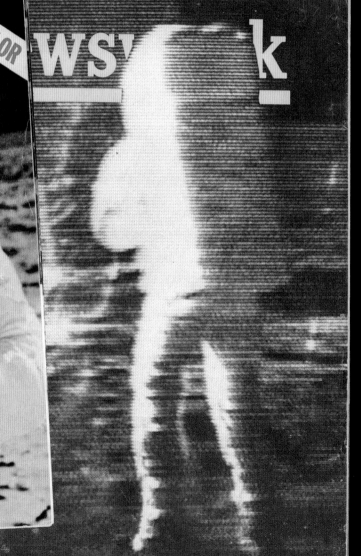

AUGUST 1, 1969

FIFTY CENTS

TIME

THE KENNEDY DEBACLE:
A GIRL DEAD, A CAREER IN JEOPARDY

AUGUST 11, 1969   50c

Newsweek

MOONWALK IN COLOR

L. ALDRIN

Newsweek

The Chappaquiddick affair, as it came to be known, was just one of a series of dark passages that summer. In early August, San Francisco's two major newspapers and the Vallejo Times Herald received the first of a series of taunting letters from a man calling himself "the Zodiac," who took credit for a series of murders and attacks (still unsolved half a century later) that terrorized California from the mid-'60s through the early '70s. Then, on the night of August 9, four drug-fueled fanatics crashed the Los Angeles home of movie director Roman Polanski, who was filming in Europe at the time, and savagely killed his eight-months-pregnant wife, actress Sharon Tate, and four others. The next night, a group of seven, including the murderous group from the night before, invaded the L.A. home of supermarket executive Leno LaBianca and his wife, murdering them in similarly-savage fashion. In both cases, the murderers left messages in their victims' blood in the houses—"PIG" and, at the LaBianca's, "Healter [sic] Skelter."

The Tate-LaBianca murders shocked and horrified the nation. It would take until December before the LAPD linked the two crimes and pieced together a case that would enable them to round up a group of followers of a career criminal and failed singer/songwriter named Charles Manson. Coincidentally, Manson had been arrested on suspicion of car theft a week after the murders, but was released due to a clerical error. He was apprehended again that fall and was in custody when the case against him and his "Family" was established.

On the other side of the country and a world away from the horror of the Tate-LaBianca murders, an ambitious music festival was scheduled to take place on a dairy farm in Bethel, NY, the weekend of August 15-17. The Woodstock Music & Art Fair was billed as "An Aquarian Exposition—3 Days of Peace and Music." It was inspired by the 1967 Monterey Pop Festival. The festival was the brainchild of businessmen John Roberts and Joel Rosenman, musician and music producer Artie Kornfeld and concert promoter Michael Lang. The group formed Woodstock Ventures early in 1969 and set about booking a roster of performers and finding a site for the event. The town of Woodstock didn't have a suitable venue, Saugerties and White Lake didn't work out and Wallkill banned the festival. With time running out, Woodstock Ventures made a deal with Max Yasgur for the use of his farm as the festival site, telling Bethel officials they were expecting no more than about 50,000 attendees, though they actually expected 200,000.

WOODSTOCK
MUSIC & ART FAIR

presents

AN
AQUARIAN
EXPOSITION

in

WHITE LAKE, N.Y.*

# 3 DAYS of PEACE & MUSIC

**WITH**

FRI. AUG. 15
Joan Baez
Arlo Guthrie
Tim Hardin
Richie Havens
Incredible String Band
Ravi Shankar
Sly And The Family Stone
Bert Sommer
Sweetwater

SAT. AUG. 16
Canned Heat
Creedence Clearwater
Grateful Dead
Keef Hartley
Janis Joplin
Jefferson Airplane
Mountain
Quill
Santana
The Who

SUN. AUG. 17
The Band
Jeff Beck Group
Blood, Sweat and Tears
Joe Cocker
Crosby, Stills and Nash
Jimi Hendrix
Iron Butterfly
Ten Years After
Johnny Winter

**ART SHOW**

Paintings and sculptures on trees will be arranged by the Hudson valley and will be displayed while on artists' giant's stable and art progresses. Artists will be glad to discuss their work, so the unspoken question in the surroundings, or anything else that might be on your mind. If you're an artist and you want to display, write for information.

**CRAFTS BAZAAR**

If you find a creative bent there's and you have your own painting a flea-level bazaar. You'll also find all the different candles, beat and most creations all over in Indian-Style camp clothes and other far ideas.

If you like playing with beads, or improvising on a guitar, or coming along, or expressing your ideas in any of the ways, please ask and see what you can give and take.

There can be music and laughter and dozens of joyous days and hot combinations or expression.

**HUNDREDS OF ACRES TO ROAM ON**

Walk around for three days without seeing a skyscraper or a traffic light. Fly a kite, sun yourself. Cook your own food and breathe unspoiled air. Come and relax and commune with the sunshine. Tents and camping equipment will be available on the camp site.

**FOOD**

**MUSIC STARTS AT 4:00 P.M. ON FRIDAY, AND AT 1:00 P.M. ON SATURDAY AND SUNDAY.**

It'll run for 12 continuous hours. Save for a few short breaks to allow the performers to catch their breath.

AUGUST
15, 16, 17.

One day $7.00  Two days $13.00  Three days $18.00

WOODSTOCK MUSIC
BOX 996, RADIO CITY STATION
NEW YORK 10019

*White Lake, Town of Bethel, Sullivan County, N.Y.

The promoters began running radio ads early in the summer, with tickets priced at $18 for the three days in advance and $24 at the gate. But, by the Monday before the festival, the gates and the fencing around them were nowhere close to being completed. By Wednesday, thousands had already arrived at Yasgur's farm, including many who didn't have tickets. By Friday, the promoters had no choice but to declare Woodstock "a free festival." With an estimated turnout of 400,000, there were massive traffic jams on all the thoroughfares leading to Bethel. Sullivan County declared a state of emergency and New York Gov. Nelson Rockefeller nearly sent National Guard troops to the festival site on Sunday. Heavy thunderstorms turned the site into a giant quagmire and facilities were at a premium.

By all rights, Woodstock should have been the disaster that Altamont was four months later, but despite all the lack of planning by the promoters and all the hardships for attendees and performers alike, somehow the festival really ended up being "3 Days of Peace and Music," as Yasgur noted when he spoke to the throng assembled on his farm. There were relatively few drug casualties, a couple of births and two documented deaths. As for the music, what most people recall came from the 3-LP set and Michael Wadleigh's documentary film of the festival, both of which were released the following year. The Woodstock memories that endure include the performances by the Who, Ten Years After, Joe Cocker, Sly and the Family Stone, Santana (prior to the release of their debut album), Arlo Guthrie and Richie Havens ("Freedom"), and, of course, Jimi Hendrix's Monday morning festival finale.

There were a number of major acts of the day who did not play Woodstock or pulled out in the weeks prior to the festival. Dylan had committed to playing the Isle of Wight Festival at the end of August. As for the Beatles, the group had stopped touring years earlier and was wrapping up its final triumph in the days surrounding Woodstock.

After considering numerous exotic locales for the cover of their new album, the Beatles opted for being photographed crossing the London street on which EMI's studios resided, Abbey Road. The photo, taken by Iain Macmillan on August 8, 1969, became one of the most iconic album covers of all time. Beatles fans visiting London make the pilgrimage to the famous crosswalk, frustrating drivers who must wait for them to have their picture taken. The ritual can now be viewed worldwide through the 24/7 web-cam trained on the Abbey Road crosswalk.

On August 20, after Lennon's "I Want You (She's So Heavy)" was remixed and edited, the Beatles participated in a sequencing session for the new album. It would be the last time all four would ever be together in a recording studio. The next day, all four attended Apple Corps' first annual meeting and the fallout from that may account for the visible lack of warmth between them during what turned out to be the last Beatles photo session on August 22 at Lennon's Tittenhurst Park estate. Pictures from the session appeared in the October 1969 issue (No. 75) of The Beatles Book and were used on the front and back covers to the group's February 1970 *Hey Jude* LP. The August 22 session was exactly seven years after Grenada TV filmed the Beatles at the Cavern in Liverpool and the last time all four would ever be seen together in public. The in-studio united front that produced the album now officially titled *Abbey Road* was all but officially gone.

That night, at the venue where the Beatles played their most famous concert, Shea Stadium in New York, the New York Mets baseball team defeated the Los Angeles Dodgers, 5-3, to move to within six games of the first place Chicago Cubs in the National League's Eastern Division. In just over a week, the Mets had sliced four games from the Cubs' lead since the low point of their season.

1969 was the Mets' eighth season and they had never won more than 72 games in a season or finished higher than ninth place in the 10-team National League. They were looked upon as lovable losers. But that August 22 victory gave the '69 Mets 69 wins with some six weeks left in the regular season. Indeed, they were in the first week of one of the great finishing kicks in baseball history, winning 37 of their last 49 regular season games, taking over first place from the Cubs in early September, clinching the division championship with a week to go in a 100-win regular season, and then winning seven of eight games in the postseason. And they were doing it all with only one truly outstanding player, 25-year-old pitcher Tom Seaver, but with a fine blend of youth and experience. By September, the Mets were winning games in ways that one might have thought came from a bad Hollywood script, including winning both ends of a double-header against a powerful Pittsburgh Pirates team by identical 1-0 scores and with light-hitting pitchers driving in the only run in each game. It was as if an ugly duckling had grown into a graceful swan.

In the very first NL Championship Series, the Mets swept the heavy-hitting Atlanta Braves in three straight games in the best-three-of-five game series, despite three home runs by the Braves' future lifetime home run champion, Hank Aaron. Then, in the World Series against the heavily-favored Baltimore Orioles, the Mets lost the first game, but won the next four with game-saving catches by Tommie Agee and Ron Swoboda, a home run by light-hitting Long Islander Al Weis and an assist from Cleon Jones' freshly-shined game shoes. The fifth and decisive game was played at Shea Stadium in front of 57,397 fans, about 1,800 more than had attended the Beatles 1965 concert. When future Mets manager Davey Johnson filed out to Jones at 3:17 PM on October 16 to seal the 5- 3 Mets' victory and end the Series, the Mets had beaten preseason odds of 100-1. As a team, they appeared on The Ed Sullivan Show the following Sunday night and, the next day, were given a ticker-tape parade down lower Manhattan's "Canyon of Heroes" that rivaled that given to the Apollo 11 astronauts two months earlier. Everything had come together for the Mets—from lovable losers to following in the footsteps of the Beatles and the first men to set foot on the moon.

The day before the "Miracle Mets" won the World Series, pamphlets were being given out outside Shea Stadium with a quote from Seaver —"If the Mets can win the World Series, we can get out of Vietnam." It was the first of two Moratorium days to protest the continuation of the war in Vietnam. There were demonstrations and teach-ins all over the U.S. and at outposts around the world. It was the first real indication that many politicians were now firmly against the war, with Sen. George McGovern speaking to a huge crowd in Boston. New York Mayor John Lindsay wanted the American flag at Shea Stadium flown at half staff that day, but was overruled by first-year Baseball Commissioner Bowie Kuhn despite the fact that the City of New York owned the venue.

The Vietnam Moratorium Committee planned a massive march on Washington for the second Moratorium Day on Saturday, November 15, preceded by a March Against Death in the streets of Washington beginning the previous Thursday. An estimated 500,000 demonstrators descended on the nation's capital, reportedly dwarfing the turnout for the civil rights March six years earlier. For the most part, the Moratorium March was more peaceful than previous anti-Vietnam demonstrations, with the enduring memory from that day being hundreds of thousands singing John Lennon's words, "All we are saying is/Give peace a chance."

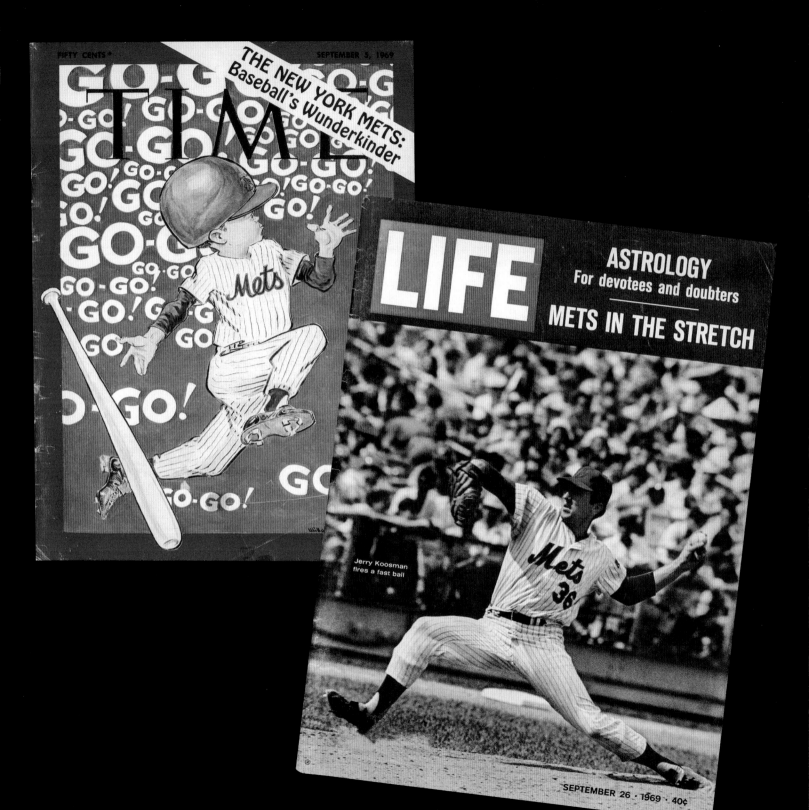

Twelve nights before the Moratorium March, though, Nixon gave a televised Oval Office address in which he asked for the support of "the great silent majority" of the American people and post-speech polls showed that a majority of Americans still supported his conduct of the war, though they didn't know that Nixon was already expanding the scope of the war into Cambodia. And three days before the Moratorium, freelance investigative reporter Seymour Hersh broke the story of the My Lai massacre.

My Lai had taken place on March 16, 1968, when somewhere between 350 and 500 unarmed South Vietnamese civilians were killed by U.S. troops, with women gang-raped and children mutilated by members of Charlie Company, on orders to kill anyone thought to be Viet Cong or Viet Cong sympathizers. Official military reports on the incident described it as a military victory and severely minimized the number of civilian casualties. It took more than a year and a half and a congressional inquiry before freelance reporter Seymour Hersh broke the story of what was actually a massacre of epic proportions. A belated follow-up U.S. Army review of the original investigation of the March '68 incident concluded with a final report issued almost exactly two years after My Lai and subsequent Army trials of 26 soldiers resulted in just one conviction, that of Lt. William Calley, Jr., who contended that he was just "following orders" from his superior, Capt. Ernest Medina. It would take decades for something resembling the full story of the My Lai Massacre to come to light.

The unfolding story of My Lai and the Vietnam Moratorium March nearly overshadowed the U.S.'s second manned lunar landing mission, Apollo 12. This mission, with a crew of Pete Conrad, Alan Bean and Dick Gordon, was even more ambitious than Apollo 11. Conrad and Bean brought the LEM Intrepid to an on-target landing in the lunar surface's Ocean of Storms, near the unmanned Surveyor 3, which had landed on the moon in April 1967. They remained on the moon for well over a full day and did two EVAs (moonwalks) of nearly four hours each. All went well, other than Bean terminating color TV transmission by inadvertently pointing the camera at the sun and then leaving several rolls of film on the lunar surface. After lifting off from the moon and re-docking with the CM Yankee Clipper, the crew remained in lunar orbit for an extra day to take photographs, including that of a solar eclipse.

The Apollo 12 mission ended successfully with splashdown in the Pacific on the afternoon of November 24 with no problems other than Bean sustaining a mild concussion and being briefly knocked out after one of the crew's film cameras konked him on the forehead during the splashdown. A very successful, if less celebrated, mission. The next one, Apollo 13, would end up being a much more perilous trip.

Apollo 12 returned to earth at roughly the halfway mark of the Rolling Stones' first American tour in nearly 3½ years. Much had changed in the rock world in that time. The short, manic shows dominated by screaming, hysterical girls had given way to longer concerts played before more cooled-out audiences. The Stones' tour set list was dominated by material from 1968's *Beggar's Banquet* and their new *Let It Bleed* LP (released as the tour came an end on December 5). The group had a new member, with Mick Taylor replacing Brian Jones, who had been dismissed from the Stones after becoming a burned-out walking drug casualty, shortly before his death from drowning in early July.

Most of the concerts were held in large arenas, with the peak of the tour being the Stones' shows at New York's Madison Square Garden on November 27 and 28. These performances provided much of the material for the 1970 *Get Yer Ya-Yas Out* album and the *Gimme Shelter* tour documentary directed by Maysles Brothers, who filmed the Beatles first U.S. visit in February 1964. While their documentary *What's Happening! The Beatles in the U.S.A.* captured the frenetic innocence of Beatlemania, *Gimmie Shelter* was a visual record of one of 1969's dark passages.

With the memory of Woodstock still fresh in mind, the Stones wanted to finish the tour with a free concert in San Francisco. Like Woodstock, though, the venue kept having to be moved, with the Altamont Speedway being settled on less than 48 hours before the December 6 date for what had grown into a one-day free festival. Along with the Stones, also on the bill were Woodstock veterans Jefferson Airplane, Santana, Crosby, Stills, Nash & Young and the Grateful Dead, plus country-rockers the Flying Burrito Brothers. Some 300,000 descended on Altamont but the spirit of Woodstock was nowhere in evidence, with the kind of crime, injuries, death and bad vibes that didn't happen on Max Yasgur's farm all too much the story here. And exacerbating the situation was the personnel hired to protect the stage—the local chapter of Hell's Angels, paid with $500 worth of beer.

As the day wore on, the drug-fueled crowd and beered-up Angels made for a combustible combination. After the Airplane's Marty Balin was knocked out by one of the Angels after trying to break up a fight at the edge of the stage, the Dead bailed out of the concert. The Stones didn't come on until after sundown and, with the atmosphere growing worse by the minute, a fight broke out during, fittingly, "Sympathy For The Devil." Next, the Angels had a confrontation with a by-now-drug-crazed 18-year-old named Meredith Hunter. After he had tried several times to reach the stage, he drew a .22 caliber revolver but was rushed by one of the Angels, who stabbed Hunter to death as the band played "Under My Thumb." Rather than risk a riot, the Stones, only vaguely aware of what had happened, finished their set and quickly exited. The Woodstock nation and its innocence had lasted less than four months.

Nine nights after Altamont, John & Yoko led an enlarged Plastic Ono Band in closing a "Peace For Christmas" UNICEF benefit at London's Lyceum Ballroom on December 15. Included in the band was George Harrison, who had been touring England with Delaney & Bonnie & Friends with Eric Clapton. It was the first time two Beatles had been on the same concert stage since the last Beatles tour three years earlier and the last time Lennon and Harrison would ever appear on the same stage.

The next day, huge billboards and posters appeared in 11 cities around the world that announced "WAR IS OVER! IF YOU WANT IT. Happy Christmas From John & Yoko." On December 19, "The Beatles' Seventh Christmas Record" was sent out to their fan club members. It was a melancholy, John & Yoko-dominated disc that showed, even more starkly than the '68 disc, that this was no longer a group, but rather four individuals pursuing their own careers.

The following week, LIFE magazine issued a special double issue cover-dated December 26, 1969, that told the story of the '60s, a Decade of Tumult and Change. The Beatles were featured on the cover and inside the magazine. This was entirely appropriate as the Beatles were not only a product of the '60s, but also had profoundly influenced the decade themselves, both musically and culturally. In February 1964, New York television reporter Gabe Pressman had sarcastically asked a bemused Paul McCartney what effect the Beatles would have on Western culture. As the decade came to end, we had the answer.

LIFE

The '60s

Decade of
Tumult and Change

TWO-IN-ONE ISSUE 60 CENTS

# 1969: The Year in Music and Film

## by Frank Daniels

Nineteen sixty-nine was a year for beautiful album covers and beautiful music. Being not quite the Hindenburg disaster that some people thought they would be, Led Zeppelin released TWO great albums that year; it was the only way to fly. Blind Faith was destined to release just one album ever, but hey, they released the same album with two different covers. The one with a topless 11-year-old strawberry-blonde girl holding a silver space ship caused a bit of controversy, so retailers were given the option of a cover featuring a photo of the band. King Crimson's *In the Court of the Crimson King* left everyone wondering what that album cover was about, but whatever they had done, it was amazing.

Glen Campbell's hot streak continued throughout the year, and one of the year's best war-themed songs was his hit, "Galveston." The singer was stationed in a faraway place, dreaming of the life he had left at home. Meanwhile, Santana had everyone wondering whether the woman he sang to would change her evil ways, all the time wondering also how many different images they "saw" in Santana's album cover. Three Dog Night had just released "One," which expressed so well the agony of breakup. The hit had people reaching for Harry Nilsson's back catalog; he was the lonely fellow who had written that song. "Now I spend my time just making rhymes of yesterday," they sang.

The Detroit scene produced a group called MC5. Some people bought the album and were astonished that they urged people to "kick out the jams" by calling them mother F-ers in the process. Others bought the same album and said, "No. He says 'brothers and sisters.'" There was some great music, though, and another superlative cover. Speaking of great covers, how about *Live/Dead*? No, that's not an album by the Zombies, but by the Grateful Dead, of course. The Walking Dead came later. While you whiled away the time becoming a party to a magnificent concert experience, you couldn't help marveling at the time and work that it must have taken to create the cover.

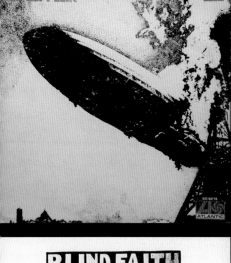

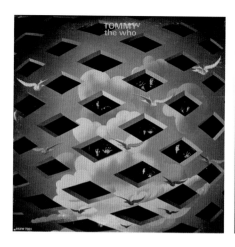  

This was also the year that the Who took the notion of a concept album to the next logical level. Since the songs together told a story, people began labeling *Tommy* as the first "rock opera," and so it was, telling the story of a child who sees something so horrific that he blocks it out—losing the ability to see, speak or hear, but gaining a special talent in the process. He "sure plays mean pinball." For you younger readers who don't recognize that word, pinball was the Fortnite of 1969. The Kinks followed with *Arthur (Or The Decline And Fall Of The British Empire)*.

The chart-topping singles of the year were all over the place, including two from bands that weren't even bands: the instant classic "Na Na Hey Hey Kiss Him Goodbye" (from Steam) and the bubble-gum hit "Sugar Sugar" by a group of comic book characters, the Archies. Since the soundtrack was running at #1 on all the major charts, cover versions from the *Hair* musical were rolling out, with the 5th Dimension's magnificent medley of "Aquarius" and "The Flesh Failures (Let the Sunshine In)" topping the charts and two others coming darn close: the Cowsills version of the title song (#2) and Oliver's "Good Morning Starshine" (#3). Sly and the Family Stone sang for peace and unity among the races with "Everyday People," while Zager & Evans warned of a bleak far-off future in "In The Year 2525 (Exoddium & Terminus)." Tommy Roe made us "Dizzy," while the Temptations lamented "I Can't Get Next To You" and the 5th Dimension had a bad case of "Wedding Bell Blues." After Diana Ross announced she was leaving the Supremes for a solo career, they issued their final single together, ironically titled "Someday We'll Be Together."

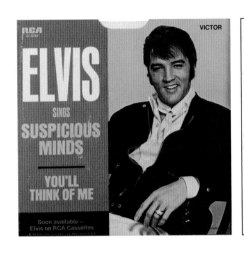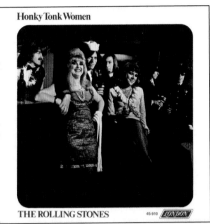

When Tommy James & the Shondells added a splash of psychedelia to their bubble-gum sound, they scored a chart-topper with "Crimson And Clover" and a number two hit with "Crystal Blue Persuasion." On the softer side, Peter, Paul & Mary were "Leaving On A Jet Plane" and Henry Mancini brought us back to the movies with his arrangement of the "Love Theme From Romeo & Juliet."

Meanwhile the new, modern Elvis Presley had us all worried about being "caught in a trap" with our "Suspicious Minds." His rendition of the depressing story of a young man's life cut short "In the Ghetto" also gave him a #3 hit. The Rolling Stones went back to the top of the pops with "Honky Tonk Women," while the Beatles continued their domination of the charts with "Get Back" and the double-sided hit "Come Together"/"Something."

We realized that there were so many sounds in the popular music of 1969 that David Bowie's shout out to Major Tom, "Space Oddity," might be on the radio sandwiched between "Lay, Lady, Lay" (from Bob Dylan's country album *Nashville Skyline*) and "Bad Moon Rising" from Creedence Clearwater Revival. And good times never seemed so good with Neil Diamond's "Sweet Caroline," still heard during seventh inning stretches at baseball diamonds throughout the land. If you spelled your name "Danger," you were hooked on the innovative comedy of the Firesign Theatre. A certain Beatle was on the album cover, and there were plenty of references to the group.

101

  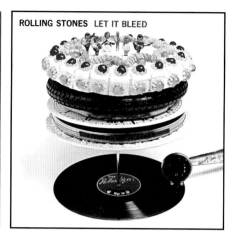

The Zombies told us it was the "Time Of The Season" for loving, courtesy of their initially neglected 1968 album *Odessey And Oracle*. By the time the single was released in early 1969, the band had broken up. The Youngbloods had only moderate success with their 1967 recording of "Get Together" (peaking at #62), but when the song was used in a public service announcement for the National Conference of Christians and Jews, it gained a wider audience and worked its way up to number five in September 1969. The Band took us "Across The Great Divide" and "Up On Cripple Creek" on their second album, while the Rolling Stones said we could *Let It Bleed* months before the Beatles gave us words of wisdom, "Let It Be." Reggae music was imported from Jamaica with Desmond Dekker's *Isrealites*. If gospel was more your bag, maybe you listened to the recording of "Oh Happy Day" by the Edwin Hawkins Singers and wondered whether the so-called Jesus Freak movement was going to produce more music like that. George Harrison reworked the song as "My Sweet Lord," producing versions by Billy Preston and himself the following year.

The biggest musical festival of the year and the decade was Woodstock. But for multiple reasons, the Beatles neither played the event nor had any of its members attend. Promoter Michael Lang wanted the Beatles, but realized that the group would have overpowered the bill and that they had stopped touring. As John was a big influence on Lang, he reached out to John through Apple's Chris O'Dell, who was friends with an acquaintance of Lang. Ms. O'Dell sent a memo about the concert to John & Yoko, who at the time were frequently at Apple. John told Chris that he was not interested in playing, but would like to go see it. But, alas, it was not to be. In May, John was barred from entering the U.S. due to his 1968 arrest in London for possession of marijuana. And, as it turned out, during the dates the mid-August 1969 festival took place, the Beatles were putting the finishing touches on their latest LP, *Abbey Road*. In a letter to Lang dated July 7, 1969, Ms. O'Dell indicated that Apple wanted to present at Woodstock: (A) The Plastic Ono Band; (B) Billy Preston; and (C) James Taylor. Apple also wanted a booth to promote Apple projects—past, present and future—and show a color film by Mr. & Mrs. John Lennon. As for the Plastic Ono Band, this would be a "series of plastic cylinders incorporated around a stereo sound system" (as depicted on the "Give Peace A Chance" picture sleeve shown on page 17). The July 12 NME reported that John and Yoko were considering attending Woodstock if the U.S. Embassy granted an entry visa to John. There was also talk of John and Yoko fronting an American-assembled group. Apparently no follow-up took place and Apple had no presence at Woodstock.

That muddy festival wound up being unduplicated, although people have tried many times. There was something about it that simply could not be repeated—and it featured perhaps the most notable recording of "The Star-Spangled Banner" anywhere, performed by Jimi Hendrix.

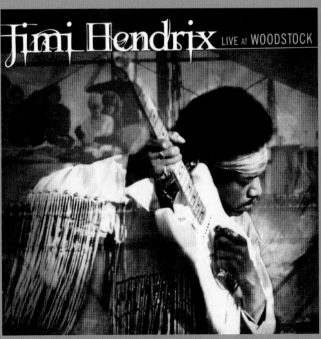

In between albums and singles, you might have taken in a movie or two in 1969. One of the most popular movies of the year was *Goodbye, Columbus*, a drama which featured the Association performing the title song, and Ali McGraw's first starring role. In a different sort of dramatic release, John Wayne won his only Oscar in one of his most heralded Westerns, *True Grit*, in which he portrayed Rooster Cogburn. Glen Campbell's recording of the title song hit #35 on the charts. Another popular Western was the musical *Paint Your Wagon*, starring Clint Eastwood, Lee Marvin and Jean Seberg. In the U.K., Marvin's recording of the film song "Wand'rin' Star" topped the charts in March 1970, incredibly blocking the Beatles "Let It Be" from reaching number one!

On the comedy side, we were treated to the "strange bedfellows" adventures of *Bob & Carol & Ted & Alice*. The only comedy that did better that year at the box office was *The Love Bug*, a Disney live-action film featuring the omnipresent Dean Jones. Jones actually appears in two roles in the movie, with the second being a cameo as a hippie uttering the line, "We ALL prisoners, chicky-baby. We all locked in." The other "star" in the film was Herbie, a Volkswagon Beetle with license number OFP 857, the same type of car that would later appear on the album cover to *Abbey Road*, with license number LMW 28IF. Goldie Hawn won best supporting actress in the comedic farce, *Cactus Flower*, which also featured Walter Matthau and Ingrid Bergman.

Two of the year's more memorable comedies involved robberies. Woody Allen made his directorial debut with *Take The Money And Run*, a mockumentary co-written by Allen (with Mickey Rose) on the life of Virgil Starkwell, an inept bank robber, played by Allen. One of the film's more memorable scenes has Virgil in a prison chain gang singing "Gonna see Miss Liza, gonna go to Mississippi." Another has his attempted robbery of a bank go wrong when a teller and the bank manager have difficulty reading Virgil's handwritten note saying he has a gun. To them, it looks like "gub." By the time it's all sorted out, the police arrive and arrest Virgil. *The Italian Job* is a British comedy caper starring Michael Caine as Charlie Croker, an ex-convict who recruits a team to steal $4,000,000 of gold in Torino, Italy. The plan involves a computer-created traffic jam that allows the robbers to escape with the gold in three Mini Coopers. It contains Caine's classic line, "You're only supposed to blow the bloody doors off!"

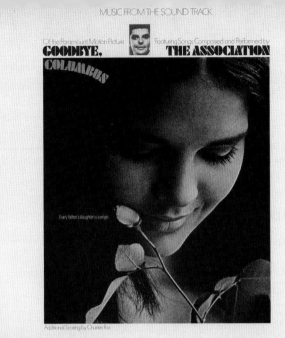

MUSIC FROM THE SOUND TRACK

STEREO
W
1786

Of the Paramount Motion Picture       Featuring Songs Composed and Performed by
**GOODBYE,**                          **THE ASSOCIATION**
**COLUMBUS**

Every father's daughter is a virgin

Additional Scoring by Charles Fox

STEREO ST-263
PARAMOUNT PICTURES Presents

**JOHN WAYNE · GLEN CAMPBELL · KIM DARBY**

IN
HAL WALLIS'
PRODUCTION

**TRUE
GRIT**

A BRAND NEW BRAND OF AMERICAN FRONTIER STORY

**Glen Campbell**
sings the Title Song
"True Grit"
Arranged and Conducted by Al Delory

**Elmer Bernstein**
conducts Themes from his Original Score
Arranged by Artie Butler

Capitol

STEREO
Bell 1201

ORIGINAL SOUND TRACK

**CACTUS FLOWER**

SCORE COMPOSED & CONDUCTED BY
**QUINCY JONES**

FEATURING ....
THE TIME FOR LOVE IS ANYTIME
("CACTUS FLOWER" THEME)
Instrumental by Quincy Jones
Vocal by Sarah Vaughan

bell

COLUMBIA PICTURES
Presents
A FRANKOVICH Production

**WALTER      INGRID
MATTHAU    BERGMAN**

in
**CACTUS
FLOWER**

Introducing GOLDIE HAWN as TONI

Co-starring
**JACK WESTON**    RICK LENZ · VITO SCOTTI · IRENE HERVEY    Screenplay by I.A.L. DIAMOND    Stage Play by ABE BURROWS    Based on a French Play by BARILLET and GREDY    Produced on the New York Stage by DAVID MERRICK    Produced by M.J. FRANKOVICH    Directed by GENE SAKS    TECHNICOLOR

MUSIC FROM THE ORIGINAL MOTION PICTURE SOUNDTRACK
COMPOSED AND CONDUCTED BY

**QUINCY JONES**
**MICHAEL CAINE ... NOËL COWARD**
**THE ITALIAN JOB**
**MATT MONRO ... ON DAYS LIKE THESE**

Several of the year's other noteworthy movies featured memorable music. *Easy Rider* was an instant classic. Peter Fonda, Jack Nicholson, Dennis Hopper and a panorama of motorcycles hum along on the open road, ushering in a renaissance for young filmmakers. Producer Phil Spector is in the movie, but he didn't handle the music; instead, viewers were treated to the Band, Jimi Hendrix, the Byrds and a theme song from Steppenwolf. That song, "Born to Be Wild," wound up giving a name—sort of—to a guitar-oriented style of rock music. "Heavy metal thunder" actually referred to motorcycles, and Rolling Stone magazine had already referred to heavy metal music in 1968, but the expression in a popular song was easy to remember.

James Bond was back in *On Her Majesty's Secret Service*, but this time played by newcomer George Lazenby. The action-packed film featured a touching love song sung by an ailing Louis Armstrong, "We Have All The Time In The World." Ironically, neither Bond's bride Tracy, who dies at the end of the film, nor Armstrong, who died two years later, had much in the way of time. *Midnight Cowboy*, starring Dustin Hoffman and Jon Voight, won the Oscar for best picture. Its theme song was Nilsson's "Everbody's Talkin'," which gave the singer his first hit at number six.

The top-grossing movie of the year was none of the above. It was a buddy drama about two historical figures, with music from BJ Thomas. That's right, *Butch Cassidy and the Sundance Kid*. The movie left everyone wondering "who are those guys" and enjoying the on-screen partnership of Paul Newman and Robert Redford. Thomas racked up a number one hit with "Raindrops Keep Fallin' On My Head," which won the Oscar for best song in a film.

So...when Apple put out *Abbey Road* that fall, it didn't come out in a vacuum. This had been a year of great transitions and triumphs. For the Beatles, *Abbey Road* had been one small step for four men, but it was also an unrepeatable step of evolution: a "giant leap," if you will. It's quite possible that one of the records that you see here, or one of the movies mentioned, brings positive feelings to mind. Maybe one of the artists who released a magnum opus in '69 influenced your favorite record. Or maybe it IS your favorite record. That was 1969: loaded with a diverse group of amazing sounds, images, people and events. The music is still fresh, even though it all happened fifty years ago.

MUSIC FROM THE SOUNDTRACK

THE JIMI HENDRIX EXPERIENCE • THE BYRDS • STEPPENWOLF
ROGER McGUINN • FRATERNITY OF MAN • THE ELECTRIC PRUNES
THE HOLY MODAL ROUNDERS

PANDO COMPANY in association with RAYBERT PRODUCTIONS presents

PETER
FONDA **easy rider** Released by COLUMBIA PICTURES DENNIS
HOPPER

JACK NICHOLSON

DUNHILL abc
STEREO
DSX 50063

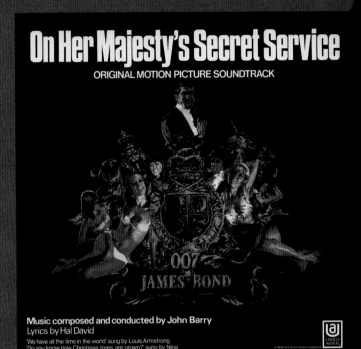

# On Her Majesty's Secret Service

## ORIGINAL MOTION PICTURE SOUNDTRACK

007
JAMES BOND

**Music composed and conducted by John Barry**
Lyrics by Hal David

'We have all the time in the world' sung by Louis Armstrong
'Do you know how Christmas trees are grown?' sung by Nina

UA UNITED
ARTISTS

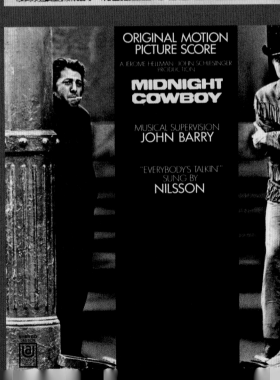

ORIGINAL MOTION
PICTURE SCORE

A JEROME HELLMAN · JOHN SCHLESINGER
PRODUCTION

MIDNIGHT
COWBOY

MUSICAL SUPERVISION
JOHN BARRY

"EVERYBODY'S TALKIN'"
SUNG BY
NILSSON

STEREO

STEREO

ORIGINAL SCORE COMPOSED AND CONDUCTED BY
# Burt Bacharach
FROM THE 20TH CENTURY-FOX PRODUCTION

A&M
RECORDS

SP 4227

PAUL NEWMAN
ROBERT REDFORD
KATHARINE ROSS IN
BUTCH CASSIDY AND
THE SUNDANCE KID

# "It's Just a Nasty Rumor"

## by Bruce Spizer

On January 7, 1967, the M1 motorway linking London to the British Midlands was covered with ice, leading to hazardous driving conditions. That evening, Paul McCartney's black Mini Cooper was involved in a crash on the M1. A rumor quickly spread throughout London that Paul had been killed in the accident. Fans were relieved to find out soon that Paul was alive and well, having answered the phone at his home in St. John's Wood. The February 1967 issue (No. 43) of The Beatles Book reported the incident on its Beatle News page, stating that Paul had been at home all day with his car safely locked up in his garage. The facts were not quite that simple, but Paul's death was indeed a "FALSE RUMOUR."

That Saturday evening, art gallery owner Robert Fraser and his assistant, Mohammed Hadjij, had dropped by Paul's house, later to be joined by Mick Jagger, Keith Richards and Brian Jones of the Rolling Stones and antiques dealer Christopher Gibbs. After a while, the gathering changed locations, first to Jagger's home and then to the Richards' residence. Paul was a passenger in Jagger's Mini Cooper, while Hadjij drove Paul's vehicle. Hadjij lost control of the car and crashed. The vehicle was a total loss and Hadjij was hospitalized.

Although Paul did not blow his mind out in a car, he was involved in a moped accident a year earlier on the evening of December 26, 1965. McCartney was in Liverpool visiting his family, when he decided to ride a rented moped to his cousin Bett's house. He was joined by a friend, Guinness heir Tara Browne, who was following Paul on a separate moped. As Paul was looking at and describing the full moon, he lost his balance and fell to the ground, chipping his tooth and splitting his lip in the process. Most Beatles fans did not learn of Paul's mishap until June 1966 issue (No. 35) of The Beatles Book, which told fans "The TRUTH about PAUL's Tooth." Ironically, Tara Browne would die in an auto crash a year after Paul's moped accident on December 18, 1966. The Daily Mail's story on his death would inspire John's opening verse to "A Day In The Life."

# BEATLE NEWS

## NEIGHBOURS

As most Beatle people know, John and Ringo are close neighbours in Weybridge, Surrey, and naturally, they frequently pop across to see each other.

John often travels across to Ringo on a motor-bicycle. It's quite a sight to see him tearing along the country lanes on his moped.

## FALSE RUMOUR

Stories about the Beatles are always flying around Fleet Street. The 7th January was very icy, with dangerous conditions on the M1 motorway, linking London with the Midlands, and towards the end of the day, a rumour swept London that Paul McCartney had been killed in a car crash on the M1. But, of course, there was absolutely no truth in it at all, as the Beatles' Press Officer found out when he telephoned Paul's St. John's Wood home and was answered by Paul himself who had been at home all day with his black Mini Cooper safely locked up in the garage.

### Moustaches All Round

All the boys have decided that a stiff upper lip is an absolute must for the New Year. Paul's moustache is growing long and black, John's is not so black but longer, George's you have already seen in photographs, and Ringo's is similar to Paul's.

Biggest surprise...

Ringo downs a pint of keg

---

# BEATLE NEWS

## FANTASTIC DEMAND FOR TOKYO TICKETS

The demand for tickets for the three Beatle concerts in Tokyo, scheduled for June 30, July 1st and 2nd, has been so fantastic the boys will be doing two extra shows there.

Over 200,000 fans have applied for tickets and there is only seating for 33,000 at the three concerts at the Budo Kan. By including two matinees on July 1st and 2nd, the boys hope to be able to give more of their fans a chance to see them.

### Manila Visit

After their visit to Japan the Beatles will be off to Manila in the Philippines. They'll play one date and they hope to find time for a brief holiday.

It isn't their first trip there. They spent 30-minutes in Manila waiting for the aircraft to re-fuel, after their Far Eastern tour.

### TV DATES

The boys thought they'd like to ... which ... with the ... le, so on ... were in ... at EMI ... ouse in

... on Top ... on June ... And the ... will see ... the Ed

...

... rmany ... won't ... ul and ... ys in ... mostly ... ve to ... e he

... will ... with

## The TRUTH about PAUL'S Tooth

Following last month's photograph of Paul, showing his broken tooth, we've had hundreds of letters asking how it happened. He went up to Wirral in Cheshire to visit his father and spent some time riding around on his scooter.

One day he fell off and struck his tooth, knocking a chip out of it. Fortunately he wasn't more seriously hurt but he easily could have been.

## MINI - BEATLES

Each of the boys now owns a Mini, as well as a pretty impressive selection of other cars. So we thought you might like to know the line-up at the last count.

John has a black Mini-Cooper with blacked out windows; a black Rolls-Royce with blacked out windows, plus a Ferrari, which he has painted matt black.

George has a black Mini-Cooper, a green Ferrari. Paul has a green Mini-Cooper plus a blue Aston Martin, and Ringo has a maroon Mini-Cooper plus a maroon Facel Vega. He is at present selling his Rolls-Royce through Brian Epstein's garage.

That was it when we checked, but we're not guaranteeing it will stay that way for long!

## CHAUFFEUR CONFUSION

There seems to be a mix-up as to who drives who where!

John's chauffeur is an ex-Guardsman called Anthony, who lives just a little way from John's house, while Alf Bicknell, the official chauffeur for the group has a flat IN John's house.

"It's quite simple really", Alf explained. "Anthony is John's personal chauffeur, but I live in John's house because the lease on my old home ran out and he offered me the flat."

Quite simple really . . . . . . . .

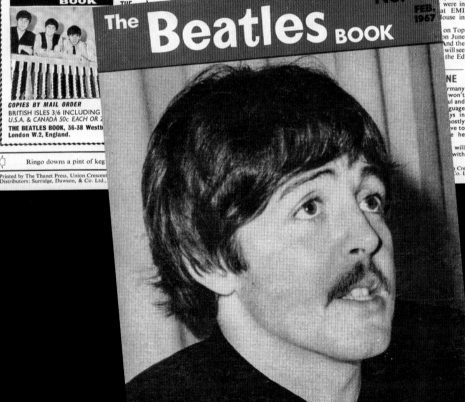

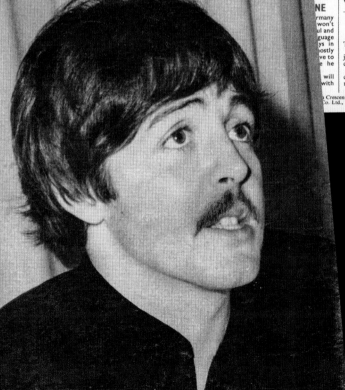

# The Beatles BOOK

**No. 43**

**FEB. 1967**

While the 1967 rumor of Paul's death was quickly disposed of, things were quite different two years later when an elaborate conspiracy theory spread in America about McCartney's death and the clues of his demise planted by the remaining Beatles in their album covers and recordings. The first published account of the 1969 rumor appeared in the student newspaper of Drake University in Des Moines, Iowa. Tim Harper's feature article, titled "Is Beatle Paul McCartney Dead?," ran in The Times-Delphic on September 17, 1969. Harper reported that there had been much conjecture on the university's campus about McCartney's present condition, with an amazing series of photos and lyrics pointing to a "distinct possibility that McCartney may indeed be insane, freaked out, even dead." [Actually, it was Harper's article that started the discussion. The "facts" had come from associate editor Dartanyan Brown, who recounted to Harper a conversation he had over the weekend at his apartment with an unknown woman, who told of secret messages in Beatles albums that suggested Paul was dead.]

Harper wrote that *Sgt. Pepper* had signaled the death of the old Beatles (the boys who made the girls scream) and the emergence of the new Beatles, who took drugs, criticized religion, studied with the Maharishi and had a new sound. The album also dropped hints that all was not well with the Beatles, particularly Paul. On the front cover, there is a hand above Paul's head. This was supposedly an ancient death symbol of either the Greeks or American Indians. [Actually neither culture, or any other for that matter, uses this symbol as a sign of death.] There was also a left-handed guitar lying "on the grave at the group's feet." Harper indicated this was significant because Paul was the only lefty in the group. [Ringo is also left-handed, but facts should never get in the way of a good rumor.] On the back cover, Paul has his back to the camera, while the others face forward. George is pointing to the printed lyric "Wednesday morning at five o'clock," which is the time some famous unnamed person "blew his mind out in a car."

Harper writes that *Magical Mystery Tour* "displayed a major idiosyncrasy." The cover has all four dressed in walrus suits, three gray and one black. Paul is the walrus, which is supposedly the Viking symbol of death. Why does the booklet refer to "4 or 5 musicians"? With *The White Album*, the mystery gets even spookier. "Revolution No. 9" has the sound of a car crash and when played backwards, one hears "Turn me on dead man" and "Cherish the dead." [The former is clearly audible.] In "Glass Onion" we are told: "And here's another clue for you all/The walrus was Paul."

# Is Beatle Paul McCartney Dead ?

**BY TIM HARPER**

Lately on campus there has been much conjecturing on the present state of Beatle Paul McCartney. An amazing series of photos and lyrics on the group's albums point to a distinct possibility that McCartney may indeed be insane, freaked out, even dead.

The Sergeant Pepper album, obviously, signified the "death" of the old Beatles who made girls

scream when they sang "yeah yeah yeah!" The new Beatles blew grass and dropped acid, criticized religion, studied under Maharishi in India, and had a new sound.

This album also started the hints that all was not right with the Beatles, especially Paul. On the front cover a mysterious hand is raised over his head, a sign many believe is an ancient death symbol of either the Greeks or the American Indians. Also, a left-handed guitar (Paul was the only lefty of the four) lies on the grave at the group's feet.

On the back of the same album, George, Ringo and John are smiling out toward the camera, but McCartney has his back turned. George is pointing toward a phrase from the song "A Day in the Life" pertaining to a certain Wednesday morning at five a.m. when some famous but unnamed person "blew his mind out in a car." The other two Beatles looking out are also indicating phrases, one about gaining the world but losing the soul and the other about Wednesday morning at five.

In the centerfold photo of the foursome they are all looking the same direction. The only difference? Paul wears a black arm band.

### Magical Mystery?

The Beatles' next album, Magical Mystery Tour, displayed a major ideosyncracy. On the front of this album all four are dressed in walrus suits, after the top tune on the record, "The Walrus." No faces are visible, but three of the walrus suits are gray; the other is black.

Inside, under the words "The Walrus," there is a phrase saying Paul is the walrus, not John, who sings the song. The walrus is supposedly the Viking symbol of death. In an introductory paragraph to the album, "4 or 5 magicians" are mentioned. Why?

Then came the group's latest album: The Beatles, with an all-white cover. With this record the whole mystery became even more spooky. On the tune "Revolution No. 9" there is a part where a lone deep voice repeats "number nine." When this is played backwards a voice quotes "Turn me on, dead man," and "Cherish the dead," and there are many sound effects, including the noise of a spectacular auto crash.

In another song on the record, "Glass Onion," the Beatles sing "Here is another clue for you all: The Walrus was Paul."

So much for the clues, even though these are only a few of the many people are pointing at. There is a good deal of circumstantial "evidence" available. For instance, Paul used to be the most flamboyant of the foursome; lately Lennon has had the spotlight.

### Imposter?

Sure, people point to Paul's recent marriage to Jane Eastman and the approaching birth of their baby, but there's a kicker: McCartney has a brother, Michael, who could possibly be helping to carry on the hoax.

Another thing: everyone knows Paul was going with English model Jane Asher, so why all of a sudden was he married to Jane Eastman? Also, at the recent Bob Dylan concert at the rock festival on the Isle of Wight, three of the Beatles attended. Paul was conspicuously absent.

Now the discrepancies arise. Why, if something is wrong with Paul, are these clues dropped? It would be just like the Beatles to perpetrate a huge put-on like this, but there just seems to be more to it, such as the phone numbers discernable when the Magical Mystery Tour cover is held up to a mirror.

### Win Island?

One of the wilder rumors has it that if a certain English phone number is called at exactly five a.m. any Wednesday (London time) and the caller tells whoever answers what there is to the mystery and

McCartney
Turn to Page 3

# Drake Times-Delphic
## "The Student Voice"

| | | |
|---|---|---|
| Volume 88 | Wednesday, September 17, 1969 | Number 2 |

Harper then provided circumstantial "evidence," claiming that Paul used to be the most flamboyant Beatle, but now it was John. Paul was dating Jane Asher, but then suddenly married Jane [sic] Eastman. All of the Beatles except Paul attended Bob Dylan's performance at the Isle of Wight Festival on August 31, 1969. This apparently supported the rumor that an impostor had replaced Paul. And Paul had a brother, Michael, who could assist with the hoax. Harper also told of a wild rumor that if you called a certain English number on a Wednesday morning at exactly five o'clock and tell the person answering the call what there is to the mystery and its particulars, the caller wins the Beatles island in the Mediterranean Sea. He admitted that we might never know the truth about this intriguing matter, but it was something to think about.

The following week, the student newspaper of Northern Illinois University, The Northern Star, ran an article titled "Something Wrong With McCartney? Clues Hint at Possible Beatle Death" on September 23. Its author, Barb Ulvilden, plagiarized (word for word, mistakes and all) and slightly edited Harper's piece. The only new "fact" added was the erroneous statement that Paul's brother Michael had dated Miss Eastman.

On Sunday, October 12, 1969, disc jockey Russ Gibb was doing his afternoon shift on Detroit's WKNR-FM. After playing a few tracks from *Abbey Road*, Gibb opened the phone lines for listeners to call in and rap with Uncle Russ. The first caller was a student at Eastern Michigan University, Tom (Zarski), who wanted to talk about Paul McCartney's death. Gibb was skeptical, but became interested when Tom told him that there were clues in the Beatles records, informing Gibb that he needed to play "Revolution No. 9" backwards to hear a special message. Gibb quickly grabbed a copy of *The White Album* and placed the fourth side on a turntable. Tom told him to play the section where the voice repeats "number nine, number nine." Gibb complied, and, to his amazement, heard the repeated phrase "turn me on, dead man, turn me, on dead man." Shortly thereafter, a young man dropped by the station with his copy of Capitol's *Magical Mystery Tour* album. During a commercial break, the man told Gibb he had a clue that proved McCartney was dead. Back on the air, Gibb followed his instructions and played the end of "Strawberry Fields Forever" so his listeners could hear what the young man claimed was Lennon saying "I buried Paul." The rest of the show was spent going over clues found in the album covers and booklets.

University of Michigan student Fred LaBour had caught part of Russ Gibb's show on his car radio and was fascinated with what he heard. He had been assigned the task of writing a review of *Abbey Road* for the school's newspaper, The Michigan Daily, and had been looking for a different approach. The clues to Paul's death provided something truly unique. The next day, LaBour went through a stack of Beatles albums, sat behind his typewriter and knocked out his "review." His editor, John Gray, was impressed and told LaBour that he would devote a full page to the piece. When asked how long he took to write the item, LaBour replied, "It's the best bullshit I ever wrote and it only took an hour and a half."

On the morning of October 14, students began grabbing copies of The Daily Michigan. By noon, all copies were gone, so two more press runs were done to meet demand. It was the talk of the entire campus. An editor's note preceded LaBour's piece "McCartney Dead; New Evidence Brought to Light." John Gray explained to readers that LaBour had been assigned to review *Abbey Road*, but while researching the album's background he chanced upon something more significant. He ended by saying "Mr. LaBour says it's all true." It wasn't and they both knew it.

LaBour's opening was designed to catch everyone's attention: "Paul McCartney was killed in an automobile accident in early November, 1966 after leaving EMI recording studios tired, sad and dejected." LaBour explained that the group was working on a new album, tentatively titled *Smile*, when bickering ensued, causing McCartney to drive off into the rainy night in his Aston-Martin. [*Smile* was never a Beatles project. It was conceived by Beach Boy Brian Wilson.] Paul was found four hours later, decapitated. LaBour then laid the basis for a conspiracy theory: "Thus began the greatest hoax of our time and the subsequent founding of a new religion based upon Paul as Messiah."

According to LaBour, when word reached the studio of Paul's death, the surviving Beatles and George Martin decided to keep the news from the public as long as possible. After all, "Paul always liked a good joke." Harrison buried Paul, Ringo conducted the service and John went into hiding for three days. Lennon then came up with the plan. They would create a false Paul, bring him into the group and slowly release clues to Paul's death in their record albums. Brian Epstein threatened to expose the plot and mysteriously died, leaving only Martin and the Beatles in the know.

The group set up a Paul look-alike contest and recruited its winner, Edinburgh orphan William Campbell, into the fold. He had minor plastic surgery and studied tapes of Paul's voice and singing style. Campbell's mustache would distract people from seeing the minor facial differences. The other Beatles grew their own facial hair to integrate him into the band. When work began on *Sgt. Pepper*, the Beatles current *Smile* album was scrapped and handed off to Beach Boy Brian Wilson, who Paul admired. When Wilson subsequently abandoned *Smile*, he was sued by Capitol Records. In a tribute to Paul, Wilson titled the next Beach Boys album *Smiley Smile*.

Lennon and Martin then went to work on *Sgt. Pepper*, crafting an album that would be an artistic and monetary success filled with clues of Paul's death. The cover depicts a grave, with yellow flowers at the bottom shaped as Paul's bass and the letter "P." In the gatefold photo, the patch on the fake Paul's sleeve reads "OPD," standing for Officially Pronounced Dead. He wears a British war medal honoring a heroic death. On the back cover, the fake Paul has his back to the camera. Paul's car accident was referenced in the opening verse to "A Day In The Life." The concept of the album was a different group, yet "the one you've known for all these years." Martin emerged as a composer, bringing in his old-time piano tunes such as "When I'm Sixty-Four" and later "Maxwell's Silver Hammer." At the end of "Strawberry Fields Forever," a single recorded during *Sgt. Pepper*, John mumbles "I buried Paul."

*Magical Mystery Tour* is also full of clues. There are numerous pictures of Paul where a hand appears behind his head—a mystic symbol of death. A picture of fake Paul on page three has a sign saying "I YOU WAS," indicating the change of identity. Page five shows policemen and surgeons, who would have been involved after Paul's death. On pages 10 and 13, Paul has black trousers and no shoes, which is how dead men are buried. The empty shoes appearing on page 13 by Ringo's drums are a Grecian death symbol. And on page 23, the picture of the group on the staircase has Paul wearing a black flower, while the others have red ones. "Magical Mystery Tour" implies this is all a hoax. The group is "dying to take you away." "The Fool On The Hill" is "perfectly still" with a "foolish grin," characteristics of a dead man. "Blue Jay Way" is full of Eastern mysticism and religious fervor, bringing in the religious nature of the plot. "I Am The Walrus" has the death passage from King Lear and "walrus" is Greek for corpse. Played backwards, you can hear "Paul is dead." With "All You Need Is Love," Lennon develops his fledgling religion.

LaBour then goes totally off the rails, stating as fact that Paul was a homosexual. In "Yellow Submarine" you hear "Paul's a queer," answered with "Aye, aye, Captain." Thus, the plotters did not need to deal with girlfriends. Paul rarely saw his dad and had few friends. Campbell was the key to the hoax, being able to play the part perfectly. A girlfriend was needed to keep females away, so Peter Asher's sister, Jane, was paid to pretend she was with Paul. When the fake Paul later married Linda, Jane was whisked out of the public eye, giving the plotters more confidence.

Campbell was then given a more prominent part in the group and allowed to use his natural voice on "Lady Madonna," leading many listeners to first think the song was sung by Ringo. Campbell's "tough guy" singing style would continue through *Abbey Road*. The pure white cover of *The White Album* showed Lennon's "further adoption of a God-like image and an ever increasing sense of the value of purity of purpose to the plot." The collage poster shows Paul lying in a pool of water, deceased, with half his head missing. Campbell's passport picture is in the lower left corner. "Back In The U.S.S.R." is a thank you to Brian Wilson for *Smile*. In "Dear Prudence" John is begging Paul to open up his eyes. Prudence was John's nickname for Paul during their Nurk [sic] Twins days. "Revolution No. 9" had chaos, religious absolution and the backwards tape "Turn me on, dead man."

All of the above lead up to *Abbey Road*, whose title was significant because "Monks live in abbeys." On the cover, John is in white, representing an anthropomorphic god, followed by: Ringo the undertaker; barefoot Paul, resurrected with a cigarette in his right hand; and George the gravedigger. They have just walked out of a cemetery [actually EMI Studios] on the left of the street. Paul is being "led out of the tomb, thereby conquering death with a little help from his friends," a "symbolic resurrection." "Maxwell's Silver Hammer" is a song of religious justice. "Octopus's Garden" is slang for a cemetery where navel heroes are buried. "I Want You (She's So Heavy)" is John trying to pull the buried Paul out of the earth. Side Two of *Abbey Road* "announces the principals upon which the religion will be based: beauty, humor, love, realism, objectivity." The medley covers interpersonal relationships, money grubbers, fad followers and a realistic view of life, "Boy, you're gonna carry that weight a long time." At the medley's end, they proclaim "the love you take is equal to the love you make." But at the very end, they joke about the Queen. "The Beatles are building a mighty church, and when you emerge from it, you will be laughing, for Paul is the Sun of God."

Although anyone reading LaBour's article should have noticed its satirical aspects and numerous outright false statements, there was enough truth mixed in to allow one to come away thinking it must be true. After all, he was right about so much and provided explanations for things many people had wondered about. Much to LaBour's surprise, details contained in his story were picked up by newspapers and radio stations throughout America. LaBour's source and inspiration for his story, Russ Gibb and WKNR-FM, added more fuel to fire by broadcasting a two-hour special titled "The Beatle Plot" on October 19.

By this time, LaBour's totally made up clues were accepted as fact. Nobody bothered to check to see if "walrus" was really the Greek word for corpse. It wasn't. But, in all fairness, Google was decades away. The total creepiness of actually hearing "Turn me on, dead man" over and over again when playing "Revolution No. 9" backwards caused many to hear things that were not there. If an important clue told us John was saying "I buried Paul" at the end of "Strawberry Fields Forever," then it must be so, even if he was really saying "Cranberry sauce." If you were supposed to hear "Paul is dead man, miss him, miss him" at the end of "I'm So Tired," you did.

The story of Paul's supposed demise ran rampart on college campuses. Word of the September 17 article in the Drake Times-Delphic spread to other universities via friends phoning each other. At Ohio Wesleyan, John Summer heard the story and became one of its most vocal proponents, initially on campus and then beyond. Even middle school and high school students were discussing the clues and really wondering if Paul was, in fact, dead.

The story moved from mid-America to the East and West Coasts. New York's WABC and WMCA picked up on the "Paul is dead" rumor, with WABC disc jockey Roby Yonge breaking format on October 21 by discussing the topic on his shift, causing the station manager to pull him off the air. But most radio stations saw the topic as ratings gold, quickly putting together their own specials discussing the clues and speculating as to whether Paul was dead or alive. By October 21, major newspapers such as The Chicago Sun-Times, The Chicago Tribune, The New York Times and The Washington Post ran stories. The ABC television network ran a two-minute story on its October 23 evening news. Local TV stations got in on the action, with Chicago's WLS chartering a private plane for Tim Harper's appearance.

In New Orleans, radio station WTIX quickly realized that the "Paul is dead" story was a ratings bonanza. According to station manager Bob Mitchell, promo man Bob Robin told the station that they needed a theme song for their planned special. Robin recruited singer Lenny Capello to write and record a suitable tribute. Years earlier, Capello had minor local hits with "Cotton Candy" and "90 Pound Weakling," and in 1970 would score a number six hit on WTIX with "Tippicaw Calley" as Lenny Damon and the Bah Humbug Band. Capello co-wrote "Brother Paul" with his writing partner Rocky Saxon and recorded the song at Traci Borges' Knight Recording Studios in Metairie, part of the greater New Orleans metro area. The song was credited to Billy Shears and the All Americans. WTIX immediately added the song to its playlist, not bothering to wait for the record to be pressed. Based on listener demand, a single was quickly issued on Silver Fox Records out of Nashville, with over 40,000 copies made. Its opening verse was: "Brother Paul, I'm crying/Are you really lying/Every night and day/Beneath the cold and lonely stone?"

In Baltimore, Bob Brady & the Con Chords recorded "The Ballad Of Paul" under the name "The Mystery Tour." It got straight to the point: "Has Paul McCartney left this world?/Has he taken his last breath?/Have John and George and Ringo/Told us of his death?" The song charted at #104 in the November 29 Billboard Bubbling Under chart. Jose Feliciano, a blind guitarist who scored a number three 1968 hit with his flamenco-influenced interpretation of the Doors "Light My Fire," also got into the act, recording "So Long, Paul." Although Billboard announced the song under his name, the disc listed the artist as "Werbley Finster." The song referenced "A Hard Day's Night" and "I Want To Hold Your Hand" and ended with "So long, Paul/We hate to see you go/So long, Paul/After making all that dough."

Capitol Records joined the fun by re-releasing the single "Saint Paul" by Terry Knight, who would soon make a fortune as the manager of Grand Funk Railroad. Knight had met with McCartney in 1968 to discuss recording for Apple, but reportedly turned down the offer. He later signed with Capitol and in the spring of 1969 recorded "Saint Paul." The lyrics referenced Apple's business troubles ("Sir Isaac Newton said it'd have to fall" and "You knew it all along/Something had gone wrong"), but also were somewhat spiritual with its opening reference to the sky and "Did I hear you call/Or was I dreaming then, Saint Paul?" Many cluesters noted that this single was on the Beatles U.S. label and that the song's publisher was Maclen Music, which published the Beatles songs in the United States.

## SILVER FOX

Shelby Singleton
Music—BMI
Crawdad Music
BMI
Produced by
Bob Robin for
Shelby Singleton
Productions Inc.

12 ‖ 1
711-767
Time 2:51
Arranged by
Bob & Staff

"BROTHER PAUL"
(P. Saxon—L. Capello)
BILLY SHEARS
AND THE ALL AMERICANS
A Division of The Shelby Singleton Corp., Nashville, Tenn. U.S.A.

## M·G·M

### SPECIAL DISC JOCKEY RECORD

NOT
FOR SALE

Cascargo Music
BMI
4:30

K14097
(106,545)

THE BALLAD OF PAUL
(Evans-Brady)
THE MYSTERY TOUR
Prod. By B.O.F. Talent Management, Inc.

MGM RECORDS—A DIVISION OF METRO-GOLDWYN-MAYER INC.—MADE IN U.S.A.

## RCA

WERBLEY FINSTER

Producer: Rick Jarrard

STEREO
PLUG
74-0290

NOT
FOR SALE

Johi Music
Pub. Co., Inc./
Cymbeline
Music Co.,
BMI
XPKS-0688
3:15

SO LONG, PAUL
(J. & H. Feliciano-Jarrard)

TMK(s) ® REGISTERED · MARCA(s) REGISTRADA(s)
RADIO CORPORATION OF AMERICA—MADE IN U.S.A.

SAINT PAUL
(T. Knight)

STEREO

PROMOTIONAL
RECORD

Maclen
Music Inc.
BMI-5:35

P-2506
(S45-72279)

A GOOD
KNIGHT
PRODUCTION

Capitol

Hey Jude
Lennon-
McCartney)
Maclen
Music, Inc.
Used by
Permission

NOT
FOR SALE

TERRY KNIGHT
Arranged & Directed
By Tom Baker

Were the Beatles themselves behind the song? After all, it was published by their Maclen Music rather than Knight's publishing company, Storybook Music. That would point to the group's involvement. However, that was not the case. When the single was initially issued earlier in the year, the label listed "Storybook Music" and did not contain the reference to "Hey Jude" that was added to later pressings of the disc. Apparently Knight heard from Maclen's lawyers after the single's release when people noticed its use of the melody of "Hey Jude." Rather than being sued, Knight gave up the publishing to Maclen, which retroactively granted permission for his use of "Hey Jude."

There was also the pun-titled "We're All Paulbearers" by Zacherias and the Tree People (led by Nashville musician Zack Van Arsdale). Its lyrics ran though some of the clues and concluded with "If it's a hoax/We're none the wiser/ Why make people cry?/We're all Paulbearers, you and I."

None of these "Paul is dead" records were big sellers as they didn't hit the stores until various times in November. By then, the rumor was beginning to lose its steam. After weeks of seclusion, McCartney resurfaced, assuring fans that all was well. This was in contrast to how he initially handled the matter.

When Paul was first told of the rumor by Beatles publicist Derek Taylor, he did not take it seriously, finding it amusing and believing it would quickly run its course. He saw no need to appear in public to reassure his fans he was alive and well, instead relying on Apple to make a statement. Paul stayed in his home in St. John's Wood with his family. When the rumor persisted, he issued a Mark Twain-style denial of his death: "I am alive and well and unconcerned about the rumours of my death. But if I were dead, I would be the last to know." Paul's remarks were published in several newspapers on October 22, but little changed. Many thought, "But if he were really alive, he would have appeared in public." Paul and his family sought seclusion at his farmhouse in Scotland, but he was tracked down by a reporter and photographer from Life magazine. Angered by this invasion of his privacy, Paul cursed at them and doused them with a bucket of water. Upon realizing how his conduct could affect his image, McCartney calmed down and agreed to answer questions and be photographed with his family. Life ran the story and pictures in its November 7 issue, with Paul and his family appearing on the cover.

# LIFE

## Paul is still with us

Paul and
his family
last week
in Scotland

NOVEMBER 7 · 1969 · 40¢

The cover of the November 15 Rolling Stone assured readers that "Paul is not dead." Inside, the magazine ran through the clues from Fred LaBour's article in the Daily Michigan, dismissing it as "the fodder for the pseudo-authenticated bullshit that makes a good rumor." Disc jockey E. Alvin Davis of KLEO in Wichita bragged that he was doing all that he could to spread the rumor even though he didn't necessarily believe it. To him, it did not matter whether it was true or not. It was entertaining and had lots of listeners talking about it. The magazine slammed the Midwest with its "cynical rumor-mongers spreading what they know to be bullshit" and noted that the canard had spread to New York, where WABC disc jockey Roby Yonge was pulled off the air for "perpetrating the nasty rumor."

Nasty or not, the rumor had a positive effect on the sales of Beatles albums. The November 5, 1969, Variety ran an article titled "Rumors of McCartney's Death Put Beaucoup Life Into 'Abbey Road' Sales." The interest generated by talk of Paul's demise and the hunt for clues not only sparked additional sales of *Abbey Road*, but also pushed three other Beatles albums back into the Billboard Top LP's chart. People were buying *Sgt. Pepper's Lonely Hearts Club Band*, *Magical Mystery Tour* and *The White Album* in hopes of learning about the clues spread throughout their covers, posters, booklets and records. While Capitol played no part in starting the rumor, the company did nothing to dispel talk of McCartney's death. When Capitol re-issued Terry Knight's "Saint Paul," it ran a full-page ad in the trade magazines with the following cryptic text: "Written in London, November, 1968/Recorded in March, 1969/Released: April, 1969/Now you understand its significance." Apparently few did. While the rumor reinvigorated Beatles LP sales, Knight's single failed to re-enter the charts (having previously charted for two weeks at No. 114 in the Billboard Bubbling Under chart in summer 1969 based on sales in Knight's home town of Detroit).

But was it just a nasty rumor or was it more complex than that? The January 1967 rumor of Paul's death was quickly disposed of and forgotten. But the 1969 "Paul is dead" story refused to die. While most people were relieved to learn that Paul was alive and well, others were not convinced, still believing that Paul had died and was replaced by a look-alike. And fifty years later, there are still those who adamantly insist that it's a fake Paul, or "Faul," that came to be on *Sgt. Pepper* and is still with us today. If you want to believe it, their arguments can seem quite convincing. This staying power shows that the "Paul is dead" story was more than just a nasty rumor—it is a conspiracy theory.

# 28 IF: The "Paul is dead" Conspiracy Theory

## by Fox Feynman

As psychology professor Christopher French told Scientific American, "Although conspiracy beliefs can occasionally be based on a rational analysis of the evidence, most of the time they are not. As a species, one of our greatest strengths is our ability to find meaningful patterns in the world around us and to make causal inferences. We sometimes, however, see patterns and causal connections that are not there, especially when we feel that events are beyond our control. … We all have a natural inclination to give more weight to evidence that supports what we already believe and ignore evidence that contradicts our beliefs. The real-world events that often become the subject of conspiracy theories tend to be intrinsically complex and unclear. Early reports may contain errors, contradictions and ambiguities, and those wishing to find evidence of a cover-up will focus on such inconsistencies to bolster their claims." (Thea Buckley, "Why Do Some People Believe in Conspiracy Theories?" SA Mind, 26:4:72, July 2015)

A conspiracy theory applies induction to the facts in evidence, but it looks at the information differently. Merely believing a different interpretation of the same facts is not a "conspiracy theory." Since no volume of opinion establishes a fact, the minority viewpoint may actually be the more truthful one. However, what we call conspiracy theories are characterized by beliefs that: (1) a group of people has deliberately concealed the truth; (2) there is secret knowledge available that reveals the truth; (3) the theory explains why things are not what someone wants, or why the world is out of control; and (4) the less probable the theory is, the more convinced we are that it has to be true.

"If my life is not working out or the people around me on the street don't do what I want or don't look how I'd like them, it's easier to imagine that there is a group or entity out there making that happen. Something totally beyond my control." (Paul Ratner, "Why Your Brain Loves Conspiracy Theories," Big Think Edge, June 17, 2018)

The conspiracy helps us cope with something that might be unacceptable or hard to deal with. There are those who believe the world is flat. Part of this belief system in modern times seems to stem from a distrust for government. When the Apollo astronauts beamed pictures of the round earth from space and later landed on the moon, some people simply refused to believe this. And so, the U.S. faked the moon landing. In the years that followed, they found perceived flaws in the pictures. They assert that no one has ever circumnavigated the globe across what they think is the edge. Never mind all the evidence or asking why you would fake it six times or how thousands in NASA and U.S. government could keep six fake landings a secret. And that is why Paul McCartney is dead.

It is October 1969. We have been hearing since 1966 that the Beatles are breaking up. This time, they haven't released a full album in almost a year. Since that time, John Lennon has released two solo singles. Both John and George have released solo albums. Ringo has been filming a movie without the others, and Paul is off somewhere by himself. You just purchased their latest album, which appears to conclude with a song entitled "The End"—containing Paul's devastating words, "And in the end, the love you take is equal to the love you make." It's about a breakup. You're in college now, but you have followed the Fab Four since they first appeared on The Ed Sullivan Show in February 1964. Their breakup would mean something for you like the lost innocence of Jackie Paper growing up in the story of "Puff (The Magic Dragon)."

The story was brewing in the papers since Tim Harper wrote about it in the Drake Times-Delphic on September 17, 1969, but now it was all starting to "Come Together." Maybe this is why Russ Gibb's broadcast from WKNR-FM in Detroit on October 12th meant so much to you. You heard a guy named Tom Zarski call in, explaining that there was a rumor that Paul McCartney was dead, and there was a secret message proving it. The phrase "number nine" from that crazy song "Revolution 9" was actually "Turn me on, dead man" when played backwards! The radio audience flipped out, and the station manager wanted Gibb to keep promoting it.

Fred LaBour, who went on to be an integral part of the band Riders in the Sky, heard a few people call into Gibb's program with what they thought were clues to Paul's death, and two days later his own article appeared. That article was a send-up. It wasn't serious. Called "McCartney Dead; New Evidence Brought to Light," it actually made fun of what he had heard on the broadcast—even making up clues. Instead of prompting people to think it was silly, LaBour's article fueled the fire. Within a week, articles were popping up everywhere about it.

You used induction. You put the information together yourself. When you listened to songs, you heard: "Turn me on, dead man" ("Revolution 9"); "I buried Paul" ("Strawberry Fields Forever"); "Paul is dead, man, miss him, miss him" ("I'm So Tired"); "He blew his mind out in a car/He didn't notice that the lights had changed/A crowd of people stood and stared/They'd seen his face before" ("A Day in the Life"); "I'm sorry that I doubted you/I was so unfair/You were in a car crash, and you'd lost your hair" ("Don't Pass Me By"); and "He hit a light pole/Better go to see a surgeon" ("Revolution 9").

These things couldn't mean that Paul was dead; therefore, he had to be dead, and you now had secret knowledge proving it. Everything you looked at, and everything you heard, fit in with that theory. If someone holds a hand over Paul's head in a photo, it means he's dead. Paul has his back to the camera on the back cover of *Sgt. Pepper.* It means he's dead. In the *Magical Mystery Tour* booklet, he wears a black flower while the others have red flowers. It means he's dead. The more ridiculous it seemed, the further down the rabbit hole you went.

Paul had been in an automobile accident in early November 1966—probably on the 8th, that "stupid bloody Tuesday." He was rushed to a hospital and was "OPD—Officially Pronounced Dead" on the morning of the 9th ("number nine")—"Wednesday morning at five o'clock." But wait! If Paul died in 1966, who sings on *Sgt. Pepper* and the records after that? It must be someone named Billy—nicknamed "Billy Shears." Yes, we've found the truth that no one wants us to know, but that the Beatles themselves have been trying to "leak" to us gently for three years with clue after clue.

Let's revisit how conspiracy theories operate: This is what people don't want us to know, but we have secret knowledge available that reveals the truth. The Beatles aren't really breaking up; Paul is dead! The more ridiculous the secret-death theory seems, the more that means it is true.

We can look at every bit of evidence in more than one way and we can find whatever we want in it. The cover of *Abbey Road* is proof positive that Paul is dead. John is dressed in white, representing an angel or a priest residing over Paul's funeral. George is in blue jeans, just like a grave digger would dress. Ringo is wearing black, so he's the funeral director or mortician. Paul is barefoot, which is how many people are buried. And aren't his eyes shut? Just like a dead man. And look, he is out-of-step with the others, meaning he is not one of the Beatles. And in "Come Together," John sings "One and one and one is three/Got to be good looking 'cause he's so hard to see." Paul was always the cute one. Now he's hard to see because he's dead. And look, this all ties in with the cover of *Yesterday And Today* where the boys are standing around a steamer trunk. If you turn the album cover sideways, it looks like Paul is lying in a coffin! And who has his hand on the lid of the coffin? Why it's Ringo, the funeral director, closing Paul's coffin! Never mind that *Yesterday And Today* came out in June 1966, five months before Paul died in the car crash. We give great weight to what supports our belief and ignore what doesn't.

And then there's the license plate on the Volkswagen Beetle parked at the side of Abbey Road. It represents Beatle Paul. The number on the plate is **LMW 28IF**. The Beatles are telling us "**28 IF M**cCartney **W**ere **L**iving." Never mind that Paul would have been 27. We can just ignore it's a year off. After all, it's only one year. Or maybe **LMW** means "**L**inda **M**cCartney **W**eeps." Never mind that Linda did not meet Paul until 1967, so why would she weep over the death of the real McCartney in 1966 when the only Paul she knew was an impostor? We can overlook that, too.

And what about that Terry Knight's "Saint Paul" single on Capitol? The song bemoaned what was happening to the Beatles: "You [Paul] knew it all along/Something had gone wrong/They [the public] couldn't hear your song of sadness in the air." It's a melancholy song that takes a musical snapshot of life in the late '60s. "I think there's something wrong/It's taking you too long to change the world," and so the Beatles were destined to break up: "Sir Isaac Newton said it had to fall."

Capitol Records released the single in April 1969 to indifference everywhere except Knight's home town of Detroit. If we fast-forward to October, people all around the country are getting requests for "Saint Paul." People are claiming that it is about Paul's death and Capitol smells record sales. They promote the single's re-release in a manner that is cleverly ambiguous. It paraphrases the line "did Judas really talk to you, or did you put the whole world on"—leaving the possibilities open that the song was, or was NOT, about Paul's death. The ad explains that the song was written in 1968, and "Now you understand its significance." Does that mean you realize Paul is dead, or are you supposed to recognize that the song was about something else entirely? Knight confronted the reality of change that was embodied in the perceived break-up of the Beatles and the struggles of Apple.

As a side point, "Saint Paul" makes passing references to Paul McCartney as the Biblical "Saint Paul." When Knight sings, "did Judas really talk to you, or did you put us on," all Bible readers should realize that the historical Paul never spoke to Judas Iscariot. Instead, it was Jesus who had appeared to Paul on the road to Damascus. Terry Knight probably changed the word "Jesus" to "Judas" so that the song would not be controversially asking Paul McCartney if Jesus had spoken to him. No need to reignite that "Beatles are more popular than Jesus" controversy again. But while Knight dodged that bullet, he may have unintentionally fueled the rumor. Although none of the lyrics are about someone's death, we can certainly interpret them that way if we wish to do so.

The speed and depth in which the "Paul is dead" story spread is also worth noting. In 1969, there was no Facebook or Twitter to share our knowledge of Paul's supposed death and the hidden clues with others. We could not go on Instagram to see images of the clues. We had to find them ourselves on our album covers. We could not go to YouTube to hear the backwards messages. We had to play our records backwards on our own turntables. (Although the Internet was over two decades away, the first message transmitted between computers at different locations took place on October 29, 1969, when UCLA student Charley Kline sent the letters "L" and "O" to a Stanford computer 350 miles away in Menlo Park, California as part of ARPANET, the Advanced Research Projects Agency Network.)

Like other famous conspiracy theories, there are still people today who believe that Paul died in a car crash and was replaced by a look-alike. There's another school of thought claiming that the "hoax" was a Beatles publicity stunt. Maybe it's a legend now, but the Paul-is-Dead theories show how important the Beatles were back then.

The Beatles

2531

Ballad of John and Yoko

Old Brown Shoe

**The Beatles**

**Old Brown Shoe**

Ballad of John and Yoko

# FAN RECOLLECTIONS

I was 13 years old in 1969. My friend Cassie's birthday was coming up and she was having a slumber party. Cassie's mom ran a preschool and was letting Cassie use the big classroom for the occasion. A whole bunch of noisy, excited 13-year-old girls arrived to find a huge, empty room with a record player set up in the middle.

For her birthday, Cassie got some great presents, but the only one that I was really interested in, being a huge Beatles fan, was the newly released *Abbey Road* LP. We all gathered around the record player to hear the brand new album.

We listened. I could hardly breathe, I was overwhelmed, it was simply stunning. I had to hear it again. As the other girls all got involved with party games and teenage girl talk, I played *Abbey Road* over and over. As the night got later, my friends, one by one, began to fall asleep. I sat next to the record player and listened to *Abbey Road* from beginning to end, again and again. From the instantly arresting "Come Together" to the passion of "Oh! Darling" and the hypnotic "I Want You (She's So Heavy)" followed by (my favorite) breath of fresh air, "Here Comes the Sun," through Side Two's majestic journey to the end, I was spellbound. After a while I looked around and saw that everyone else in the room had fallen fast asleep. I was the only one awake; I had stayed up the entire night listening! I put the needle back on Side Two as I sat in the middle of the room with my friends sleeping quietly all around me. I watched the sunrise as I listened to "Here Comes The Sun."

Although sadly I have no pictures from that magical evening, the above photo shows me holding my sleeping bag under my arm for a slumber party of a different kind. It is a still from The Brady Brunch episode "The Slumber Caper," which aired in October 1970, exactly one year after my *Abbey Road* slumber party. I played the role of Jenny, who unfairly gets uninvited and then later re-invited to Marcia's slumber party. Holding the pail and covered in flour is Robert Reed, who played the father, Mike Brady.

In 1982, when I married Laurence Juber, I walked down the aisle to "Here Comes The Sun."

Hope Juber

Finally! The wait was over! When the student newspaper, The Daily Tar Heel, announced that the local record shop in downtown Chapel Hill had copies of *Abbey Road*, I think I left skid marks down Franklin Street going to claim my copy!

It was Fall of '69. The album became the sound track of my four years at the University of North Carolina. Spring is beautiful on the UNC campus. I remember walking to class, passing open dorm windows and hearing "Here Comes the Sun" or "Come Together." Because spring ushers in a new beginning, I had hopes that the incredible music offered on *Abbey Road* would not be the Beatles last album. How could it be? Their vocals on songs such as "Because" were so beautiful and they were so "together" as a band. Certainly this couldn't be "The End."

*Abbey Road* IS my favorite album. I play it when I wish to remember those halcyon days in Chapel Hill. Consistently, whenever I close my eyes and listen to this album, I can almost smell the azaleas and roses, and feel the gentle breeze blowing through my dorm windows as I played *Abbey Road* over and over.

Gene Flanagan

On the morning *Abbey Road* was released, I was in my car on my way to work. I was listening to music on the car radio when the DJ announced a song from the new Beatles album. The song "Oh! Darling" started playing. Paul had not finished singing the first lyrics when I pulled over and stopped at the side of the road. This was the first I had heard of the album and I couldn't believe what I was hearing. The song wasn't anything like the Beatles had done previously. And Paul's voice wasn't anything like I had heard from him before. It was awesome. I sat there, in my car, as morning traffic passed by listening to this remarkable song until it finished. The song was incredible; it just blew me away. As I resumed my drive to work, I remember shaking my head, thinking, "The Beatles have done it again! A No. 1 album!"

The next day I bought a copy of *Abbey Road* on 8 track cartridge and played it, for weeks, every time I got in the car. I am 76 years old and have been a lifelong Beatles fan. And while it is impossible for me to choose a favorite Beatles song or album, if I was forced to choose—if it was a matter of life or death—I would have to pick "Oh! Darling" and *Abbey Road* as my all-time favorites.

Larry Borders

I remember the anticipation of the *Abbey Road* album release. Music City in Kenmore Square, Boston announced it was flying someone in from the U.K. with 50 copies of the British pressing of the LP, which was being released earlier than in America. It was first come first served and I was number one in line having waited six hours for the store to open! So, it's possible that I might have been one of the first in the country to own a store copy. My vinyl copy is the U.K. glossy cover version (PCS-7088) with a plain black inner sleeve. Pretty darn cool.

John Giglio

I was just turning 12 in October 1969 when I went with my hard saved pocket money to a warehouse store (there were not many record stores at that time in Switzerland), where I bought my first ever longplay record, *Abbey Road* by the Beatles.

I played it to death on the record player of my parents, which was part of their radio equipment in the living room. You had to lift the top to play the record. Although I bought may other Beatles records in the coming years, *Abbey Road* was my first and still is my favorite Beatles album.

Marcel Reichmuth

I graduated high school in June of 1969. The latest Beatles controversy exploded just in time for the festivities. Many Top 40 stations around the country were puzzled about what to do with "The Ballad Of John And Yoko." They certainly wanted to play the latest Beatles single, but lots of stations feared offending their communities by airing the song complete with the line "Christ you know it ain't easy."

The two great AM Top 40 stations in my hometown of Worcester, Massachusetts solved the problem, each in a different way. WORC 1310 simply spliced out the offending word. WAAB 1440 had a different solution. They dropped a metallic sounding "No-No" over "Christ." It may be hard to believe in these raunchy times that such measures were even necessary, but at least listeners in Central Massachusetts were able to hear the song on their radios.

*Abbey Road* was released at the end of September 1969, just about two weeks after I started my first full-time radio job. The Beatles were about half the reason I wanted to be a DJ. The other half was how much I loved Top 40 radio.

The Beatles had already been my favorite band for five years by this time. I was beyond excited that I'd be playing their newest songs on the radio, except it turned out I wasn't going to unless I took it upon myself. WTWN in St. Johnsbury, Vermont was a little station located exactly in the middle of nowhere. No record promo people ever got near the place and the station's older management was happy with its large MOR (middle of the road) library. So, as the new young jock, if I wanted to play the hits for two hours every night on my shift, I would have to go out and buy the records myself, thus reducing my $80 a week salary. No problem. The thrill of playing the Beatles on the radio was worth every penny.

Clyde Anderson

Shortly after *Abbey Road* was issued in the fall of 1969, my very cool sixth grade teacher, Mr. Lambrous, told the class that we were going to have a "relax and hang out day" the following day. He asked us to bring our favorite albums to school. He would bring his portable phonograph player so that we could all listen to the records.

My friends and I thought it would be the perfect time to bring the new Beatles *Abbey Road* album to share with him and the class. And sure enough, we did just that. Needless to say, the entire class loved it! Even Mr. Lambrous loved it! The turntable was positioned right by the open sunshiny window of the classroom as the weather was so nice in Arizona in the fall. Even those who passed by were rockin' to the album and began forming a small crowd outside the window! We played the album through a couple of times by demand. What an incredible time-stamped memory this has always been for me.

Looking back on the quality of the album now, it's hard to believe that the band was going through a bit of personal discord at the time they were involved in what would be their last recording sessions as a group. The fact *Abbey Road* turned out so beautifully is a testament to the magic and chemistry of the band as a single unit. Indeed, a chemistry that transcended even their own humanity when united. It's truly no wonder that *Abbey Road* remains their all time best selling studio album. It certainly deserves the accolades it continues to receive.

Perry Cox

I remember that by the time the *Abbey Road* LP was released, the "establishment" was finally coming around. Even shoe stores here in Buffalo, New York had a couple dozen copies by the cash register!

John Bonato

Born in 1965 in Sydney, Australia, I was a little young for any serious recollections of *Abbey Road* when it came out (although my older brother, a rabid Rolling Stones fan, purchased it upon release, so I was certainly exposed to it). However, I do have an interesting recollection of "The Ballad Of John And Yoko."

Having discovered the Beatles in a big way in the 3rd grade (1973) via weekday morning re-runs of the Beatles cartoon series, and a year or two later beginning guitar lessons inspired by their music, I set about acquiring Beatles albums whenever and however possible. One of the first ones I owned was *Hey Jude*, which included "The Ballad Of John And Yoko."

Coming from a Catholic family, it was pretty soon pointed out to me that that particular song was not to be played in our house due to its blasphemous chorus lyric, so I complied (to an extent—it was such a fun and easy song to play on an acoustic guitar!). My older brother told me that, when it had come out in 1969, the biggest radio station in Sydney at the time—2SM—had edited the offending word out, since that particular station was owned by the Catholic Church.

I found this hard to believe and had never heard the song on the radio since becoming "Beatle-aware;" that was, until December of 1980, when 2SM (like every other rock/pop radio station in Sydney) was saturated with Beatles and Lennon music. Sure enough, the song eventually came on the radio, and I finally heard what my brother had been talking about: at each chorus, in place of the Lord's name, they had gone to the trouble of editing in an up-down strum of an E-chord on 12-string acoustic guitar! Bizarre as it sounds, it actually worked, and I can imagine that, over an AM transistor radio in 1969, someone unfamiliar with the lyrics would have been none the wiser.

Michael McIntosh

1969 was a great year for rock albums. Between September and December alone the following albums came out: *Led Zeppelin II*, *In The Court Of The Crimson King* by King Crimson, *Volunteers* by Jefferson Airplane, *Monster* by Steppenwolf, *To Our Children's Children's Children* by the Moody Blues, *Willie And The Poor Boys* by Creedence Clearwater Revial and *Let it Bleed* by the Rolling Stones. The thing to do then (at age 14) was to get together with friends and LISTEN to these albums from start to finish, half of the time in some hushed state of near-reverence.

*Abbey Road* came as a bit of a surprise on its release, at least to me, in that I don't recall much in the way of advance hype for the album. What I do remember most was just how magnificent it sounded at the time, particularly after the so-so singles that preceded it. The music, the harmonies, the overall sound, the imaginative production. And what a mind-blower that second side suite was. Purely from an audio perspective, this was taste of what was to come in the '70s with advances in analog recording and mastering. And it STILL sounds great on my vintage Japanese pressing.

Robert Woods

I was already a huge Beatles fan, starting with the Ed Sullivan Show appearance and first hearing "I Want To Hold Your Hand" over my parents' car radio. I heard that *Abbey Road* was coming out, but I was surprised to hear it played in its entirety on a local non-commercial college radio station WFMU in East Orange, New Jersey. I was immediately knocked out by the diversity of the music played over the album. I remember the Side Two medley in particular and "Come Together" of course. The radio DJ gave a mention to "Maxwell's Silver Hammer." In retrospect, John Lennon would not have been pleased!

John Fox

On the 11th September 1969 I was 16 years old! BBC Radio Stoke on Trent played "Fixing a Hole" for me at 7:30 am on that Thursday morning in celebration of my birthday. Strange how many years later I would become BBC Radio Stoke's local Beatles "expert" to be called upon about any Beatles news items. But at that time I was eagerly awaiting the new Beatles album, *Abbey Road*. My Beatles scrapbooks were growing all the time, as I was buying every available music paper that I could afford: New Musical Express, Record Mirror, Melody Maker and, of course, The Beatles Book Monthly, plus any girls magazines I could borrow from the girls at school.

I was already known at school for being a Beatles nut! It helped because my friends brought me all their stuff too. This was our last year at Grammar School, we were in the Fifth Form, and next year we would all, hopefully, be off to Britain's First Purpose Built Sixth Form College, which was to be opened by PM Harold Wilson. Long hair was well and truly in, and all ours got longer, much to the disgust of some members of staff, who still wore gowns. Our Head Teacher still wore his gown and mortar board; we were almost Public School!

New LP's were regularly seen around school, mainly in the hands of the Fifth and Sixth Formers, who could go into the Main Hall at dinner time and play them on the Hi-Fi System and blast them out, overlooked by a reluctant teacher on duty. This is where *Abbey Road* had its first public play as far as I'm concerned.

But wait a minute, let's go back before the release date, to Friday 19th September: BBC 2's Late Night Line Up Show. At about 11:00 pm that night I sat and watched, in glorious black and white, as *Abbey Road* was played on the TV, along with some very strange film footage.

We had BBC2 because we had Rediffusion, Britain's first Cable TV, which meant we had NO interference with reception. Colour would have to wait!

The main thing I remember about the show was the cartoon that accompanied "Maxwell's Silver Hammer." It was done in a Capt. Pugwash or Crystal Tipps and Alistair style of cut outs with limited animation. There was also footage of dancers, the record playing and weird things going on, which I thoroughly enjoyed. I was raving about it back in school on the following Monday morning.

I watched it again on Saturday 10th October, so it must have been recorded. It appears to have long since vanished as I have asked many, many times over the years if anyone else remembers seeing it. I seem to have been in a minority.

The album was finally released on Friday 26th September, and I bought my copy on Saturday 27th, from Sherwins in Hanley Stoke on Trent. I still have my first copy, in perfect condition. Being a collector since the age of 9 in 1963, and being a bit OCD, it went straight into a plastic pocket. It wasn't my copy that was played at school the following week in the Main Hall. I didn't take my precious things into school for obvious reasons!

So what did I think of *Abbey Road* you might ask? Well, in my opinion, it was just perfect; they could do no wrong. I loved every bit of it and still do. I have lots of copies these days, for various reasons, but interestingly enough, my copy was only ever initially heard by me in mono even though it was a stereo disc. The reason being that my record player was mono, with the lid coming off and housing the one and only speaker. I didn't get a stereo record player until September 1970.

Off course "Something" was the new Beatles single, released on 31st October that year. Strangely not a number one, but that's probably because we all had both tracks on the album, and the Beatles didn't normally release tracks from albums as singles in the U.K. Of course, I did buy the single too. Why wouldn't I?

Garry Marsh

(C) 1997 Vincent Ruello
Vocalist Purple Cream

The above item is the only known surviving piece of memorabilia from the *Abbey Road* album launch broadcast on BBC2's Late Night Line-Up on Friday, September 19, 1969. Apparently all video footage from the show was lost or recorded over by the BBC. It is not an animation cell, but rather a one of a kind drawing in pen, pencils and texta (colored felt-tip pens) most likely created by John Lennon. It has wobbly separated heads that Philip Jenkinson, a film archivist and presenter on Late Night Line-Up, made to dance and wobble to the film clip for the song "Maxwell's Silver Hammer," one of the more memorable segments from the *Abbey Road* special. It was presented to Rowan Ayers, the creator and producer of Late Night Line-Up, and was signed by each of the Beatles in early 1970, making it one of the last items signed by the group. Ringo thanked Rowan and requested that the producer give his regards to two of the show's presenters, Joan Bakewell and "Tony what's is name" (Tony Bilbow). John, the presumed artist, signed the work with "a peace from John Lennon." George offered "Hare Krishna" greetings, while Paul just signed his name.

July 20, 1969: Astronauts walk on the moon!

September 26, 1969: The Beatles walk across the road!

My first impressions of *Abbey Road* at age 11:

• The department store in Dayton, Ohio has racks and racks of the new Beatles album. Wow! Just a photo on the front cover—no type, not even the name of the album!

• John has a new look: white shoes, white suit, and on top of that suit—a lion's head! Can't see much of his face with his reddish mane and full bushy beard. Like a cool Jesus.

• Walrus gumbo? (Later learned it was gumboot.)

• Doesn't everybody say 1 and 1 and 1 is 3?

• I'll have to look up Pathaphysical and Polythene.

• Ringo wrote another song!

• The stereo sounds great on headphones.

• My eyes always pop open when "I Want You (She's So Heavy)" abruptly ends.

• I've heard the moog before on the Monkees' "Daily Nightly," now the Beatles are using it.

• George's songs are fantastic on this album.

• Questo Abrigado—what language is this?

• "Always shouts out something obscene." Funny.

• The songs on Side Two really run right into one another.

• There's a secret unlisted song after Side Two ends that's missing its last note!

• Hey—both sides of this album end unexpectedly.

• Beatles have done it again! I love *Abbey Road*.

Mark Helfrich

I remember listening to *Abbey Road* in 1969 and thinking how much music had progressed since I bought my first record, Ricky Nelson's "Young World," seven years earlier. I was excited about the future possibilities for music. Everything sounded terrific in this song cycle. Unfortunately, 1969 was the last GREAT year for music. It never got that good again. *Abbey Road* is a masterpiece.

Maury Mello

The weekend that *Abbey Road* was released, I went to a Bingo Night at my high school in West Haven, Connecticut. One of the prizes was *Abbey Road*, which made me determined to win as I did not have money to buy it being 13 years old. I scored enough points to guarantee a prize, but the person before me with one extra point selected *Abbey Road*. I was devastated! I tried to persuade him to take my *Blood, Sweat And Tears* LP that I took as my prize, but he would not budge. I went home disheartened. I finally got my copy of *Abbey Road* on Christmas Day and played it over and over again for the next month! After almost 50 years, I still have my original copy of *Abbey Road* that I received on Christmas in perfect condition!

John Schiraj

I had been a massive Beatles fan since December 1963 when I first heard "I Want To Hold Your Hand" on the radio. I was 14 years old in 1969, living in a suburb of Cleveland, Ohio. I had been taking guitar lessons for about a year. (I still have my 1967 Gibson N-25 acoustic.) I absolutely loved (and still love!) *Abbey Road*. In addition to buying the LP, I bought the guitar book for it. My lifelong friend, who was 18 and my guitar teacher, and I practiced for weeks and put together a show at our church after a dinner. The highlight of our act was "Here Comes The Sun," with me singing and playing rhythm and him on lead guitar.

Of course, we did not realize this would be their last recorded album. When *Let It Be* came out in 1970, we didn't know it had actually been recorded before *Abbey Road*—it was years before I figured that out!

The Beatles broke up at the top of their game, leaving us with a classic album that stands the test of time!

Nancy Cuebas Riley

I was living in rural Australia and was 15 years old when *Abbey Road* was released. I was an avid John Lennon fan and was torn between wanting the Beatles to go on forever, but also seeing John's more avant garde solo activities with the Plastic Ono Band as signs that the dream was starting to fracture. Like many fans at the time, I looked for every reassurance that the band would continue from what I saw as credible Beatles sources. I watched Australia's TV rock program Countdown and read every edition of the monthly Beatles Book and Go Set (Australia's version of Rolling Stone). I also tuned into the Beatles hour every Thursday night on Brisbane radio 4BC.

I remember that the release of *Abbey Road* was somewhat of a surprise after the seemingly many false starts of the then titled *Get Back* album.

I ordered a copy on its Australian release date in October 1969 from my local record and electrical retailer and waited with great anticipation. While I loved the album, it did not "grab me" like *Sgt. Pepper* or *The White Album*. I think that after the largess of the double disc *White Album*, a single disc album of Beatles music was always going to fall short somewhat. It was also not the breakthrough in terms of style that its predecessors certainly were, but all the same it was by far the best new music in what was a period of high quality popular music making.

In hindsight, it is probably in my top three or four Beatles albums, especially in terms of sound and production, and has worn well over the past 50 years. "Come Together," "Something," "The End," "Oh! Darling" and "Here Comes the Sun" are proven chart toppers in favourite Beatles song polls, so I probably underestimated *Abbey Road*'s importance at the time. Most importantly, perhaps I just knew that the end was near.

Tim Goodacre

I was born in the USSR 36 years ago in Georgia (you remember the place from the song, right?). As we all know, western groups were not so welcome in that country until the break-up in 1991. While growing up in the USSR for a 7-year-old kid it was very difficult to get anything new in terms of western music. The only Beatles albums that I could put my hands on were *A Hard Day's Night* and the USSR-only compilation *A Taste of Honey*. One day I was given a flimsy 3-song blue vinyl disc containing three songs: "Come Together," "Something" and "Octopus's Garden." This was my first introduction to the music of *Abbey Road*. Later that year I got another 3-song vinyl with additional songs from the album: "Here Comes The Sun," "Because" and "Golden Slumbers"/"Carry That Weight"/"The End." I was blown away by Paul's voice on "Golden Slumbers." It was a magical song for me. At that time I did not know those songs were from one album.

Later, in 1992, after the Soviet break up, a private company in Russia released the entire Beatles catalog, including *Abbey Road*. It was the very first time I got the full album and listen to it entirely. I was already 10 years old. I was blown away immediately. I had never listened to anything like it before. Since then I became a big Beatles collector and possess *Abbey Road* albums from the United Kingdom, Germany, Japan, etc., but that very first Russian album that my family bought me was the first ever time I listened to that Masterpiece. I still keep it my collection (on the wall) as a great memory from my childhood. My dream came true when on June 19, 2004, I went to London for the very first time and walked across the crossing. Unforgettable feeling. I also had the privilege to take a picture with the original sign on Abbey Road, full with graffiti. Unfortunately the sign is no longer there, but I still have the picture, which brings me even more warm memories to my heart.

Yaakov Edisherashvili

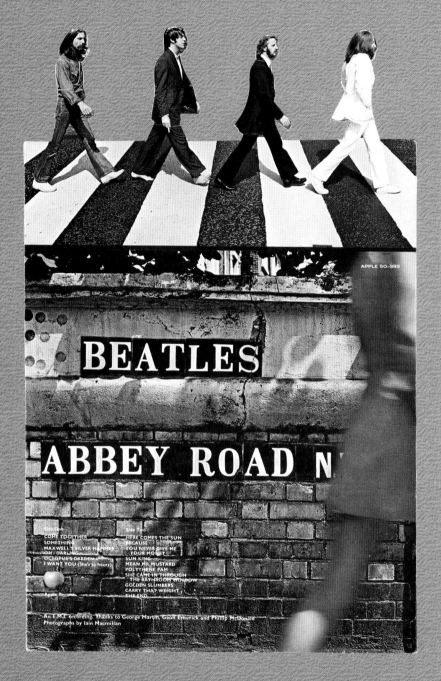

Capitol prepared multiple in-store displays for Abbey Road, including a floor display consisting of a cropped enlargement of the front cover attached to a record bin and a 12" x 19" cardboard counter display combining the back cover with die-cut figures of the Beatles from the front cover.

When I discovered the Beatles in the late '70s as a middle schooler, it was impossible for a young teen on an allowance to afford all of the records at once. The common practice was to borrow and tape friends' albums.

My friend Donna lent me her *Abbey Road*, and I carefully put on Side One. It would have been very bad manners to scratch a friend's album. I lay back over the footboard of my bed, letting the music wash over me. Songs like "Something" were familiar to me. "I Want You (She's So Heavy)" was not. During that last piece, with my eyes closed, I drifted to the hypnotic ending. Until it stopped. I jumped to my feet in one move, certain that something terrible had happened to the record and it was my fault. The tone arm was already calmly returning to its cradle.

I stood and processed the intention of it, and then I laughed. Who can cut a song mid-measure, get away with it, and have it be the perfect ending? Only the Beatles.

Karen Duchaj

I purchased *Abbey Road* in September of 1969. I remember sitting on the floor in the living room of my home in Kewanee, Illinois and experiencing the record through my parents' console stereo.

The first side of the album was what I had come to expect from a Beatles album, several individual songs that were good. However, Side 2 was the real surprise. When "You Never Give Me Your Money" crossfaded dreamily into "Sun King," I sensed something different was happening. I soon realized this was a medley, something different for the Beatles. It included the only time John, Paul and George would trade guitar solos on a Beatles album and Ringo's one Beatles drum solo. When the ending of "Golden Slumbers"/"Carry That Weight"/"The End" was finished, I thought, "What a perfect way to end

a great album." Little did I know that that really was "The End." That album turned out to be the last time John, Paul, George and Ringo would ever work together.

Michael Rinella

The first song I heard on the radio from *Abbey Road* was "Come Together." The DJ didn't say who it was until it was over, but I knew it was the Beatles. I wasn't aware they had a new album coming out. The lyrics were typical John Lennon word play, but the music was great. It wasn't long before I made a bee-line to my local record store to see if they had the new album. I was disappointed with the cover after such elaborate packaging for *Sgt. Pepper*, *Magical Mystery Tour* and *The White Album*, but the music was sublime. Even with Ringo's throw-away tune "Octopus's Garden" and one of my all time least favorite Beatles songs, "Maxwell's Silver Hammer," the rest of the album ranks right up there with their best.

As far as the singles from that era are concerned, I liked the flip sides more. "Get Back" was alright, but I loved John's "Don't Let Me Down." His heart on his sleeve approach spoke to me. And "The Ballad Of John And Yoko" was OK, but after a few listens became tiresome. I preferred George's "Old Brown Shoe" with its drivin' beat and rockin' guitar solo in the middle. I played it to death. What needs to be said about "Something" b/w "Come Together"? A killer double A-sided single. The only drawback was like two other previous Apple singles—it didn't have a picture sleeve. Why not!!!

David Rauh

October 1969, a fall Friday night. I was walking the streets of Coventry in Cleveland Heights. All I could hear is the sound of *Abbey Road* blaring from all the open windows.

Edward Fagan

*Abbey Road*, what a swan song!!! We couldn't have known it at the time, but this was to be the last set of recordings of that band from Liverpool, who thrilled us with each new release since 63/64. What better way for the Beatles to go out as a band—On Top. They would never face the fate of many other bands who decline as they age. The Beatles left us longing for more. This explains the hundreds of millions of dollars they were offered for a reunion. Luckily they never succumbed to that temptation. Instead, they went on to create many excellent solo compositions.

The release of *Abbey Road* coincided with the rumor that Paul McCartney had died in a auto accident in 1966 and that the barefoot, out-of-step Paul and VW Beetle 28IF on the cover was evidence of his death.

As far as the music was concerned, it was fantastic. George had fully come into his own with possibly the best two tracks on the album, "Something" and "Here Comes the Sun." Paul worked his magic with the fantastic medley on Side Two. John had his bits as well: the Chuck Berry-inspired "Come Together," the abrupt ending of "I Want You (She's So Heavy)" and the beautiful three part harmonies of the gorgeous song "Because."

Look at the cover someday when you are listening to the album. The Beatles were saying goodbye to us as they were symbolically walking away from the studio. The sixties had finished and a new segment of their lives was about to begin.

John Bezzini

I first heard of *Abbey Road* from WIBG radio station in Philadelphia, PA. They announced a release date of October 1, 1969. I had to wait until the following Monday to buy it. That was when I would get paid from my paper route. So, with money in hand I rode my bike the five miles to the High Street Record store in Burlington, NJ.

The owner of the store, Danny, always put a copy of the latest Beatle release away for me. He KNEW I would be on my way! Anyway, I get to the store, lock my bike to a tree out front and enter. Danny saw me locking my bike. When I entered the store Danny was standing there with a copy of *Abbey Road* in hand. He said "I pulled this out of the box for you as soon as I opened it. I knew you would be coming!" Well, he was RIGHT! Danny was GREAT! I rode my bike home as quick as I could and parked myself in front of my record player. I must have played it over 50 times in a row! What a GREAT recording. I still have it and every once in a while I play it. It still sounds as great as the first listen! And I can still see Danny standing there smiling!

John Reeder

For my 14th birthday, my mother bought me a record player. The only records she had were Tom Jones albums, *A Hard Days' Night* (with a broken spot on the edge) and *Meet the Beatles!* I didn't have records of my own, so we went to a store to pick out two. I chose the new Steve Martin album, *A Wild And Crazy Guy*, but didn't really know what other album to choose. My mom suggested *Abbey Road*, which I agreed to, not really knowing much about it. I played it until the grooves were gone. I loved that album! Mom made jokes that I was possessed by it, but she was glad I liked the Beatles as much as she did. From that point forward, I was hooked. When anyone asked me what I wanted for my birthday or Christmas, it was always a Beatles album that I didn't have. When I became old enough to work, I bought Beatles albums on payday. From my introduction to *Abbey Road*, I now have quite a collection of their music and memorabilia, including a Hofner bass guitar signed by Sir Paul! Oh, and every book written by Bruce Spizer!

Shelly Trent

Over spring break my senior year of high school, I found a used LP of *Abbey Road*, which was the first Beatles album I ever bought. I wasn't very familiar with the group, but was seeing a girl who liked them. You know how that goes. I played the album once and didn't really care for it, except maybe "Here Comes The Sun." A couple weeks later, I decided to play it again, and suddenly it became my favorite album. I listened to it every day for a month or two! By graduation, I had dozens of Beatles LPs & 45s. And although in general I was initially less of a fan of George's songs, "Here Comes The Sun" remains my favorite Beatles song.

Jeff Morris

My friend worked at the BX (base exchange) on Randolph Air Force Base in San Antonio, Texas when they received their shipment of *Abbey Road* albums. He called me and said "You need to come down here, I am going to hold the new Beatles album for you because they'll all be gone before the end of the day."

I went down and he handed it to me and I was in awe! No print of any kind on the front cover, just a great picture of a group that had changed in appearance so much in the past 6 years. I went home and did not hesitate to put it on the turntable. I played it for a few weeks straight and liked it more and more with each play. What great memories!!!

Danny Harnett

The first Beatles single I ever heard was "Penny Lane"/"Strawberry Fields." I was six years old. My family owned a restaurant that had a jukebox. There were lots of Beatles records. I fell in love with them! I had many forty-fives.

But the first Beatle album I ever bought was when I was 8 years old. I saved up my money, and bought *Abbey Road*. I thought "Come Together" was a cool song. "Something" was absolutely mesmerizing. And "I Want You (She's So Heavy)" was so heavy. The second side of the album also invoked emotions in my eight-year-old little self. The Beatles are my favorite, ever. Their music and lyrics span Across The Universe.

Beth Carbone Evangeliste

My story about how I became a Beatles fan starts with *Abbey Road*. Actually, how it started was that I was already a Monty Python fan. Eric Idle hosted an episode of Saturday Night Live in 1976, and this was repeated in February 1977. I was 10 years old. On the episode, there was a running gag where Eric repeatedly came out with a guitar and made an attempt at singing "Here Comes the Sun" with a yelling voice. His "singing" was absolutely horendous. After the show, I asked my parents, "What does the real song sound like?" They said, "You can listen to it right now. We have the album in the rack over there. It's called *Abbey Road* and has the Beatles crossing the road."

I went to the record rack and found *Abbey Road* and played "Here Comes the Sun." As soon as I played it, I said to myself, "I know this song!" Afterwards, I decided to flip the record over to hear what else was on the album. The first track was "Come Together." As soon as I heard that song, I said, "I've heard this, too!" The next song was "Something," and I said to myself, "I've heard this, too!" I wasn't familiar with "Maxwell's Silver Hammer" or "Oh! Darling," but I did recognize "Octopus's Garden." I then said to myself, "That's not right!" I couldn't believe so many songs I had heard before could appear on just a regular album and not a Greatest Hits album. Of course, I wanted to hear more and very soon became a hardcore Beatles fan thanks to *Abbey Road*.

Mark Arnold

I graduated college in June 1969. I went to Europe with my friend, Bob, for two months. The first stop was 3 Savile Row, where I met John Lennon, shook his hand, talked with him and took some photos. He signed a piece of Apple stationery. I walked around London all evening saying I shook one of THEIR hands. I said to Bob that I wanted to work for the Beatles. Upon returning to the States I learned of this "little" music festival was only 13 miles from where I was staying in the Catskill mountains. Yes, it was Woodstock and I was there the entire weekend. It opened my eyes to so many new artists and bands and cemented my thoughts about working in the music/Beatles world.

When summer ended, I tried to get a job at Capitol Records. They had none to offer. So I was out of college, money spent, see no future, pay no rent (I lived at home). On October 1, I went to Sam Goody in Paramus, NJ hoping to get a job selling (Beatles) records at the largest record store in the NY Metro area. Fate stepped in that day as I went to apply for a job. There it was, right on the counter, the new Beatles album, *Abbey Road*. No writing on the cover, just the Beatles crossing some street we never heard of. Of course, I immediately purchased the album, forgetting about the job for a day. I went home and listened to it non stop all day and late into the night. I had no idea this was going to be their final album. Neither did anyone else at the time.

The next day I went back to Sam Goody and got the job of selling records at $2.00/hour. By the end of the day, they offered me a managerial job, which I later accepted. Working there was the first huge step in my journey that led me back to John Lennon, in 1974, who really liked my idea of a Beatles fans' convention, saying, "I'm all for it. I'm a Beatles fan, too!" 45 years and 131 FESTS later, we are still bringing Beatles fans from all over the world together.

I still have one burning question for Paul. How did he know my personal situation at that very moment in time? After leaving Liverpool, he was never out of college, money spent, see no future, pay no rent! Fifty years later, that crosswalk is the most photographed on the planet, EMI Studios officially changed its name to Abbey Road Studios decades ago, and *Abbey Road* is considered one of the greatest albums of all time, by ANYONE! "Love You, Love You, Love You, Love You!" Words that ended the album *Abbey Road* and also their career as the Beatles.

Mark Lapidos

I have been a Beatles fan and collector since the beginning. I was the right age to experience Beatlemania. It was everything they say it was and more! Over the years, I have assisted both Bruce Spizer and Perry Cox with their wonderful books.

*Abbey Road* was released in October of 1969. Did I run right out and purchase a copy to be worn out on my turntable as all my other Beatle albums before it? NO! I was smack dab in the middle of South Vietnam fighting a war, so I had to wait till I got home to buy the album. It became one of my favorites, so as a sideline to my Beatle collecting, I started collecting everything *Abbey Road*.

I collected the albums, tapes, 45s from the album. I collected the album from every country I could find. I had a flimsy-covered copy from Asia that I took to the language department of The Ohio State University. Turns out it was written in Chinese. But I needed more. So, I started collecting memorabilia. I collected sheet music issued for all of the songs from the LP, even "The End," song books, the large stand-up display, the 8-track bin, rare posters. But that wasn't enough. I started collecting albums that mimicked *Abbey Road*'s cover, such as the Red-Hot Chili Peppers wearing only socks while crossing! I bought George Benson's *The Other Side Of Abbey Road*.

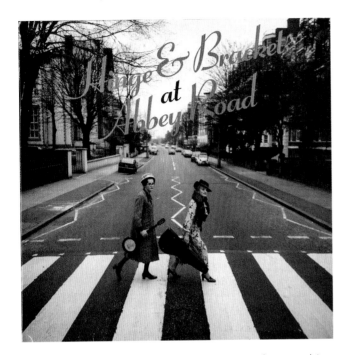

I bought all the books on *Abbey Road* in my thirst for knowledge. One, written by Brian Southall, was about the studio and titled *Abbey Road*. The book contained a picture of two old ladies making the crossing titled *Hinge & Bracket At Abbey Road*. This was a time before the internet, so I was in a quandary as how to obtain one of these records. I wrote to Brian at EMI and asked for information. To my pleasant surprise I received a letter from him on EMI stationary and a copy of the Hinge & Bracket LP. I have also collected statues of the Abbey Road crossing. Well, that's my story and I'm sticking to it.

Mark Galloway

Winter 1969: at the dawn of my fourteenth birthday, I saw the movie *Yellow Submarine* at the theatre. Then, in May, with money I received as a gift for my birthday, I bought the new Beatles' single "Get Back," followed in June by another 45 of the Fab Four, "The Ballad Of John And Yoko." These stereo discs sounded better on my parents' stereo console, but I kept my Shine ED100 mono record player. In July, I enjoyed the Apple single "Give Peace a Chance." At the time, I thought that Plastic Ono Band was a pseudonym for the Beatles; I later learned from various articles that John carried on his musical desires with Yoko Ono and other musicians. I was sure then that the Beatles were ancient history. My older brother made me discover new albums: Deep Purple's third album, Jethro Tull's *Stand Up* and, above all, Led Zeppelin. These groups changed my vision of pop music and influenced me to grow my hair as long as possible!

On Friday, October 3, I went to the Woolworth store of Centre Domaine in Montreal, Quebec. In the music section, I noticed a nameless, untitled album with a cover showing four long-haired dudes crossing a street. I took the album and looked at its back. What a shock: Beatles, Abbey Road N; Apple logo. Un-be-lie-va-ble!!! I was holding a new LP from my fetish group in my hands. I was jubilant, imagining new harmonies from John and Paul. The song that impressed me the most: "I Want You (She's So Heavy)." And what could I have said about Side Two (from the fantastic multiple voices "Because" to the unlisted "Her Majesty"), except that it was a logical continuation of *Sgt. Pepper*, and that it demonstrated unquestionably the progressive side of the Beatles. The girls at the time loved "Something."

In December, during Christmas break, thanks to my new General Electric Trimline portable stereo, I organized a music listening session with my friends, where they went through my top 5 albums: *Abbey Road*, *Led Zeppelin II*, *Stand Up*, *Deep Purple* and King Crimson's first LP. John, Paul (no, he was not dead!), George and Ringo were the darlings of the day. We were all ready to dive into the '70s with the Beatles!

Normand Tremblay

I remember my Uncle Billy playing his new *Abbey Road* album after its release. My uncle was a big Beatles fan and became a drummer, with past desires of darkening his hair and trying to grow his nose like Ringo's. My grandparents watched me as a small child and I would find things to do, like sorting out my uncle's records. I made sure everyone knew the Beatles album belonged to my uncle by writing his name on the *Abbey Road* sky.

Years later, my love for the Beatles came into focus. Times had changed as my uncle moved out and got into country music. Grandma handed me the same original *Abbey Road* album left behind. The songs I remember when newly released like "Come Together," "Here Comes the Sun" and "Something" all came back to me in a new and exciting way. My uncle passed away unexpectedly when I was a teenager. It is great to have this *Abbey Road* album with his name in the sky where I trust we will meet again someday. Thanks for the original LP, Uncle Billy!

Dr. Jennifer Sandi

I became interested in the Beatles thanks to my eighth grade chorus class in 1985. After a student brought in a cassette copy of *20 Greatest Hits*, I had to get all their albums, eventually buying *Abbey Road* on cassette (clear shell, I remember it well). Although I didn't know it at the time, the cassette switched the opening tracks on each side, with "Here Comes The Sun" opening Side One and "Come Together" on Side Two. Imagine my surprise when I later learned that the version I grew up on differed from the vinyl LP! When I bought the CD, I had to adjust to "Here Comes The Sun" not beginning *Abbey Road*.

I recall my initial impressions of the album—it was such a change from their earlier material. "I Want You (She's So Heavy)" baffled me with the static-filled ending. "Maxwell's Silver Hammer" contained such dark humor. But it also exudes optimism ("Here Comes the Sun") and straight-forward rock and roll ("The End"). It sounded more modern to my mid-80s ears, as the production was so clean. All these years later I still marvel at its mastery and the masterpiece of the medley. Most of all, I still imagine the four of them playing "The End," knowing that their days as a band were numbered and wanting to go out on top. They certainly accomplished just that.

Kit O'Toole

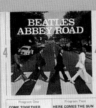

# Capitol relieves nervous tension 3 ways.

**1**  **2**  **3**
**On Record**  **On 8-Track**  **On Cassette**

Capitol actually relieved nervous tension five ways in 1969. In addition to releasing *Abbey Road* on vinyl, 8-track and cassette formats, the company also issued the album on reel-to-reel tape and 4-track. The cassette version switched the opening songs on each side to bring the running times of the two sides closer. The 8-track had drastic alterations to accommodate the format's four programs: (1) Come Together • Maxwell's Silver Hammer • Oh! Darling • Her Majesty; (2) Here Comes The Sun • Because • Something • Octopus's Garden; (3) I Want You (She's So Heavy) • You Never Give Me Your Money; and (4) Sun King • Mean Mr. Mustard • Polythene Pam • She Came In Through The Bathroom Window • Golden Slumbers • Carry That Weight • The End.

145

# A Fan's Notes:
## On the Way to *Abbey Road*

by Bill King (originally published in Beatlefan #90 Sept-Oct 1994)

Images and sounds from the summer and fall of 1969 come tumbling out of my memory like a pop culture cornucopia: "Honky Tonk Women" … one giant leap for mankind … "Questions 67 and 68" … Dylan joining the Man in Black on TV … Woodstock.

Ah, yes, Woodstock. I was there. No, I wasn't up to my ears in sex, drugs, rock 'n' roll and mud on Max Yasgur's New York farm. But, I was in a little town called Woodstock, in Georgia's Appalachian foothills, where my family was "roughing it" for a week in a rustic cottage—complete with color TV to stay in touch with the rest of the world, which seemed to be going mad.

So it is that my memories of Woodstock and the Manson Family killings forever are entwined with images of us sitting at the breakfast table, trying to pick tiny bones out of the catfish we'd snagged in Lake Allatoona.

It was as if the spicy social and cultural gumbo that was the '60s was boiling over in the latter days of summer as my senior year of high school approached. Already in July, we'd had the wild contrast of the investiture of the Prince of Wales in an ancient ceremony and the modern marvel of man walking on the moon—both telecast live around the world via satellite.

A few days after the moon landing, Teddy Kennedy, who earlier that year was the fifth most admired man in America in a Gallup Poll, had gone on national TV to try explain Mary Jo Kopechne's death in his car at Chappaquidick.

And then, during that jam-packed week we were at the lake, we watched reports on the bizarre and bloody murders of actress Sharon Tate and her friends, followed by the similar slaughter of an L.A. grocer and his wife the next day. Northern Ireland erupting as Catholics and Protestants took their age-old hatred into the streets, prompting the introduction of British troops. The gathering of more than 400,000 blissed-out folks at that other Woodstock, for a three-day rock fest that became a cultural watershed. And Hurricane Camille tearing up the Gulf Coast, killing 283 people.

We didn't know it, but another cultural upheaval was taking place in London, where the Beatles were burning out in a creative supernova. The day before Sharon Tate was butchered, the Fab Four strolled across a certain zebra walk that was to be immortalized on one of the most famous album covers of all time.

Even for those of us who lived it, 1969 seems like another world … a world where the hot new home entertainment item was the 8-track tape; the hottest new band was Creedence Clearwater Revival; Johnny Cash was pioneering country crossover; adolescent boys were falling in love with Olivia Hussey of *Romeo & Juliet*, while Henry Mancini had an unexpected chart-topper with the film's love theme; and Hollywood was courting the burgeoning youth market with *Goodbye Columbus*, *The Wild Bunch* and *Midnight Cowboy*. *I Am Curious (Yellow)* was testing pornography laws across the country.

TV's tame answer that fall to all this sexual license fell way short of Broadway's nudity-laced *Hair* and *Oh! Calcutta!* Nonetheless, some ABC affiliates were nervous about airing the comedy anthology *Love, American Style*. The networks were on a youth kick, with cool teens and caring teachers addressing relevant concerns in *Room 222* and Aaron Spelling trying to follow up on his *Mod Squad* success with *The New People* about a group of college kids stranded on a Pacific island who must start all over. And there was a goofy new sitcom: a story of a lovely lady with three girls who met a man named Brady with three boys of his own.

As school got underway, the upcoming nationwide Vietnam Moratorium Day anti-war protest was argued in Current Affairs class; we still watched *Dark Shadows* when we got home; and, in the latter half of September, tracks from the *Abbey Road* LP showed up on the radio. Stations in a few cities also began playing tracks from the Beatles abortive *Get Back* album, taken from acetates that had leaked out.

On September 22, my 17th birthday, the Beatles were seen on TV in a disjointed promo film for "The Ballad Of John And Yoko" (with a drum beat replacing each mention of "Christ"). The event was the star-loaded premiere (with Tom Jones, James Brown, Janis Joplin, Oliver, Buck Owens, Three Dog Night and Crosby, Stills, Nash & Young) of ABC's *The Music Scene*, a hip but ultimately short-lived variation on *Your Hit Parade*.

Reflecting on the events of 1969, I am swept back to a time when outrage still was tempered with hope; a heady mix of anything-goes and lingering innocence made life a thrilling adventure; there seemed to be no limits to what we could do, and when, not coincidentally, the Beatles were at the apex of their musical and cultural influence, a presence so powerful and pervasive that it crossed almost all socio-economic boundaries.

Back then, the Beatles occupied a sort of pop culture Mount Olympus. No mere stars, their every move triggered worldwide interest and trends. Their lyrics and album covers were examined for meaning, in the uniquely '60s belief that these rock 'n' roll demigods must know something we didn't.

This resulted not only in that ludicrous media uproar in the fall now known as the Paul-is-dead hoax, but also in the revelation at the Manson trial a few months later that Crazy Charlie considered the Beatles to be higher beings who were sending him messages through their music. "Helter Skelter," he believed, foretold an impending race war and was the alert for him to get on the right side by slaughtering some pigs. In reality, it used playground imagery as an analogy for sex.

Back then, the Beatles were so unbelievably hip that we figured anything they did must be hip, even if it didn't appear so on the surface. I remember the first time I heard *Abbey Road*. A group of us gathered at a schoolmate's house to work on a Senior English class report, and it wasn't long before our attention wavered from Joseph Conrad, and we adjourned to Mary's basement bedroom to listen to the new Beatles LP, which I hadn't yet scraped together the bucks to buy.

We listened in awe as Mary guided us through *Abbey Road*. I'll never forget her preface to "Maxwell's Silver Hammer," which today is viewed in the same light in which the Beatles themselves saw it—as the "corny" one. However, Mary, who was known as one of the school's artsy intellectuals, imbued the track with some unknown quasi-mystical meaning beyond the comprehension of us mere mortals. "This one is too far out," she said breathlessly as the song began. And, you know, listening to the tale of Maxwell Edison and his deadly silver hammer in the wake of the summer of '69 ... well, it did seem that way.

# Why Don't We Do It In Abbey Road?— Yet Another Iconic Cover

The naming of a Beatles album and the design of its cover was often an evolving process. For the group's first album, George Martin's initial idea was to have the group pictured at the London Zoo by the insect section in keeping with the proposed album title, *Off The Beatle Track*. This idea was abandoned when the zoo's director objected. Instead, the album was named *Please Please Me* for the group's first big hit single, "Please Please Me," and its cover was shot in the center stairwell to EMI House in Manchester Square, London.

The group's follow-up to *Rubber Soul* went through several possible titles. The first idea was *Abracadabra*, but that title had reportedly been used. Ringo suggested poking fun at the name of the new Rolling Stones LP, *Aftermath*, by calling it *After Geography*. John's idea was *Beatles On Safari*. Paul's suggestion, *Magic Circles*, eventually evolved into *Revolver*. Robert Freeman's proposed cover featuring a montage of photos of the faces of the group's members was rejected and replaced by Klaus Voormann's pen and ink drawing of the heads of the band members mixed with a collage of photos of the group's members.

In its early stages, the next album was cynically titled *One Down, Six To Go*, in honor of the band's new contract with EMI (meaning one LP done, six left to do). It, of course, became *Sgt. Pepper's Lonely Hearts Club Band*. The group considered naming its 1968 double album after the Henrik Ibsen novel *A Doll's House*, but was forced to come up with another title when the British progressive rock band Family released its debut album in July 1968 with the title *Music In A Doll's House*.

Mal Evans' diary listed several titles considered for what would be the last album recorded by the Beatles, including: *Four In The Bar*; *Turn Ups*; *Inclinations*; and *All Good Children Go To Heaven*. However, the name given the most serious consideration was *Everest* (or perhaps another pun title, *Ever Rest*). The idea came from Paul's fondness of the image of Mt. Everest appearing on the pack of Everest brand cigarettes smoked by engineer Geoff Emerick.

Apparently, the group considered taking a plane to Tibet and being photographed with Mt. Everest in the background. While this would have made for a stunning cover, it was not very practicable, particularly since the group was heavily involved in finishing its new album. Understandably, they couldn't be bothered to make the time-consuming trip, leading someone (probably Paul) to suggest why don't we do it in the road outside the studio. Rather than traveling 4,500 miles to the foothills of the world's tallest mountain, the group would walk about 450 feet from the front door of EMI Studios.

The cover image of the Beatles walking through the zebra crossing (crosswalk) evolved from a sketch by Paul, which was refined by Scottish photographer Iain Macmillan. On the morning of August 8, 1969, the Beatles arrived for the photo session. While a policeman held up traffic, Macmillan stood on a step-ladder and shot six pictures of the Beatles walking across the road. They were shot both walking away from and walking to the studio. After reviewing the six color transparencies, Paul selected the fifth photo, with the band in near-matching stride heading away from studio.

Three of the Beatles wore suits designed by Tommy Nutter, while George was casual, wearing blue jeans and a blue denim shirt. Paul wore sandals in the first two pictures before removing them for the final four. He held a cigarette in his right hand for the fifth photo.

The white Volkswagen Beetle appearing on the left (studio) side on the street was there by happenstance, having been parked there by a man living in the block of flats next to the studio. The fifth and sixth photos have a black police van parked on the right side of the road. Its license number, SYD 724F, was added to the front plate of the white Rolls Royce appearing on the cover of the 1997 Oasis album *Be Here Now*. There is a man standing on the sidewalk by the police van, often identified as Florida tourist Paul Cole. However, some elements of his story of the incident have led some to believe he is not the mystery man. The three men on the sidewalk standing by the right gate of the studio parking lot were returning from lunch while on a decorating job they were doing in the building. They have been identified as Alan Flanagan, Steve Millwood and Derek Seagrove.

The third photo has a line of four vehicles, headed by a London Taxi, stopped to allow for the photo to be taken. The fourth photo has a red double-decker bus that appears to be bearing down on the group. The sixth photo has a bus in the background picking up passengers after it has passed through zebra crossing.

Although Macmillan's sketch of the album cover envisioned that the title *Abbey Road* would be printed over the blue sky at the top of the picture, designer John Kosh opted for a pure cover photo with neither the band's name nor album title. While the group's name did not appear on the cover of either *Rubber Soul* or *Revolver*, this was the first time a Beatles front cover would have no text. EMI expressed concern for marketing reasons, but the Beatles held firm and backed Kosh.

The back cover features another picture taken by Macmillan, who searched for the area for a suitable street marker sign. He selected a gray-colored brick wall near the corner of Alexandra Road, which had "ABBEY ROAD N.W.8" in black tiles with white letters. (After the wall was taken down in the 1970s, a woman living in a flat across the street rescued the "A," "B," "E" and "Y" tiles.) Although Macmillan was upset when a woman in a short blue dress walked in front of his camera lens during one of his shots, he later realized that her intrusion made for a more interesting picture.

Macmillan's photo of the wall was augmented by the addition to the upper part of the wall of "BEATLES" in the same style of block letters as the street name. The song titles appear in white in the lower left area, along with credits and thanks to George Martin and the Abbey Road engineers who worked on the project. There is also a small green Apple logo.

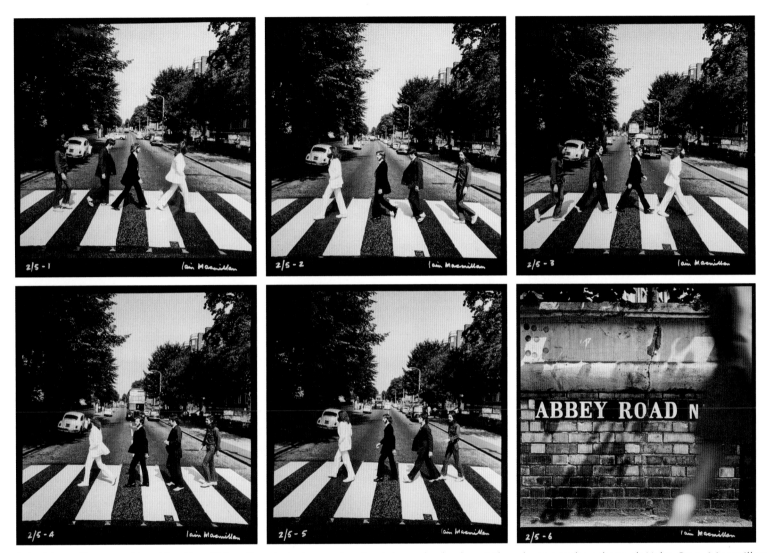

Iain Macmillan was hired for the *Abbey Road* photo session by John, who had met the photographer through Yoko Ono. Macmillan later printed limited editions of all six photographs taken for the front cover. Each of the photographs was limited to 25 copies. He also printed a limited set containing the five alternate front cover shots plus the unaltered back cover image (prior to the addition of the BEATLES tiles and text). This set was limited to five copies and is shown above, left to right, starting with the top row, in chronological order of when the pictures were taken. Due to the small number produced, all of these Iain Macmillan signed and numbered prints are highly collectible, with complete sets commanding a substantial premium.

Although the front cover to *Abbey Road* is one of the iconic images of the sixties, initial reaction to the cover was muted at best. Writing in Rolling Stone, Ed Ward opened his review of the album by mocking its cover: "Eeeeeeeeeeeeck, it's the Beatles. Look. Look. They're crossing Abbey Road in London." To Ward and doubters of the Beatles, it was just an unimaginative picture of the group walking across a street.

For those who believed or suspected Paul was dead and replaced by an impostor, the cover was full of hidden clues. John was dressed in white, representing an anthropomorphic god or angel. Ringo was dressed as an undertaker, while George wore the clothes of a gravedigger. As for Paul, he was barefoot (some people are buried without their shoes) and holding a cigarette in his right hand even though the real Paul was left-handed. And Paul had his eyes shut (just like a dead man) and was out of step with the others. Some articles reported the "funeral procession" was shown leaving a cemetery, when in reality they were walking away from EMI Studios on Abbey Road. Even the license plate on the VW Beetle was supposed to provide a clue or two, including **28IF** meaning that Paul would be 28 if he were alive (although he was 27 at the time).

Others could easily relate to the cover. The Beatles were crossing a street in a crosswalk, something very ordinary that all of us did. And if you were in London, you could actually walk across the very same street. And then, people started doing just that. Sometimes alone, sometimes in groups of four, Beatles fans recreated the famous walk across the zebra crossing, holding up traffic while getting their picture taken.

And with the proliferation of smart phones, it has become that much easier for fans to have their picture taken as they mimic the famous stroll taken by their heroes.

The cover to *Abbey Road* has been parodied many times. Booker T. & the M.G.s paid homage to the Beatles album with *McLemore Avenue*, its 1970 LP named after the location of Stax Studios in Memphis and containing mostly instrumental versions of 13 tracks from *Abbey Road*. The Heshoo Beshoo Group, a jazz combo from South Africa, mimicked the cover on its 1971 album *Armitage Road*. The vocal quartet New York City took its turn in 1974 with *Soulful Road*. The latter two albums do not contain any songs associated with the Beatles.

In 1988, EMI put together a five-song EP of early tracks recorded by the Red Hot Chili Peppers timed for the American band's upcoming U.K. tour. Although no Beatles songs were included on *The Abbey Road E.P.*, its cover featured the foursome pasted over the crosswalk wearing nothing but strategically placed socks. On the other side of the spectrum is *Snoopy's Beatles*, a 1995 collection of a dozen Beatles songs with children's voices and toy instruments. Rapper Chub Rock got into the act with his 1997 album *The Mind*. The 2001 CD *Jive Bunny And The Master Mixers Play The Music Of The Beatles* is a non-stop 24-song medley of Beatles songs performed by sound-alikes. Beatallica's 2013 album *Abbey Load* parodies the album cover and provides recordings of Beatles songs done in the style of Metallica, including *Come Together* and the Side Two medley.

Paul got into the act himself with his 1993 album *Paul Is Live*. The title itself mocks the Paul is dead rumor that was fueled by "clues" on the *Abbey Road* cover. The original cover was modified by the removal of the Beatles and addition of Paul and Arrow, an offspring of Paul's sheepdog, Martha. In contrast to the original cover, Paul is wearing shoes, has his left foot forward (rather than his right) and is using his left hand, this time holding a leash rather than a cigarette. The license plate is changed from **28IF** to **51IS**, meaning Paul is 51.

ARMITAGE ROAD
the heshoo beshoo group

New York City
SOULFUL ROAD

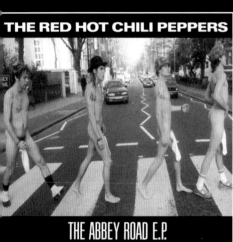

THE RED HOT CHILI PEPPERS

THE ABBEY ROAD E.P.

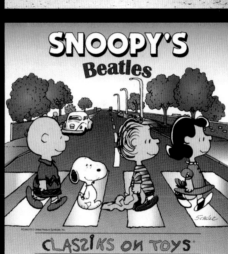

SNOOPY'S
Beatles

CLASSIKS ON TOYS

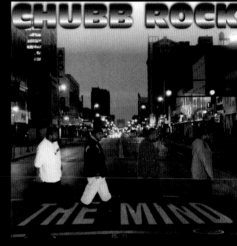

CHUBB ROCK

THE MIND

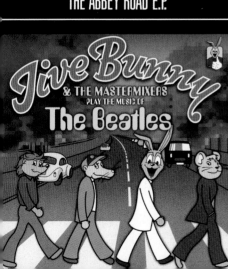

Jive Bunny
& THE MASTERMIXERS
PLAY THE MUSIC OF
The Beatles

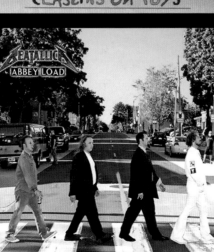

BEATALLICA
ABBEY LOAD

paul is live

# BEATLES
## NATIONAL LAMPOON
### THE HUMOR MAGAZINE
### OCTOBER 1977
### PRICE $1.25

IND
34490

**NEW EMINEM * AUDIOSLAVE**

**3 DIFFERENT SIMPSONS COVERS**

# Rolling Stone
### SPECIAL COLLECTORS' EDITION

## THE SIMPSONS MAKE ROCK HISTORY

**PLUS: WARREN ZEVON, U2, DAVE GROHL AND THE BEST NEW VIDEO GAME EVER!**

# The Recording Sessions

The recording of songs for the Beatles album named after the location of their favorite recording studios did not begin at EMI Studios, 3 Abbey Road. In fact, when the sessions started for what would be the last album recorded by the group, they thought they were working on tracks to complete an LP begun in January 1969.

The Beatles spent the first month of the year rehearsing and recording at Twickenham Film Studios and their Apple headquarters at 3 Savile Row. George Martin scaled his involvement back a bit, supervising the sessions, but not always being present as producer. Although the Beatles hired Glyn Johns as the balance engineer, his role expanded to that of producer when Martin was not there. At the end of the month the sessions came to an end, with Ringo starting the filming of *The Magic Christian* and Johns heading to America to produce a Steve Miller LP. By this time, the Beatles thought they had finished about eight songs worthy of release. The plan was to record additional tracks to complete the album.

On February 22, the Beatles were back in the studio as Ringo had a day off from filming. They decided against recording at Apple as their studio was undergoing renovations. Perhaps because Abbey Road was not available on short notice, they returned to Trident Studios with George Martin as producer and Glyn Johns as engineer. They ran through 35 takes of "I Want You," a song initially worked on at Apple. Although they did not know it at the time, they had begun work on an entirely new album. Two of the songs recorded in January, "Get Back" and "Don't Let Me Down," would be issued on a single, with the rest eventually released on the album *Let It Be*.

In mid-April, John knocked off a new song he was anxious to record. Although George and Ringo were not available, he booked a session at Abbey Road with George Martin for April 14. He and Paul completed "The Ballad Of John And Yoko," which would be the group's rush-released follow-up single to "Get Back."

Two days later, on April 16, the entire band got together at Abbey Road to begin work on two George songs, "Old Brown Shoe," which would be the B-Side to their new single, and "Something." Martin served as producer, but the remaining sessions held at the studio through May 2 would have his assistant, Chris Thomas, in charge. During this time, the group also worked on "I Want You (She's So Heavy)," "Oh! Darling" and "Octopus's Garden."

The next sessions were at Olympic Studios on May 5 and 6, with Martin as producer and Johns as engineer. The group added overdubs to "Something" and began work on "You Never Give Me Your Money" before taking another break from recording.

When recording resumed on July 1, the Beatles returned to Abbey Road with George Martin fully in charge. This development surprised Martin, who had grown frustrated with the rising tensions during the *White Album* and *Get Back* sessions, as well as Lennon's new no overdubs "play it till we get it right" recording philosophy. In an interview in the July 1987 issue of Musician, Martin recalled:

"I never thought we would get back together again, and I was quite surprised when Paul rang me up and asked me to produce another record for them. I said, 'If I'm really allowed to produce it, I will. If I have to go back and accept a lot of instructions I don't like, I won't do it.' But Paul said they wanted me to produce it as I used to, and once we got back to the studio it really was nice."

While the atmosphere in the studio was much more relaxed than it had been earlier in the year, the *Abbey Road* sessions were not quite a return to the past. As had been the case with *The White Album*, some of the sessions took place with less than all four Beatles present. John missed the initial July sessions due to a car crash in which he and his family were injured. Yoko, who was pregnant, was ordered by her doctor to remain in bed until she recovered. When John arrived at Abbey Road on July 9, he had a double bed brought into the studio so Yoko could be by his side.

From July 1 through August 25, the Beatles made full use of the studio, spending considerable time embellishing the tracks. Under Martin's supervision, often with Geoff Emerick as engineer, the group produced their most polished effort. According to Martin:

"*Abbey Road* was kind of *Sgt. Pepper Mark II*—the last thing we ever did—and Paul went along with the idea, but John didn't. So it became a compromise, with one side of the album very much the way John wanted things—'Let it all hang out, let's rock a little'—and the other being what Paul had accepted from me: to try to think in symphonic terms, and think in terms of having a first and second subject, put them in different keys, bring back themes and even have contrapuntal work. Paul dug that, and that's why the second side sounds as it does."

# Come Together

Recorded: July 21 (basic track) & July 22, 23 & 29 (Abbey Road Studio 3) & July 25 & 30 (Studio 2) (overdub sessions)
Mixed: August 7

Producer: George Martin
Engineers: Geoff Emerick, Phil McDonald & John Kurlander

John: Lead vocal; hand claps; tambourine; electric guitar
Paul: Backing vocal; bass guitar (Rickenbacker); electric piano
George: Rhythm and lead guitar (Les Paul)
Ringo: Drums; maracas

The album's opening track, "Come Together," was written by John shortly before the Beatles began their July 1969 sessions at Abbey Road. John got the title for the song from Timothy Leary, who visited John and Yoko in early June 1969 at the couple's second and final Bed-In for Peace held at the Queen Elizabeth Hotel in Montreal, Canada. Timothy and his wife Rosemary sang on the chorus of John's hotel room recording of "Give Peace A Chance" and were mentioned in the lyrics of the song. Leary, who was an outspoken proponent of LSD, asked Lennon to write a song titled "Come Together—Join The Party" for his bid to become governor of California. John quickly responded with lyrics such as: "Come together right now/Don't come tomorrow, don't come alone/Come together right now over me." Lennon recorded a demo for Leary, who adopted it as his campaign song and had the tape played on California radio stations. Joe Roberts Jr. prepared a psychedelic poster incorporating the theme. After being imprisoned for possession of marijuana in late 1969, Leary dropped out of the gubernatorial race, which was won by Ronald Reagan (later to become President of the United States).

Meanwhile, unbeknownst to Leary, John reworked and expanded the song for recording with the Beatles. When Leary later heard the Beatles version of "Come Together" on the radio, he felt a bit miffed, but admitted that "the new version was certainly a musical and lyrical improvement over my campaign song."

John's improved arrangement of the song opens with him repeatedly singing "Shoot me," an idea borrowed from "Watching Rainbows," an uncompleted song from the *Get Back* sessions. While these words took on a morbid twist when John was shot and killed in 1980, their meaning in 1969 was most likely drug related as John was shooting heroin at that time.

The song's opening line, "Here come old flat top, he come groovin' up slowly," is similar to a line from Chuck Berry's "You Can't Catch Me," "Here come a flat top, he was movin' up with me." Although Lennon's "Come Together" has a totally different feel than the Berry rocker, he was sued for copyright infringement by the song's publisher. A settlement was reached when John agreed to record three songs controlled by the publisher. He satisfied this requirement by recording Lee Dorsey's "Ya-Ya" and Chuck Berry's "You Can't Catch Me" and "Sweet Little Sixteen" for his *Rock 'n' Roll* album.

The remainder of the lyrics are Lennon at his nonsensical best—phrases that sound good, but may or may not mean anything. There are obvious references to himself such as "He Bag Production, he got walrus gumboot, he got Ono sideboard." The line "He shoot coca cola" is most likely an acknowledgment of John's drug habit of shooting heroin and cocaine. There are probable references to George in the first verse: "He one holy roller, he got hair down to his knees." The final verse appears to cover Paul. "He roller coaster" most likely refers to Paul's "Get Back," which an Apple ad described as "a song to rollercoast by." The "muddy water" and "mojo filter" references probably reflect Paul's fondness for Muddy Waters' guitar riffs. The "Got to be good looking, 'cause he's so hard to see" line seems to poke fun at Paul's reputation as the "cute" Beatle. Whether "He got early warning" was John intimating Paul had bad breath is not known.

The Beatles recorded eight takes of "Come Together" on July 21, 1969, at Abbey Road. These performances feature live vocals from John, backed by Paul on his Rickenbacker bass, George on his Les Paul guitar and Ringo on drums. Take 1, which is on *Anthology 3*, reveals how the song sounded before the addition of echo and overdubs. On the finished master, John's vocal is given heavy echo treatment, but on Take 1 his voice is pure and playful. John can clearly be heard singing "shoot me," while on the master the "me" is lost in the mix. Because he did not play guitar or piano, John was able to clap his hands to accentuate the beat, most often used to accompany him singing "shoot me." During the song's instrumental break, John plays tambourine and sings some of the lyrics from the first verse. He also plays tambourine towards the end of the song.

The first take also reveals slight lyrical variations and that John had yet to come up with an acceptable last line for the final verse. Although the song would be refined during the next few days, Take 1 is a fascinating first performance that demonstrates the magic the band was still capable of delivering without studio wizardry or, in the case of the *Get Back* sessions, excessive rehearsals.

The *Abbey Road* anniversary edition contains another fine runthrough, Take 5. Prior to the track, John says "I get very involved." Once again, John delivers another entertaining guide vocal and improvises with vocals over where he knows the guitar solo will later be recorded. When the song breaks down, John jokingly sings "He's got Doris Duckers" and comments on "teenage lyrics" and other humorous asides.

Because "Come Together" was recorded on a four-track tape machine, the best performance (Take 6) was copied to an eight-track to allow for overdubs. The eight-track tape was identified as Take 9. On July 22, Lennon re-recorded his lead vocal and added a guitar part. At John's request, Paul provided "swampy and smoky" piano fills. Maracas were added during the middle and ending instrumental portions of the song. Additional vocals were recorded on July 23 and 25, including Paul's backing harmony during the latter session. George contributed his double-tracked lead for the instrumental break and guitar solo for the song's ending, as well as the tone-pedal guitar chords leading into his solo, on July 29 and 30. The song was mixed for stereo on August 7.

## Something

Demo Recorded: February 25 (Abbey Road; Ken Scott engineer)
George: Vocals; electric guitar; piano

First band version recorded: April 16 (Abbey Road, Studio 3)
George: Electric guitar
John: Bass
Paul : Drums
George Martin: Piano; producer
Engineers: Jeff Jarratt; Richard Lush

Master version recorded: May 2 (Studio 3); May 3 (Olympic); July 16 (Studio 2); August 15 (Orchestra Studio 1; console Studio 2)
Mixed and edited: August 19

Producer: George Martin (except May 2); Chris Thomas (May 2)
Engineers: Jeff Jarratt & Nick Webb (May 2); Glyn Johns (May 3); Phil McDonald & Alan Parsons (July 16 & August 15); Geoff Emerick (August 15)

George: Lead vocal; rhythm and lead guitars (Les Paul); hand claps
Paul: Backing vocal; bass guitar (Rickenbacker); hand claps
John: Piano
Ringo: Drums; hand claps
Billy Preston: Hammond organ

Outside musicians: 12 violins; 4 violas; 4 cellos; string bass

George began writing "Something" during the recording of *The White Album*. The song's opening line, "Something in the way she moves," came from the title to a selection on James Taylor's first album, *James Taylor*, released by Apple in December 1968 in the U.K. and in February 1969 in the U.S. George composed "Something" on piano in an empty studio while waiting for Paul to complete his overdubs. Chris Thomas, who served as producer for some of *The White Album* sessions, recalls George playing his new composition on harpsichord prior to recording "Piggies" on September 19, 1968.

Harrison, while playing his Fender Telecaster through a Leslie speaker, presented "Something" to the group towards the end of the *Get Back* sessions on January 28, 1969. After teaching the band the chords, George led the group and Billy Preston through a few loose rehearsals of the song. The lyrics were not finished, with Harrison looking to complete the second line. John advised George to "just say whatever comes into your head each time...until you get the word," and used "attracts me like a cauliflower" as an example. Following Lennon's advice, George sang "pomegranate" to fill the empty spot. Although Harrison had arranged the song's bridge, its lyrics were also incomplete. While John often ignored George's offerings for Beatles albums, he showed interest in the song and added backing vocals.

George recorded a demo of "Something" at Abbey Road on February 25, 1969. This recording, featuring George on vocals, electric guitar and piano, is on the *Abbey Road* anniversary edition. (It previously appeared on *Anthology 3* in a difference mix with just electric guitar and vocal.) The demo contains the following extra lyrics not present on the finished master: "You know I love that woman of mine/And I need her all of the time/You know I'm telling you/That woman, that woman don't make me blue."

The Beatles first serious attempt at "Something" took place at Abbey Road on April 16, 1969, with 13 instrumental takes being recorded. The performances featured Harrison on guitar, George Martin on piano, John on bass and Paul on drums. Ringo was unavailable due to filming of *The Magic Christian*.

Apparently dissatisfied with the instrumental track from April 16, the group returned to the song on May 2 for a session at Abbey Road produced by Chris Thomas. The remake performances were designated Takes 1 through 36, with the final take being the best. The backing track featured George playing rhythm guitar on his Les Paul played through a Leslie speaker, John on piano, Paul on bass, Ringo on drums and Billy Preston on Hammond organ.

AR-2400

◄STEREO►

**Apple** RECORDS

# カム・トゥゲザー
## COME TOGETHER

# サムシング

◆ ビートルズ

## SOMETHING

**THE BEATLES**

東芝EMI株式会社　　¥500

At this stage, the song had a long and monotonous coda consisting of George's lead guitar, Paul's bass, Ringo's drums and John's piano, which is similar to the style of piano he would play on "Remember" from his *Plastic Ono Band* album. The coda inflated the song's running time to 7:48, nearly four minutes longer than the 3:00 finished master. Once again, no vocals were recorded.

Additional work was done on the backing track on May 5 at Olympic Studios, with George Martin serving as producer and Glyn Johns as engineer. Harrison added his lead guitar solo and fills, and Paul re-recorded his Rickenbacker bass onto Take 36.

The remaining work on the song was done at Abbey Road with George Martin at the helm. On July 11, George recorded his lead vocal onto Take 36. The song was given a reduction mix down and edited down from 7:48 to 5:32, eliminating much of the instrumental coda. An early mono mix of Take 37 has John's piano (which all but disappears in the final mix) and Preston's organ prominently featured, and Ringo's excellent drumming buried deeper in the mix.

On July 16, the following overdubs were added: a new Harrison lead vocal; Paul's backing vocals; and hand claps from George, Paul and Ringo. Two reduction mix-downs, numbered Takes 38 and 39, were made, with the latter marked the best.

On August 4, Harrison, assisted by engineers Phil McDonald and Alan Parsons, prepared a rough stereo mix of the song from Take 39 for the purpose of cutting an acetate. The acetate was given to George Martin for preparation of an orchestral score.

On August 15, George re-recorded his guitar solo for the instrumental break and assisted George Martin with the recording of the orchestra, which consisted of 12 violins, four violas, four cellos and one string bass. The recording session took place in Studio One, with the proceedings monitored by the engineers in the control room of Studio Two. The *Abbey Road* anniversary edition contains Martin's lovely orchestral score in isolation, allowing listeners to fully appreciate the beauty of strings. "Something" was mixed for stereo on August 19 and edited down to 3:00, completely deleting the unnecessary instrumental coda.

"Something" was written by George for his wife, Pattie. The recording originally had two parts: a guitar-driven vocal section and a piano-dominated instrumental coda bearing no resemblance to the vocal section. A little over a year later, Eric Clapton recorded a song he wrote for Pattie, "Layla," which also contained a guitar-driven vocal section followed by a piano-dominated instrumental coda. But in its case, the effective instrumental section was retained.

# Maxwell's Silver Hammer

Recorded: July 9, 10 & 11 (Studio 2); August 6 (Room 43: Moog)
Mixed: August 12 & 14; edited on August 25

Producer: George Martin
Engineers: Phil McDonald & John Kurlander (July 9, 10 & 11);
Tony Clark & John Kurlander (August 6)

Paul: Lead and backing vocals; piano; guitar; Moog
George: Backing vocals; bass guitar (Fender Bass VI); electric
guitar overdubs (Telecaster)
Ringo: Drums; hammer & anvil; backing vocals

George Martin: Hammond organ

"Maxwell's Silver Hammer," like "Ob-La-Di, Ob-La-Da," is a song that Paul wanted released as a single. According to John, Paul "did everything to make it into a single." The numerous takes and overdubs on the track prompted Lennon to state that the group "spent more money on that song than any of them in the album." John did not participate in its recording as his arrival for the July sessions was delayed due to an auto accident. The final master is a slick, clever and catchy tune that many fans love and others abhor.

The upbeat vaudeville arrangement and cheery vocals belie the horrendous murders committed by the song's protagonist with his silver hammer. The lyrics are not intended to glorify a killer. In Barry Miles' *Many Years From Now*, Paul explained "Maxwell's Silver Hammer was my analogy for when something goes wrong out of the blue, as it so often does, as I was beginning to find out at that time in my life. I wanted something symbolic of that." He has also stated, "Just when everything is going smoothly, 'bang bang' down comes Maxwell's silver hammer and ruins everything." The line about Joan studying "pataphysical science" refers to "pataphysics," a term coined by avant-garde French playwright Alfred Jarry to describe a branch of metaphysics.

Although Paul began working on "Maxwell's Silver Hammer" in October 1968, it was too late to be considered for *The White Album*. He introduced the tune to the band during the *Get Back* sessions on January 3, 1969, leading the group through several stop-and-start rehearsals of the song he dubbed "the corny one." During the initial runthroughs, Paul played bass. The *Let It Be* film contains a segment with McCartney calling out the chords for John and George. Paul later followed Harrison's suggestion and switched to piano, moving George to the Fender Bass VI. At this stage, Paul had only written one and a half verses and the chorus.

The Beatles returned to "Maxwell's Silver Hammer" on January 7, working on the song's structure and adding new elements such as whistling to open and close the song and to fill instrumental breaks. George worked out a vocal harmony to accompany Paul on the chorus, and Mal Evans was given the task of striking a hammer on an anvil at appropriate times. Portions of these rehearsals appear in the film. The group continued fine-tuning the song the next day, with John joining Paul and George on the chorus, and Mal Evans perfecting his hammer part.

A few pitiful runthroughs of the song took place on January 10 after George quit the group. Paul played bass and sang as if he were drunk. The Beatles did not perform the tune during the Apple basement sessions.

The first proper recording of "Maxwell's Silver Hammer" took place at Abbey Road on July 9. The backing track of Paul on piano and guide vocal, George on Fender Bass VI and Ringo on drums was recorded in 16 takes, with the final take (designated 21 as there were no Takes 6 to 10) being selected as the best. *Anthology 3* contains Take 5, with Paul vocalizing the instrumental passages and singing nonsense syllables for the first few lines of the third verse. The anniversary edition contains Take 12, preceded by Paul discussing the drumming with Ringo. Towards the end of the session, two guitar parts (most likely Paul on his acoustic guitar and George on his Telecaster) were overdubbed onto Take 21. Additional overdubs were made the next day, including Paul on piano, George Martin on Hammond organ, Harrison on Telecaster through a Leslie speaker, Ringo on hammer and anvil, Paul's lead vocal, and backing vocals by Paul, George and Ringo. The next day, Paul added an additional vocal, and George overdubbed another Telecaster part. At this stage, the song contained a seven-second instrumental introduction.

On August 6, Paul added five Moog synthesizer parts during tape reductions designated Takes 22 through 27. Stereo mixes were made that day and on August 12. On August 14, a stereo mix was made on an edit piece, which was then edited into Remix 34. The song's instrumental introduction was edited off the master tape on August 25, leaving Paul's vocal to start the song. According to engineer Alan Parsons, this was initially done to allow an experimental opening of the song where tape echo was applied to a tape running backwards so that when played forward it made the opening vocal go "Jo-Jo-Jo-Jo-Joan was quizzical." The effect sounded cheap, so the idea was dropped. Paul decided not to add the instrumental opening back to the front of the song.

# Oh! Darling

Recorded: April 20 (backing track); July 17, 18 & 22 (vocal overdub not used); July 23 (lead vocal); August 8 & 11 (All sessions in Abbey Road Studio 3 except August 11 in Studio 2)
Mixed: August 12

Producer: George Martin (except Chris Thomas on April 20)
Engineers: Jeff Jarratt (April 20); Phil McDonald & Alan Parsons (July 17 & 18); Geoff Emerick, Phil McDonald & John Kurlander (July 22 & 23 & August 11); Tony Clark & Alan Parsons (August 8)

Paul: Lead and backing vocals; piano
John: Backing vocal; guitar
George: Backing vocal; bass (Fender Jazz)
Ringo: Drums
Billy Preston: Hammond organ (not on finished master)

Paul's "Oh! Darling" also made its debut during the *Get Back* sessions. The song is a graceful piano-driven number with influences drawn from Fats Domino, Little Richard, New Orleans rhythm and blues, Louisiana swamp pop and doo-wop vocal groups.

Although McCartney played a bit of the tune on piano during his January 3 and 6 warm-ups, the band did not attempt the song until January 7. The two runthroughs from the day have Paul on piano, John on electric guitar, George on the Fender Bass VI and Ringo on drums. McCartney, joined by John and Ringo, played a bit of the song the next day during an equipment change. He also worked the tune into his morning piano warm-up on January 9. Paul did a complete solo performance of the song towards the end of the Twickenham sessions on January 14. This version, which makes use of a Binson echo unit, has McCartney delivering an Elvis-styled rendition, complete with sneering vocal asides and a spoken passage during the bridge. A brief segment of Paul singing the introduction of the song from an early Twickenham session appears in the *Let It Be* film.

When the Beatles returned to "Oh! Darling" on January 23, Billy Preston had joined the sessions. The group played the song twice, with Paul on bass, John and George on electric guitars, Ringo on drums and Preston on electric piano. The same lineup did a 6½-minute extended performance on January 27, featuring Paul and John on vocals. When the song appears to have ended, John announces that he's just heard that Yoko's divorce has gone through and states "Free at last." As John sings "I'm free...this morning, Baby told the lawyer it's OK," the band falls back into the song. *Anthology 3* contains a 4:07 edit of this performance.

During the final *Get Back* session of January 31, Paul led the band through two runthroughs of "Oh! Darling" between takes of "Let It Be." These performances featured Paul on piano, John on Fender Bass VI, George on Telecaster, Ringo on drums and Billy Preston on Hammond organ. John joined Paul on the vocals during parts of the song.

The first serious attempt to record "Oh! Darling" took place at Abbey Road on April 20 with Chris Thomas serving as producer. The studio recording sheet listed the song as "Oh! Darling (I'll Never Do You No Harm)." The backing track was recorded in 26 takes, with Paul providing a guide vocal over his piano, John on guitar, George on bass and Ringo on drums. Billy Preston played Hammond organ on some of the takes, but not on Take 26, which was selected for the finished master. The *Abbey Road* anniversary edition contains Take 4, with Paul's guide vocal and Preston's Hammond organ.

On April 26, Paul overdubbed a lead vocal, which was subsequently erased. Stereo mixes of Take 26 were made on May 1. No additional work was done on the song until mid-July, when Paul re-recorded his lead vocal during four separate sessions in which he recorded only one take each. These attempts took place on July 17, 18, 22 and 23, with Paul singing over Take 26. Engineer Alan Parsons recalls Paul doing these vocals each day at 2:00 in the afternoon. McCartney was apparently satisfied with his July 23 performance, as no more attempts were made and this vocal appears on the finished master.

In the *Anthology* book Paul gave the following explanation: "When we were recording 'Oh! Darling' I came into the studios early every day for a week to sing it by myself because at first my voice was too clear. I wanted it to sound as though I'd been performing it on stage all week." Paul told engineer Alan Parsons, "five years ago I could have done this in a flash," perhaps recognizing that his days of knocking out a gritty rock 'n' roll song in a single take were gone. Paul had previously recorded two songs associated with Little Richard in single takes five years earlier back in 1964 with "Long Tall Sally" and "Kansas City."

On August 8, Paul overdubbed lead guitar and tambourine (not heard in the mix). Paul, John and George added their vocal harmonies on August 11. The song was mixed for stereo the following day, with Remix 9 from Take 26 selected for the album.

The song's backing vocals were somewhat buried in the mix. The 2019 remix brings them more to the front allowing for a greater appreciation of the fine doo-wop style singing on the song.

日本だけで実現したゴールデン・レコード!!

AR-2520
STEREO

# オー・ダーリン
OH DARLING

# ヒア・カムズ・ザ・サン
HERE COMES THE SUN

☆ ビートルズ

Apple
RECORDS

株式会社  ￥ 400

"Oh! Darling" was released as a single in Japan in June 1970. The picture insert packaged with the single shows the Beatles getting ready to cross Abbey Road for what would become one of the most iconic album covers of all time.

## Octopus's Garden

Recorded: April 26 (Abbey Road Studio 2); July 17 & 18 (Studio 3)
Mixed: July 18

Producer: Chris Thomas (April 26); George Martin (July 17 & 18)
Engineers: Jeff Jarratt & Richard Langham (April 26);
Phil McDonald & Alan Parsons (July 17 & 18)

Ringo: Lead and backing vocals; drums; bubbling sound effects
Paul: Backing vocals; bass guitar (Rickenbacker); piano
George: Backing vocals; lead guitar (Stratocaster)
John: Rhythm guitar (Casino)

"Octopus's Garden" is Ringo's second solo composition on a Beatles album. Ringo got the idea for the song during his late August 1968 "vacation" from the group, when he traveled to Sardinia. While on Peter Sellers' yacht, Ringo was told that octopus go round the ocean bed, pick up stones and shiny things and build gardens in front of their caves. The beauty of these images and his desire to get away from the pressures of the Beatles ("I just wanted to be under the sea, too") inspired him to write the song.

The *Let It Be* film contains a charming segment from January 26, with Ringo introducing "Octopus's Garden," which was far from complete, to George. (Ringo had briefly played the tune three days earlier prior to the arrival of George and Paul.) Harrison, standing with his acoustic guitar, strums and sings along. Ringo, who is also standing, plays some basic chords on piano. As the song moves forward, George stops and reaches down to the piano to show Ringo some new chord changes. When George Martin arrives, Harrison flashes a grin and suggests that he and Ringo take it from the top. The rehearsal continues, and when John arrives, he moves over to the empty drum kit to fill in for Ringo, who is still on piano. The segment not only shows Harrison's uncredited contributions to the song, but also his genuine eagerness to help Ringo with his song writing.

The actual recording of "Octopus's Garden" took place at Abbey Road on April 26 during a session produced by Chris Thomas (although the recording sheet identifies the producer as "Beatles"). The group went through 32 takes with Ringo on drums and guide vocal, George on his Stratocaster through the Leslie, John on his Epiphone Casino and Paul on his Rickenbacker bass. *Anthology 3* contains Take 2, which demonstrates that the band had the arrangement worked out from the start. Without its embellishments, the song has country & western feel to it.

The *Abbey Road* anniversary edition contains Take 9, complete with studio banter. Although it is a spirited performance, it breaks down before completion.

Overdubs were added to Take 32 nearly three months later on July 17 and 18. These included Ringo's lead vocal with artificial double tracking, Paul's piano, additional drums, and backing vocals from Paul, George and Ringo. The instrumental break with George's guitar solo was augmented with special effects, including Ringo blowing through a straw into a glass of water for bubbling sounds, and Paul and George singing at a high pitch through a Leslie speaker. At the end of the July 18 session, the song was mixed for stereo. With its underwater fantasy theme and special effects, the finished master is reminiscent of "Yellow Submarine," which was also sung by Ringo.

## I Want You (She's So Heavy)

Recorded: February 22 (Trident); April 18 & 20 & August 8 & 11 (Abbey Road Studio 2)
Mixed and edited: August 20

Producer: George Martin (February 22 & August 8 & 11); Chris Thomas (April 18 & 20)
Engineers: Glyn Johns and Barry Sheffield (February 22); Jeff Jarratt & John Kurlander (April 18 & 20); Geoff Emerick, Phil McDonald & John Kurlander (August 8 & 11)

John: Lead and backing vocals; guitars (Casino); Moog
Paul: Backing vocal; bass guitar (Rickenbacker)
George: Backing vocal; guitars (Les Paul)
Ringo: Drums; conga drums; crash cymbals
Billy Preston: Hammond organ

"I Want You (She's So Heavy)" was written as a passionate plea by John for Yoko. It is another song that dates back to the *Get Back* sessions.

John introduced the "I Want You" part of the song to the group on January 28, 1969. An early runthrough of the song opens with John matching his "I want you" vocal with his distorted guitar. This funky, bluesy version of the song prominently features Billy Preston on piano and response vocals, and is nearly five and a half minutes long. When the group returned to the song later that day, Billy Preston shifted to organ and no longer provided vocals. John alternated between "I want you" and "I need you" verses and someone (possibly George) added a shaker. The next take featured

John and George jamming on guitar. The following day, the Beatles ran through a mainly instrumental jam of the song. John played the distorted riff on his guitar and briefly sang an off-mike guide vocal. Billy Preston added keyboards and some improvised "I had a dream" vocals.

During the rooftop concert, John briefly played the song's riff. The following day, between recording Paul's ballads, the group returned to the song with John and George on guitars, Paul and Billy Preston on keyboards and Ringo on drums, with Paul occasionally providing vocals.

The group's first proper recording of "I Want You" took place on February 22, 1969, during what would turn out to be the first session for the *Abbey Road* album. Ironically, the session took place not at EMI's Abbey Road studios, but rather at Trident. With George Martin as producer and Glyn Johns as engineer, the group recorded 35 takes of the song with John and George on electric guitars (with John playing the lead guitar riff), Paul on bass guitar, Ringo on drums and Billy Preston on keyboards. John sang lead while playing guitar on all but one take, which was sung by Paul.

The *Abbey Road* anniversary edition contains an incredible version of the song. It opens with the band warming up on their instruments and studio banter between John and George Martin. They agree that Take 4 sounded good up to the break. John then announces, "My boys are ready to go!" And are they ever. After Glyn Johns asks them to play softer as the neighbors are complaining, the group knocks out an energetic performance (Take 32) of the song highlighted by John's passionate vocals and Preston's organ playing.

The next day a master track was formed by editing the first part of Take 9 with the middle eight from Take 20 and the remainder from Take 32.

On April 18, back at Abbey Road with Chris Thomas serving as producer, John (on his Casino) and George (on his Les Paul) overdubbed several guitar parts onto the edited master. After a reduction mix-down (designated Take 1), John and George added more guitar. According to engineer Jeff Jarratt, "They wanted a massive sound so they kept tracking and tracking, over and over." Hammond organ and conga drums were overdubbed two days later.

John returned to the song on August 8 at Abbey Road with George Martin producing. Going back to the Trident master of February 23, John overdubbed sounds from the white noise generator of Harrison's Moog synthesizer, and Ringo added drums (primarily crash cymbals).

On August 11, John, Paul and George recorded their harmony vocals onto Take 1 from April 18. The vocals included the trio singing "she's so heavy" over and over again. It was at this session that the song received its full title of "I Want You (She's So Heavy)." When John could not decide whether he preferred the August 8 version of the Trident master or the recently completed master, he had the "she's so heavy" vocals copied from the new master track onto the August 8 version of the Trident master.

The song was finally completed on August 20, when both masters were remixed and then edited together. The opening 4:36 is from the designated Take 1 (with the multi-tracked guitars from April 18 and the "she's so heavy" vocals from August 11) and the remainder of the track is from the Trident master (with the white noise and crash cymbals from August 8). The edited master originally ran over eight minutes, but John opted for a sudden surprise ending at 7:44. According to engineer Alan Parsons, "We were putting the final touches to that side of the LP and we were listening to the mix. John said 'There! Cut the tape.' Geoff [Emerick] cut the tape and that was it. End of side one!"

"I Want You (She's So Heavy)" is one of the most interesting and complex songs in the Beatles catalog. It was recorded at two studios (Trident and Abbey Road) under the supervision of two producers (George Martin and Chris Thomas) and seven engineers (Glyn Johns, Barry Sheffield, Jeff Jarratt, John Kurlander, Tony Clark, Alan Parsons and Phil McDonald). At 7:44, it is the longest released song by the group ("Revolution 9" not really being a "song"). And while its lyrics are brief and simple, John sings the words with great passion, sometimes matching the scorching intensity heard on "Twist And Shout."

The song is also one of the group's noisiest tracks, with its tape hiss during the early stages of the song, multiple distorted guitars throughout and white noise from the Moog and crashing cymbals during the song's climatic ending. The first part of the song features a bluesy instrumental backing with changing rhythms. This is in sharp contrast to the last 3:07 of the track, which repeats the same riff over and over again, building with a sound conjuring images of powerful waves crashing with growing strength onto a rocky shore-line. Just when the listener thinks the song will never end, it stops with a harsh and jarring suddenness. On vinyl record, the abrupt end to Side One of *Abbey Road* is as effective as the completely opposite long sustained chord that ends "A Day In The Life" on *Sgt. Pepper's Lonely Hearts Club Band*.

## Here Comes The Sun

Recorded: July 7, 8 & 16, August 6, 11 & 19 (Abbey Road Studio 2 except Studio 3 on July 16 & August 6 and Studio 1 on August 15)
Mixed: August 19

Producer: George Martin
Engineers: Phil McDonald; Geoff Emerick (Aug 11, 15 & 19); John Kurlander (July 7&8, Aug 11); Alan Parsons(July 16, Aug 6, 15 & 19)

George: Lead and backing vocals; acoustic guitar (Gibson J-200); Moog; hand claps
Paul: Backing vocals; bass guitar (Rickenbacker); hand claps
Ringo: Drums; hand claps
Embellishments: Harmonium

Outside musicians: 4 violas; 4 cellos; string bass; 2 clarinets; 2 alto flutes; 2 flutes; and 2 piccolos

The second side of *Abbey Road* opens with George's "Here Comes The Sun," which is recognized as one of the album's highlights. In his book, *I Me Mine*, Harrison states that he wrote the song "at the time when Apple was getting like school, where we had to go and be business men." It was spring of 1969, and the long English winter had finally ended. One bright morning George decided to play hooky from Apple and went to visit his friend Eric Clapton at his countryside house in Ewhurst, Surrey. Inspired by the liberation from winter ("by the time spring comes you really deserve it"), as well as his escaping from Apple ("The relief of not having to go see all those dopey accountants was wonderful"), George wrote the upbeat song "while walking around the garden with one of Eric's acoustic guitars." The lyrics were finished during a June 1969 vacation in Sardinia.

The backing track to "Here Comes The Sun" was recorded in 13 takes on July 7 with George on his Gibson J-200 acoustic guitar (played with a capo on the seventh fret) and guide vocal, Paul on his Rickenbacker bass and Ringo on drums. The *Abbey Road* anniversary edition contains Take 9 of this sparse backing track with Harrison's guide vocal. George then re-recorded and added acoustic guitar onto Take 13. The following day, he recorded his lead vocal. Backing vocal harmonies by George and Paul were double-tracked with the pair singing twice rather than relying on artificial double tracking. At the end of the session, Take 13 was given two tape reduction mixes to free up additional tracks. The second, designated Take 15, was superior and became the basis for the finished master.

On July 16, hand claps (from George, Paul and Ringo) and harmonium were superimposed onto Take 15. Harrison added acoustic guitar parts on August 6 and 11. On August 15, George Martin recorded the orchestral score, consisting of four violas, four cellos, one string bass, two clarinets, two alto flutes, two flutes and two piccolos. Harrison completed the track on August 19 by adding a few Moog synthesizer overdubs. The song was then mixed for stereo.

## Because

Recorded: August 1, 4 & 5 (Abbey Road Studio 2)
Mixed: August 12

Producer: George Martin
Engineers: Phil McDonald, Geoff Emerick & John Kurlander

John: Harmony vocals; guitar (Casino)
Paul: Harmony vocals; bass guitar (Rickenbacker)
George: Harmony vocals; Moog
Ringo: Hand claps (to keep time; not in final mix)
George Martin: Electric harpsichord (Baldwin)

Harrison's upbeat track is followed by the dreamy three-part harmonies of "Because," which Lennon based upon Beethoven's "Moonlight Sonata." According to John, Yoko was playing the sonata on piano, and he asked her if she could play the chords backwards. He then wrote "Because" around them.

The Beatles began work on "Because" on August 1. The group recorded 23 takes with George Martin on a Baldwin spinet electric harpsichord matching notes with John on his Casino. Ringo kept the beat with hand claps to guide the musicians. Paul added bass on his Rickenbacker. The *Abbey Road* anniversary edition contains Take 1 of the instrumental backing track complete with Ringo keeping time. At the end of the performance, John says, "I love it." And who are we to disagree?

John, Paul and George then added their three-part harmony onto Take 16, which was deemed the best backing track. On August 4, the three recorded their vocals two more times, thus providing a rich triple-voice three-part harmony. Harrison added two Moog synthesizer parts on August 5. The song was mixed for stereo on August 12. *Anthology 3* contains a special remix that isolates the thrice-recorded three-part harmony vocals of John, Paul and George without the instrumental backing.

## You Never Give Me Your Money

Recorded: May 6 (Olympic); July 1, 11, 30 & 31 (Abbey Road Studio 2) and July 15 & 30 & August 5 (Studio 3)
Mixed: August 14 & 21

Producer: George Martin
Engineers: Glyn Johns & Steve Vaughan (May 6); Phil McDonald (all other sessions); Geoff Emerick (July 30 & 31 & August 5); John Kurlander (all sessions except May 6 & July 1 & 15); Chris Blair (July 1); Alan Parsons (July 15)

Paul: Lead and backing vocals; piano; bass guitar (Rickenbacker)
John: Backing vocals; guitar (Casino)
George: Backing vocals; guitar (Telecaster through Leslie speaker)
Ringo: Drums
Embellishments: Chimes; tambourine; sound effects (tubular bells, birds, chirping crickets and bubbles)

The *Abbey Road* medley begins with Paul's "You Never Give Me Your Money," a song consisting of three segments of its own. In Barry Miles' *Many Years From Now*, Paul states that the first part of the song was him "directly lambasting Allen Klein's attitude to us: no money, just funny paper, all promises and it never works out. It's basically a song about no faith in the person." Next up is a nostalgic bit about being out of college with money spent, which leads into an optimistic escape ("Soon we'll be away from here/Step on the gas and wipe that tear away") inspired by Paul and Linda's hitting the road to get away from it all.

The song's backing track was recorded on May 6, with Paul providing a guide vocal and piano, John playing a distorted guitar part on his Casino, George on his Telecaster through the Leslie and Ringo on drums. The Beatles ran through 36 takes, with Take 30 designated as the best. Several takes ended with an extended jam, with at least one take lasting over five and a half minutes. The anniversary edition contains Take 36, with a very different vocal from Paul.

Paul recorded his lead vocal on July 1 and added bass on July 11. Additional overdubs to Take 30 were made on July 15, including backing vocals from Paul, John and George, as well as chimes for the end of the song and tambourine. It was during this session that the song's nursery rhyme ending ("One, two, three, four, five, six, seven/All good children go to heaven") was recorded. The song was given a reduction mix and more vocals on July 30.

It was on this day that the first attempt to compile the songs of the medley took place. For this initial attempt, the crossfade from "You Never Give Me Your Money" into the medley's second song,

"Sun King," consisted of an organ note. After listening to the initial edit of the medley, Paul decided against using the July 30 embellishments. The next day, he superimposed piano and bass to Take 30.

On August 5, Paul mixed a series of tape loop sound effects, including tubular bells, birds, chirping crickets and bubbles, onto a four-track tape for use during the crossfade of "You Never Give Me Your Money" into "Sun King." Take 5 of the sound effects was incorporated into the stereo remix and crossfade of the tracks on August 14. An improved mix of the crossfade was made on August 21.

## Sun King

Recorded: July 24 & 25 (Abbey Road Studio 2)
Mixed: August 14 & 21

Producer: George Martin
Engineers: Geoff Emerick & Phil McDonald; John Kurlander

John: Lead and backing vocals; guitar (through Leslie speaker)
Paul: Backing vocals; bass guitar (Fender Jazz)
George: Backing vocals; guitar
Ringo: Drums
George Martin: Organ

According to John, "Sun King" came to him in a dream (most likely after reading Nancy Mitford's biography on France's Louis XIV, the Sun King). The song's chord progression is similar to that of the dreamy-sounding Fleetwood Mac instrumental "Albatross" (which was released as a single in late 1968 and topped the British charts in early 1969). Although "Sun King" was not properly recorded during the *Get Back* sessions, John did play bits of the song on January 2, 3 and 10. The song's brief opening lyrics consist of little more than "Here comes the Sun King" and the sentiment that everybody's laughing and happy. The song concludes with a nonsensical string of foreign and foreign-sounding words and phrases such as "Mundo paparazzi mi amore" and "tanta mucho que can eat it carousel."

"Sun King" (titled "Here Comes The Sun-King") was recorded as a single selection with another John song, "Mean Mr. Mustard," in 35 takes on July 24. The backing track consisted of John on his Casino through the Leslie and guide vocal, George on guitar, Paul on Fender Jazz Bass and Ringo on drums. The following day, Lennon recorded his lead vocal and backing vocals along with McCartney and Harrison. George Martin added organ. The track was mixed for stereo on August 14 and 21. The anniversary edition contains Take 20, with studio banter and an off-mike Lennon guide vocal.

## Mean Mr. Mustard

Recorded: July 24 & 25 (Abbey Road Studio 2)
Mixed: August 14 & 21

Producer: George Martin
Engineers: Geoff Emerick & Phil McDonald; John Kurlander

John: Lead and backing vocals; guitar (Casino); piano
Paul: Backing vocals; bass guitar (Fender Jazz)
George: Backing vocals; guitar
Ringo: Drums
Embellishments: Maracas; tambourine; bongos

"Mean Mr. Mustard" was started by John during his visit to Rishikesh, India in 1968. It was reportedly inspired by an article John read about a man who stored money up his rear end. John cleaned this up with the line "Keeps a ten bob note up his nose." Although Lennon's composition was part of the May 1968 rehearsals held at Harrison's Esher home, the song was not recorded during the *White Album* sessions. The Esher demo, which appears on *The White Album* deluxe edition, contains a double-tracked Lennon vocal. Both verses were complete, although Mr. Mustard's sister was named Shirley. When the song was recorded for *Abbey Road*, John changed her name to Pam to serve as a link to "Polythene Pam."

"Mean Mr. Mustard" was played a few times during the *Get Back* sessions. The most complete performance took place on January 8, with John on piano, George on guitar and Ringo on drums. The song was also performed on January 14, 23 and 25.

As detailed above, "Mean Mr. Mustard" was recorded as a single track with "Sun King" in 35 takes on July 24. The backing track consisted of John on his Casino through the Leslie speaker and guide vocal, George on guitar, Paul on Fender Jazz Bass and Ringo on drums. The following day, Lennon recorded his lead vocal and backing vocals along with McCartney and Harrison. John also overdubbed piano. Other embellishments to Take 35 included bongos, maracas and tambourine. As noted above, the track was mixed for stereo on August 14 and 21 as part of a crossfade with "You Never Give Me Your Money."

The *Abbey Road* deluxe edition contains Take 20 of the song, which has John messing around on his guide vocal. At this stage, he is still singing "sister Shirley." John also sings "God save the Queen" in reference to the line "Takes him out to look at the Queen." The Beatles had previously performed a brief version of "God Save The Queen" during their January 30, 1969, rooftop concert.

## Polythene Pam

Recorded: July 25 & 30 (Abbey Road Studio 2); July 28 (Studio 3)
Mixed: August 14

Producer: George Martin
Engineers: Geoff Emerick & Phil McDonald; John Kurlander

John: Lead vocal; acoustic 12-string guitar (Framus Hootenanny)
Paul: Backing vocal; bass guitar (Rickenbacker)
George: Backing vocal; guitars (Les Paul and Telecaster)
Ringo: Drums
Embellishments: Maracas; tambourine; cowbell

The medley's next song is John's "Polythene Pam." The name of the character is a slight modification of the nickname of a young Beatles fan, Pat Hodgett, who began seeing the group in the early sixties. She was called Polythene Pat because she had a habit of eating polythene. The weird wardrobe was inspired by an August 8, 1963, encounter with a woman introduced to Lennon by Royston Ellis, a British beat poet. In his Playboy interview, John stated that Ellis told him that his girlfriend Stephanie "dressed up in polythene. She didn't wear jackboots and kilts, I just sort of elaborated. Perverted sex in a polythene bag. Just looking for something to write about."

"Polythene Pam" has the same pedigree as "Mean Mr. Mustard." John wrote the song in India, recorded a double-tracked demo and decided against recording the song for *The White Album*. The demo has a line not in the recorded version: "Well it's a little absurd, but she's a nice class of bird." John, aided and abetted by Paul, ran through an impromptu performance of the song during the *Get Back* sessions on January 24.

To facilitate the intended medley concept, "Polythene Pam" and "She Came In Through The Bathroom Window" were recorded as a single track on July 25. The band recorded 39 takes, with John on 12-string acoustic guitar, Paul on his Rickenbacker bass, George on his Les Paul guitar and Ringo on drums. Lennon and McCartney provided guide vocals for their separate songs. Although Take 39 was deemed the best, Ringo redid his drum part and Paul re-recorded his bass. Proper lead vocals were also recorded.

On July 28, Take 39 was embellished with additional vocals, acoustic guitar, electric guitar, tambourine, maracas and cowbell (and possibly piano, though not in the mix). A reduction mix, designated Take 40, was made at the end of the session to allow for additional overdubs. These were made on July 30 and included vocals, guitar and percussion. The track was mixed on August 14.

## She Came In Through The Bathroom Window

Recorded: July 25 & 30 (Abbey Road Studio 2); July 28 (Studio 3)
Mixed: August 14

Producer: George Martin
Engineers: Geoff Emerick & Phil McDonald; John Kurlander

John: Lead vocal; acoustic 12-string guitar (Framus Hootenanny)
Paul: Backing vocal; bass guitar (Rickenbacker)
George: Backing vocal; guitars (Les Paul and Telecaster)
Ringo: Drums

Embellishments: Maracas; tambourine; cowbell

Paul's "She Came In Through The Bathroom Window" was inspired by a break-in to McCartney's house in St. Johns Wood by a group of Apple Scruffs (female fans who constantly hung around waiting for the Beatles by their studios, Apple headquarters and sometimes their homes). Diane Ashley used a ladder found in Paul's garden to climb into an open bathroom window on the second floor of his home. The line "Tuesday's on the phone to me" refers to Paul receiving a call from a neighbor about the incident. At the end of a rehearsal of the song on January 9, Paul reenacts the phone call: "Hello, this is Tuesday speaking. Is that Paul? I'd like to have a word with you." John continues with "I've got something of interest in the garden."

Although the song may have been started as early as Spring 1968, Paul was still working on the lyrics when he and Linda spent two weeks in New York after completion of *The White Album* in mid-October 1968. During the cab ride to Kennedy Airport to head back to London at the end of the month, Paul noticed the driver identification panel displayed in the cab. The driver's photo and name, Eugene Quits, appeared above the phrase "New York Police Dept." McCartney had his guitar with him and came up with the line "And so I quit the police department and got myself a steady job."

Paul played "She Came In Through The Bathroom Window" to the group at Twickenham on January 6, 1969, with a series of run-throughs during which he taught John and George the chords. The group further rehearsed the song on January 7, 8 and 9 with the line-up of Paul on bass, John on piano, George on his Telecaster through the Leslie and Ringo on drums. During rehearsals on January 9, the band turned in a few humorous performances. After a German count-in, John sings the song with a thick Cockney accent, and Paul provides off-the-cuff responses. During a later performance, the vocal shenanigans continue with the following exchange:

John: Get a job, cop!
Paul: And got myself a proper job.
John: Bloody 'bout time too, if you ask me.
Paul: And though she tried her best to help me.
John: You bloody need it, too.
Paul: She could steal, but she could not rob.

"She Came In Through The Bathroom Window" was both rehearsed and recorded during the Beatles initial Apple basement session held on January 21, 1969. *Anthology 3* contains one of these performances, followed by Paul favorably discussing John's classical-sounding piano part. When the song was recorded six months later for the *Abbey Road* album, John would be on guitar rather than piano. Although the group further rehearsed the song on January 29, these performances were not taped on Apple's eight-track recorder.

"She Came In Through The Bathroom Window" was recorded as a single track with "Polythene Pam" on July 25. The band recorded 39 takes, with John on 12-string acoustic guitar, Paul on his Rickenbacker bass, George on his Les Paul guitar and Ringo on drums. Lennon and McCartney provided guide vocals for their separate songs. Although Take 39 was deemed the best, Ringo redid his drum part and Paul re-recorded his bass. Proper lead vocals were also recorded.

On July 28, Take 39 was embellished with additional vocals, acoustic guitar, electric guitar, tambourine, maracas and cowbell (and possibly piano, though not in the mix). A reduction mix, designated Take 40, was made at the end of the session to allow for additional overdubs. These were made on July 30 and included vocals, guitar and percussion. The track was mixed on August 14.

The *Abbey Road* anniversary edition contains Take 27 of the "Polythene Pam"/"She Came In Through The Bathroom Window" recording. The track is preceded by Paul discussing the drumming with Ringo. John comments that it sounds like Dave Clark, a reference to the leader and drummer of the Dave Clark Five, whose "Glad All Over" single knocked the Beatles "I Want To Hold Your Hand" from the top of the British charts in 1964. Although Clark played drums in concert, he used session drummer Bobby Graham on the group's recordings. Had Pete Best remained the Beatles drummer, George Martin would have insisted the group use a studio drummer for the recordings. As for Ringo's drumming on "Polythene Pam," it is quite active, demonstrating no need for a session drummer.

## Golden Slumbers

Recorded: July 2, 3, 4, 30 & 31 (Abbey Road Studio 2, except July 30 Studio 3) and August 15 (Orchestra Studio 1; console Studio 2)
Mixed: August 18

Producer: George Martin
Engineers: Phil McDonald (all sessions); Geoff Emerick (July 30 & 31 and August 15); Chris Blair (July 2, 3 & 4); John Kurlander (July 30 & 31); Alan Parsons (August 15)

Paul: Lead and backing vocals; piano; guitar
George: Backing vocals; bass guitar (Fender VI); guitar (Telecaster)
Ringo: Backing vocals; drums; timpani (possibly Paul)

Outside Musicians: 12 violins, 4 violas, 4 cellos and 1 string bass, 4 horns, 3 trumpets, 1 trombone and 1 bass trombone

The medley continues with two of Paul's songs, "Golden Slumbers" and "Carry That Weight," which were also recorded as a single selection. The first song was derived from a lullaby written by Thomas Dekker as part of his 1603 play, *The Pleasant Comodie of Patient Grissill*. While visiting his father in 1968, Paul came across the tune in a songbook owned by his stepsister Ruth (most likely *St. Nicholas Songs*, published 1885). The lyrics to Dekker's lullaby are:

> Golden slumbers kiss your eyes;
> Smiles awake you when you rise.
> Sleep pretty wantons do not cry,
> And I will sing a lullaby.
> Rock them, rock them, lullaby.

Because Paul was unable to read the music added by W.J. Henderson, he created his own melody. He also changed a few of the words and added some of his own lyrics.

The rhythm track to "Golden Slumbers"/"Carry That Weight" was recorded in 15 takes on July 2, with Paul on piano and guide vocal, George on Fender Bass VI and Ringo on drums. The next day, Takes 13 and 15 were edited to form the backing track for the master. The following overdubs were then added: a McCartney lead vocal; Harrison's Telecaster through the Leslie; rhythm guitar by Paul; a second McCartney lead vocal. Because these embellishments used up the remaining empty tracks, two reduction mixes were made at the end of the session, with Take 17 being the best.

An overdub was added during a brief session held on July 4. Overdubs made on July 31 included a vocal from Paul, drums by Ringo and timpani part (played by Ringo or Paul). George Martin's score of 12 violins, four violas, four cellos, one string bass, four horns, three trumpets, one trombone and one bass trombone was added on August 15. The *Abbey Road* anniversary edition contains the orchestral score on its own.

## Carry That Weight

Recorded: July 2, 3, 4, 30 & 31 (Abbey Road Studio 2, except July 30 Studio 3) and August 15 (Orchestra Studio 1; console Studio 2)
Mixed: August 18

Producer: George Martin
Engineers: Phil McDonald (all sessions); Geoff Emerick (July 30 & 31 and August 15); Chris Blair (July 2, 3 & 4); John Kurlander (July 30 & 31); Alan Parsons (August 15)

Paul: Lead and backing vocals; piano; guitar
George: Backing vocals; bass guitar (Fender VI); guitar (Telecaster)
Ringo: Backing vocals; drums; timpani (possibly Paul)

Outside Musicians: 12 violins, 4 violas, 4 cellos and 1 string bass, 4 horns, 3 trumpets, 1 trombone and 1 bass trombone

"Carry That Weight" is another of Paul's songs dealing with his growing dissatisfaction with Apple under Allen Klein. In Miles' *Many Years From Now*, Paul talked about things "getting crazier and crazier and crazier. Carry that weight a long time: like forever!" McCartney stated that the song was about the bad atmosphere at Apple, a "serious, paranoid heaviness" that was "very uncomfortable."

Paul introduced "Carry That Weight" during the *Get Back* sessions on January 6. He performed piano renditions of the "Golden Slumbers"/"Carry That Weight" medley on the mornings of January 7 and 9. Ringo sang with Paul on the chorus of "Carry That Weight" during the January 9 runthrough.

The backing rhythm track to "Golden Slumbers"/"Carry That Weight" was recorded on July 2. During "Carry That Weight," Paul reprises the opening to "You Never Give Me Your Money," but with different lyrics. The instrumentation of the backing track is the same for both of the songs. The only difference in the vocals is the "Carry That Weight" chorus, which was added by Paul, Ringo and George on July 3. Everything else is the same. The songs were mixed on August 18. The *Abbey Road* anniversary edition contains the first three takes of the songs, starting with Paul briefly singing and playing "The Fool On The Hill" (Take 1) before leading into Take 2, which breaks down, restarts as Take 3 and breaks down again.

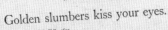

# Golden slumbers kiss your eyes.

W. J. HENDERSON.

From "The Pleasant Comodie of Patient Grissill." 1603.

*Allegretto.*

*legato*

*cres.*

1. Gold - en slum - bers kiss your eyes, Smiles a - wake you when you rise; Sleep, pret - ty wan - tons, do not cry, And I.... will sing a lul - la - by, I.... will sing a lul - la - by, I.... will sing a

*piu presto*

*mf*

*p*

Copyright, 1895, by The Century Co.

23

177

.  do.............

I will sing a lul - la - by.
(*Omit 2d time, see next page.*)

*colla voce*  *p*

*cres.*

are care, and care must

ll sing a lul - la - by.

*mf*  *mf*

178

Rock them, rock them, lul - la - by! Ah, lul - la - by! Ah,

*cres...............mf*  *p — mf*  *p*

*D. S.* rall - en - tan - do  *a battuta*

- by!...... I will sing a lul - la - by.

*after repeat.*

*D. S.* *p* *colla voce*

*dim.*

*pp*  *FINE.*

179

## The End

Recorded: July 23 and Aug 5, 7 & 8 (Abbey Road Studio 3 except Aug 8 Studio 2); Aug 15 (Orchestra Studio 1; console Studio 2); and Aug 18 (Studio 2)
Mixed: Aug 21; edited Aug 25

Producer: George Martin
Engineers: Geoff Emerick & Phil McDonald (all sessions); John Kurlander (July 23 & Aug 5,7 & 8); Alan Parsons (Aug 15 & 18)

Paul: Lead and backing vocals; bass guitar (Rickenbacker); piano; guitar (Telecaster)
John: Backing vocals; guitar (Casino)
George: Backing vocals; guitar (Telecaster)
Ringo: Backing vocals; drums; timpani (possibly Paul)

Outside Musicians: 12 violins, 4 violas, 4 cellos and 1 string bass, 4 horns, 3 trumpets, 1 trombone and 1 bass trombone

The medley concludes, appropriately enough, with a song titled "The End." Following Shakespeare's practice of placing a rhyming couplet at the end of a scene, Paul came up with "And in the end, the love you take is equal to the love you make." A fitting conclusion of which the Bard himself would be proud.

Recording of "The End" (under the working title "Ending") began on July 23, with a backing track of John on his Casino, Paul on Rickenbacker bass and Ringo on drums. The group went through seven takes before selecting Take 7 as the best. This recording features Ringo's drumming more prominently than on any other Beatles song. For the first time, Ringo was given a solo. In contrast to the long and often tedious drum solos of the late sixties, Ringo provided an effective solo lasting just over 15 seconds. In addition, his drums were recorded onto two separate tracks, thus allowing for different parts of his drumming to be placed left, right and center in the stereo mix. Ringo's solo is similar is style to the 2:30 drum solo by Ron Bushy on Iron Butterfly's 1968 heavy metal epic recording of "In-A-Gadda-Da-Vida," which runs over 17 minutes long.

Later that evening, the group added an extension to Take 7, which originally lasted for only 1:17. The backing track for the add-on features Paul on piano, John on his Casino, George on his Telecaster through the Leslie and Ringo on drums. At this stage the song was less than two minutes long, but this would be extended to 2:41 with additional overdubs. The final edit would shorten this by 36 seconds.

On August 5 and 7, the group recorded their vocals, with Paul singing lead. John, Paul and George also superimposed guitar parts on August 7. The most interesting passage begins at the 53 second mark, with the three guitarists trading solos three times over John's previously recorded churning rhythm guitar. Each solo is played for two bars and runs for approximately four seconds. Paul leads off with a tight rocking Telecaster solo, followed by George's wailing Telecaster and John's distorted Casino. The exchanging solos reach a boiling point 1:29 into the song, where Paul's piano takes over and leads into the concluding vocal couplet. The following day, Paul added bass and Ringo added drums.

George Martin's orchestral score, consisting of 12 violins, four violas, four cellos, one string bass, four horns, three trumpets, one trombone and one bass trombone, was recorded on August 15. Paul added four seconds of piano preceding his ending vocal on August 18. The stereo mixing and crossfade joining of the track to the end of "Golden Slumbers"/"Carry That Weight" took place on August 18, 19 and 21, with Remix 4 selected for the master tape of the album. On August 25, "The End" was edited down to its final running time of 2:05.

*Anthology 3* contains a newly-created mix of "The End" that starts during the opening moments of what is Ringo's drum solo on the released version of the song. The new mix reveals that guitar and tambourine parts were recorded over the drum solo, but that these additions were deleted from the final mix. The new mix has the guitar parts and orchestra more to the front. It lasts about a minute and a half, but is extended for another 80 seconds with an edit of the final chord from "A Day In The Life."

The *Abbey Road* deluxe edition contains Take 3, which, like all other initial performances of the song, is lacking the piano extension added for Paul's concluding couplet.

## Her Majesty

Recorded: July 2 (Abbey Road Studio 2)
Mixed: July 30

Producer: George Martin
Engineers: Phil McDonald & Chris Blair

Paul: Lead vocal; acoustic guitar (Martin D-28)

Although "The End" is the final piece of the medley, it is not the album's last song. As explained below, the medley is followed by 14 seconds of silence and a 23-second tune titled "Her Majesty."

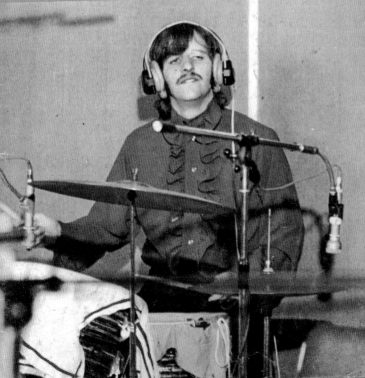

The End of The Beatles Book came with the magazine's 77th issue, cover dated December 1969 and issued a month or so after the release of *Abbey Road*. The back cover featured a photo from the band's final photo session held on August 22, 1969, at Tittenhurst, John's home in Sunninghill near Ascot, Berkshire.

Paul McCartney described the song, which was written at his farm in Scotland towards the end of 1968, as mildly disrespectful, but tongue-in-cheek, "almost like a love song to the Queen." He sang and played the song on piano at Twickenham on January 9, 1969. On January 24, Paul played the song on acoustic guitar, stretching it out for over two minutes by singing the same verse five times, with scat vocals for the first few lines of the second and fourth verses. Ringo joined in on drums, and John played some rudimentary slide guitar on the Hofner Hawaiian Standard lap-steel guitar.

The song was recorded at Abbey Road in three takes as a solo McCartney song on July 2, with Paul singing live over his Martin D-28 acoustic guitar. As Paul had only written a single verse, the track lasts only 22 seconds. The *Abbey Road* anniversary edition contains all three takes of the song.

"Her Majesty" nearly didn't appear on the album. The song was mixed and edited into the medley on July 30 between "Mean Mr. Mustard" and "Polythene Pam." In all likelihood, the tune was placed after "Mean Mr. Mustard" to tie in with that song's line "Takes him out to look at the Queen." When the tape of the medley was played back, Paul realized that "Her Majesty" did not fit in. Although McCartney instructed engineer John Kurlander to cut the "Her Majesty" segment from the tape and throw it away, Kurlander had been taught never to throw anything away. After Paul left the studio, Kurlander picked the tape up off the floor, added about 20 seconds of leader tape to the end of the medley and stuck "Her Majesty" onto the end of the leader tape.

The following day, Mal Evans brought the tape to Malcolm Davis at Apple Studios to cut lacquers of the medley for the group. Davis, who had also been taught never to throw anything away, copied the tape complete with the long gap of silence followed by "Her Majesty." Upon hearing the acetate, Paul liked the surprise effect of the song popping up after the apparent end of the medley.

When the master tape for the album was banded (placing the songs in order) on August 20, "Her Majesty" was placed at the end of the tape after 14 seconds of silence. Because Paul wanted to duplicate the random nature of "Her Majesty" exactly as it appeared on the July 31 acetate, he had the engineers use the actual piece of tape cut from the medley on July 30 rather than make a clean mix from Take 3 of the song. Thus, "Her Majesty" begins with the crashing final chord of "Mean Mr. Mustard" and ends abruptly without its closing chord (which was cut off as it blended with the opening chord to "Polythene Pam" in the test medley).

## The Medley and LP Banding Session

Both Paul and George Martin take credit for the idea for the medley; however, John was the first one to comment publicly about it. In the May 3, 1969, issue of NME, John stated "Paul and I are now working on a kind of song montage that we might do as one piece on one side." This shows that the idea for the medley predates the May 6 recording of Paul's "You Never Give Me Your Money," which by itself is like a medley of three song fragments. Although John later chastised the medley, he did contribute three of its eight songs.

On July 3, the group recorded "Golden Slumbers" and "Carry That Weight" as a single track. Similarly, "Sun King" and "Mean Mr. Mustard" were recorded as a single track on July 24, as were "Polythene Pam" and "She Came In Through The Bathroom Window" on the following day. "The End" was begun on July 23.

Although only a few of the medley's components were complete by July 30, a test of the medley (then called "The Long One" or "Huge Melody") was made that evening. The running order of the 15:30 medley was the same as the released version, except that "Her Majesty" was placed between "Mean Mr. Mustard" and "Polythene Pam." The medley test is included on the *Abbey Road* deluxe edition (shown as "The Long One"). The test edit demonstrated that, for the most part, the songs flowed together well. An exception was "Her Majesty," which was dropped from the lineup when Paul realized the song did not fit in. The tape also revealed that the crossfade from "You Never Give Me Your Money" into "Sun King" needed embellishing. This was solved by mixing in sound effects of tubular bells, birds and chirping crickets. Extensive mixing, crossfading, editing and joining of the medley's components took place on August 14, with additional work done on August 20 and 21.

The banding session for the album took place on August 20, with all four Beatles in attendance. This was the last time the entire group was together at Abbey Road. The master tape produced during the session varied from final master in two ways: "Octopus's Garden" preceded, rather than followed, "Oh! Darling;" and, Side One and Side Two were reversed. Had the decision not been made to switch the sides, the album would have opened with "Here Comes The Sun" and closed with the abrupt ending to "I Want You (She's So Heavy)." While this would have worked, the final master's running order, with "Come Together" as the opening track and the medley, along with "The End" and the surprise appearance of "Her Majesty," as the closer, is more effective.

The engineer's notes on the tape box containing Capitol's New York master tape warned that there was "distortion in spots, on original." After the entry for the song "I Want You," the engineer wrote "(audible hiss in intro" and "Note: Music ends abruptly)." After the title of the final track, "The End," he noted there was a 15-second pause before a track identified as "No Title."

# Get Back

Recorded: January 23, 24, 27, 28 and 29 (Apple basement studio);
January 30 (Apple rooftop concert)
Mixed: April 7 (mono & stereo) from Jan 27 & 28 performances

Producer: George Martin (Jan 27, 28, 29 & 30)
Engineers: Glyn Johns; Alan Parsons (except January 24);
Neil Richmond (January 24)

Paul: Lead vocal; bass guitar (Hofner)
John: Backing vocal; lead guitar (Casino)
George: Backing vocal; rhythm guitar (Telecaster)
Ringo: Drums
Billy Preston: Electric piano (Fender Rhodes)

The "Get Back" single was released about a half-year before *Abbey Road*. The song was recorded during January 1969, as part of the sessions that would eventually form the basis for the *Let It Be* movie and its soundtrack album. From January 2 through January 14, the group was filmed by director Michael Lindsay-Hogg on a Twickenham Film Studios soundstage in London rehearsing new material and loosely performing some of their favorite oldies. On January 21, the Beatles resumed work on the project in a make-shift studio in the basement of Apple's Savile Row headquarters. Recording and filming continued through the end of the month. Although the sessions were full of tension, bickering and overall bad vibes, the initial songs issued from the project gave listeners no indication of the troubled conditions under which they were recorded.

The genesis of "Get Back" dates to the morning of January 7, when Paul introduced the song prior to John's arrival. McCartney's initial rendering of "Get Back" consisted of thumping bass and loose scat vocals. Although George played a few open chord notes at the start, this embryonic performance was essentially all Paul. George joined Paul for the next attempt, which opened with Paul singing the chorus and some incomplete lyrics that would later serve as the second verse. Although Ringo did not play drums, he sang with Paul on the choruses and later verses.

The first real runthrough of "Get Back" was performed as a simple rocker with Ringo supplying a straightforward beat and George adding some wah-wah guitar fills. Paul sings the song in the style of Apple recording artist Jackie Lomax, perhaps realizing that the "get back to where you once belonged" chorus is similar to the "get back to where you should be" line from Lomax's recording of George Harrison's "Sour Milk Sea." Paul acknowledges his Lomax imitation by shouting, "C'mon Jackie!" during the second chorus.

The group returned to the song two days later on January 9, this time with John present and accounted for. Early run-throughs sound more like a jam than a finished song, but elements of the story line, such as references to Arizona and California, begin to appear. Paul then switches direction by temporarily changing the lyrics to political satire aimed at Parliament member Enoch Powell, who was in the news at that time spouting his beliefs that too many nonwhite citizens of the British Empire were immigrating to England and taking away limited jobs. Before launching into this political version of the song, Paul sings "Don't want no black man. Don't dig no Pakistanis taking all the people's jobs." The song's improvised lyrics include references to Puerto Ricans and Mohicans for the United States verse, and Pakistanis for England. The group jams behind Paul, who shouts "get back" over and over again in a voice that mocks the hatred behind Enoch Powell's beliefs. After a few political versions of the song, the band returned briefly to the song's original story line, with Jo and Theresa serving as the principal characters.

The following day, January 10, the band spent a significant portion of the morning session working on "Get Back." Prior to the start of band rehearsals, Paul performed the song on piano. After McCartney switched to bass, he led the group through a raucous version of "Get Back." At Paul's suggestion, the song was rearranged to open with crashing guitars (somewhat reminiscent of the start to "A Hard Day's Night") and a building drum roll from Ringo. The band performed several rocking run-throughs, with some incorporating bits of the "No Pakistanis" lyrics from the previous day. One of the more spirited performances features John joining Paul on the verses, a jamming wah-wah guitar solo and a Ringo drum fill leading into a third verse, which was later discarded. This verse contains references to living in a council flat (government-subsidized housing) and statements from the candidate for Labour (one of Britain's political parties). The verse about Loretta is essentially complete, but serves as the first rather than second verse. The middle verse features Jo Jo, Arizona and California, but is not in final form.

Although the group's progress with "Get Back" gives the impression that things were finally coming together for the band, things were about to fall apart. Shortly after the group's break for lunch on January 10, George announced he was quitting the group and walked out of Twickenham.

On January 13, the three remaining Beatles returned to "Get Back," with Paul refining the lyrics. Loretta's last name alternated between Marsh and Marvin after Paul rejected John's "suggestion" of "Sweet Loretta Meatball." Although the group completed a few rocking takes of the song, Ringo's drum fills during the breaks threw the band's timing off. John's guitar solos, which borrow elements from Dale Hawkins' "Suzie Q," range from passable to pitiful.

By the time the Beatles returned to "Get Back" on January 23, George had rejoined the band and the sessions had moved to the basement of Apple's Savile Row headquarters. In addition, Billy Preston was providing keyboards. Preston, who the Beatles met in 1962 when he was in Little Richard's touring band, was invited to the sessions by George. His presence not only added musical depth to the band's live performances, but also helped the group to behave in a more civil manner.

Most of the day's session was devoted to "Get Back." Although the group did not perfect the song, its structure, lyrics and instrumentation were taking shape, including Ringo's galloping snare drum part, George's chopping rhythm guitar, John's guitar solos and Billy Preston's electric piano fills and solo.

The group continued to rehearse the song on January 24, at first without Preston, who did not arrive until mid-afternoon. The most interesting version recorded that day has back-to-back performances of the song, complete with spirited improvisations from Paul during the final coda.

On January 27, the group ran through over 30 takes of "Get Back." During one of the early performances, Paul sings the first verse with Japanese characters and cities; however, most of the versions of the song recorded this day were serious attempts at a suitable master take. The performances are fairly similar, with the main differences being the tempo, John's guitar solos and the codas. During one of the codas, Paul sings, "it's five o'clock, your mother's got your tea on." He ends another with the "One, two, three o'clock, four o'clock rock" opening line from Bill Haley's "Rock Around The Clock." On the take that would later be chosen for the single and the *Let It Be* album, the group fails to play a coda, causing Harrison to comment, "We missed that end, didn't we?"

Due to the flubbed ending of this performance, the group continued work on the song. The later recordings are entertaining, but do not match the perfection of the master. The most interesting of the bunch has Paul singing pseudo-German lyrics until he switches to pseudo-French for the final chorus. During an instrumental break, Paul once again acknowledges the Jackie Lomax influence on the song by saying, "Yah, that's good Jackie" in a German accent.

The Beatles recorded additional takes of "Get Back" on the following day. The extended coda from one of these January 28 performances was put to good use. A segment containing the first 35 seconds of the coda was edited to the end of the January 27 performance chosen for the single. A later segment of the coda was used as the "Get Back" reprise that ends both unreleased *Get Back* albums and the *Let It Be* film. The full coda runs 1:22 and ends with John singing: "Shoot me when I'm evil, shoot me when I'm good, shoot me when I'm hungry, and shoot me when I'm...." The later performances of the song are ragged and have Billy Preston on organ rather than electric piano.

On January 29, the Beatles rehearsed the songs slated for the rooftop concert, including "Get Back." Because Billy was not present, John vocalized Preston's piano solo.

The next day the Beatles, accompanied by Billy Preston on electric piano, gave their last public performance on January 30. The impromptu concert was staged on the roof of Apple headquarters and included three complete performances of "Get Back," two of which appear in the *Let It Be* film. The group's final take on the song was the closing number to the concert and the film. This historic performance, complete with Paul's ad-libbed reference to playing on the rooftops, is included on *Anthology 3*.

On March 10, 1969, Glyn Johns made stereo mixes of January 23 and January 27 performances of "Get Back." These mixes were transferred to an acetate for the Beatles to review.

On March 26, "Get Back" was mixed for mono at Abbey Road by EMI engineer Jeff Jarratt. The finished master combines the January 27 coda-less performance previously mixed by Glyn Johns with the first 35 seconds of a coda recorded on January 28. An acetate of this mix was played on Easter Sunday (April 6) on BBC 1 by disc jockeys John Peel and Alan Freeman. Because Paul was not satisfied with the mix, the song was remixed for mono on April 7 by Glyn Johns and Jerry Boys at Olympic Sound Studios. This is the mix used on the British single. Johns and Boys also prepared a stereo mix for the American single. Paul was the only Beatle who attended these sessions. George Martin was most likely not present. The 2003 album *Let It Be... Naked* contains a remix of the January 27 master without the added coda.

## Don't Let Me Down

Recorded: January 22, 27, 28 and 29 (Apple basement studio);
January 30 (Apple rooftop concert)
Mixed: April 7 (mono & stereo) from January 28 performance

Producer: George Martin (Jan 28, 29 & 30)
Engineers: Glyn Johns; Alan Parsons (all except January 22)

John: Lead vocal; rhythm guitar (Casino)
Paul: Backing vocal; bass guitar (Hofner)
George: Backing vocal; lead guitar (Telecaster)
Ringo: Drums
Billy Preston: Electric piano (Fender Rhodes)

"Don't Let Me Down" was written by John as an expression of his love for Yoko Ono. In late 1968, he recorded a demo containing most of the elements of the finished song.

John introduced "Don't Let Me Down" on January 2, 1969, as his initial offering for the *Get Back* project. The first run-throughs, with John playing chords and George adding some lead guitar lines, took place without Paul. After McCartney arrived, he rearranged the song and suggested that it open with the title being sung twice. The group continued rehearsing the song the following day.

When the band returned to the song on January 6, much time was spent on the middle eight. The group experimented with different rhythms, lyrics, harmonies, falsetto voices and call and response vocals, none of which proved satisfactory. The only new idea to survive the day's extensive and frustrating rehearsals was John's decision to add a guitar introduction to the song. And while much of the time devoted to the song was unproductive, the group did work its way through a few near-satisfactory performances that showed the song's potential.

At this stage, the instrumentation of the song was still open to discussion, with consideration being given to adding piano. Although George was willing to play bass to allow Paul to move to piano, John wanted the song to have two guitars. During the initial rehearsals of the song, and for the next few days, George used a wah-wah pedal to alter the sound of his guitar.

On January 7, the group continued work on the middle eight. Performances from the next two days show the band making progress in spite of John's constant inability to remember the lyrics.

Prior to the start of rehearsals on January 10, Paul played "Don't Let Me Down" on piano. By the time the group returned to the song that afternoon, George had quit the band. The performance by the remaining Beatles was an embarrassing mess.

The group rehearsed "Don't Let Me Down" in Apple's basement studio on January 21. During one of the performances, John lapses into laughter and Little Richard improvisations. Another run-through is tighter, but once again spiked with inappropriate vocal ad-libs. George is no longer using his wah-wah pedal and is playing his rosewood Fender Telecaster through a Leslie speaker.

Billy Preston joined the *Get Back* sessions on January 22. On his first take of the song, Preston starts tentatively, but quickly falls into a groove with his blues-sounding electric piano riffs. John plays organ on this performance, perhaps to help Billy learn the chords to the song. After a few rehearsals, the group performs a fairly solid rendition of the tune, although John has trouble with the lyrics to the first verse and gets a bit silly during the second bridge. As the song reaches what had previously been its end, John says "Take it, Billy," and the band starts up again with Preston taking a piano solo while John ad-libs "Can you dig it?" and "I had a dream this afternoon." When the song comes to a halt, John says the song's title and the band adds a brief coda. One of the later takes from this day was selected by Glyn Johns for the unreleased *Get Back* album.

When the Beatles returned to the song on January 27, they rehearsed specific sections and recorded two full takes. While the song was starting to come together, there were still vocal glitches.

By January 28, the band had finally mastered the song, turning in two near perfect performances. The best of these was selected to serve as the flip side to "Get Back," although part of John's vocal from another take was dropped in to cover up some flubbed lyrics during the first verse. In addition, some vocal ad-libs and screams by John and Paul from another take were added to the end of the song.

The following day the group, without Billy Preston, rehearsed "Don't Let Me Down" for the rooftop concert. To avoid straining his vocal chords, John sang in a deeper and more relaxed voice. Paul stopped the song early on to work on his harmony part with John. During some of the choruses, John sang the title to "Keep Your Hands Off My Baby," a 1962 hit for Little Eva that was recorded by the Beatles for the BBC. Towards the end of the song, John calls out, "Go Bill," and does a brief vocalization of the missing pianist's solo.

The group played the song twice during the rooftop concert. During the first, John forgot the opening lyrics to the second verse, forcing him to ad-lib some gibberish. When the group returned to the song later in the show, John muffed the lyrics to the first verse. The earlier take of the song is tighter and appears in the film. *Let It Be... Naked* contains an edit of the two rooftop performances.

J 006-04.982

ESTEREO-MONO

EMI

ODEON

the beatles

# ALL TOGETHER NOW

The above Spanish picture sleeve to EMI's "All Together Now" single on Odeon features a photo from

## The Ballad Of John And Yoko

Recorded: April 14 (Abbey Road Studio 3)
Mixed: April 14 (stereo)

Producer: George Martin
Engineers: Geoff Emerick; John Kurlander

John: Lead vocal; acoustic guitar (Jumbo); lead guitar (Casino); tapping back of acoustic guitar
Paul: Backing vocal; drums; bass guitar; piano; maracas

In mid-March of 1969, John and Yoko decided to get married. They headed to the port of Southampton with visions of having the ceremony take place at sea. This plan fell through and the couple flew to Paris hoping to wed in France. After their attempt at a quick wedding in Paris failed, John asked Peter Brown, the Beatles personal assistant, to check out other possible locations. While John and Yoko were honeymooning down by the Seine, Peter Brown called to say they could get married in Gibraltar near Spain. The wedding took place on March 20.

After the ceremony, the couple returned to France and went from Paris to the Amsterdam Hilton to stage their week-long Bed-In for peace. This was followed by a lightning trip to Vienna, where they held a press conference (and ate chocolate cake) while inside a large white bag. On April Fool's Day, the newlyweds caught the early plane back to London, where they held a press conference at Heathrow Airport. John and Yoko sent acorns to heads of state throughout the world, asking each leader to plant an acorn for peace. All of these events were covered extensively by the men from the press.

"The Ballad Of John And Yoko" chronicles the chaotic events surrounding the couple's wedding. John accurately describes the lyrics as both a "piece of journalism" and a "folk song." He jokingly dubbed the song "Johnny B. Paperback Writer." On April 14, 1969, John dropped by Paul's house for help in completing the song. That afternoon they headed over to Abbey Road to record what would be the next Beatles single. Because Ringo was busy filming *The Magic Christian* and George was out of the country, John and Paul were the only Beatles in the studio.

They went through 11 takes with Lennon on lead vocal and acoustic guitar, and McCartney on drums. It was a good-natured and productive session. Prior to Take 4, John called out to Paul, "Go a bit faster, Ringo!" to which Paul replied, "OK, George!" This studio banter is included on the *Abbey Road* anniversary edition followed by Take 7. Take 10 was determined to be the best backing track. After

Paul added bass, John overdubbed two guitar parts on his Epiphone Casino. Paul then contributed piano and backing vocals for the bridge and last two verses. The track was further embellished with Paul shaking maracas and John thumping the back of his guitar.

Although George normally handled the lead guitar parts on the Beatles recordings, his absence gave John another opportunity. His playing is excellent throughout, particularly on the song's coda, which resembles the lead guitar from "Lonesome Tears In My Eyes." That song, written by Johnny and Dorsey Burnette and Paul Burlison and Al Mortimer, was recorded by the Johnny Burnette Trio and released in 1956 on the LP *Johnny Burnette And The Rock 'N' Trio*. The Beatles, with John on lead vocal, recorded the song on July 10, 1963, for the July 23 BBC radio program *Pop Goes The Beatles*. The performance was officially released in late 1994 on *Live At The BBC*.

"The Ballad Of John And Yoko" was mixed for stereo at the end of the session. No mono mix was made because the single was to be issued in stereo in both the U.S. and England, making the disc the group's and EMI's first British stereo 45.

The finished master is an infectious rocker with clever, but controversial, lyrics. John knew that the song's chorus would cause problems, particularly coming from the man who previously said the Beatles were more popular than Jesus. In a note to Apple promo man Tony Bramwell, Lennon gave the following instructions: "No pre-publicity on Ballad Of John & Yoko especially the Christ! bit—So don't play it round too much or you'll frighten people—Get it pressed first." The song was originally titled "The Ballad Of John And Yoko (They're Gonna Crucify Me)." John wisely dropped the subtitle.

## Ain't She Sweet/Who Slapped John?/Up A Lazy River/Be-Bop-A-Lula

Same recording session and personnel as "Sun King" (July 24)

Between takes of "Sun King"/"Mean Mr. Mustard," the Beatles jammed on four songs associated with Gene Vincent. Three were from his 1956 *Bluejean Bop!* LP: "Ain't She Sweet" (a 1920s standard written by Ager and Yellen and recorded by the Beatles in Hamburg, Germany in 1961); "Who Slapped John?" (co-written by Vincent); and "Up A Lazy River" (a standard from 1930 written by Hoagy Carmichael and Sidney Arodin). The Beatles also played a bit of "Be-Bop-A-Lula" (co-written by Vincent). This rockabilly classic was a top ten hit on Billboard's pop (#7), R&B (#8) and C&W (#5) charts and a number 16 hit in the U.K. *Anthology 3* contains "Ain't She Sweet."

## Old Brown Shoe

Rehearsed: January 27 & 28 (Apple)

Demo Recorded: February 25 (Abbey Road; Ken Scott engineer)
George: Vocal; piano; lead guitar

Recorded: April 16 & 18 (Abbey Road Studio 3)
Mixed: April 18 (stereo)

Producer: George Martin (January 27 & 28; April 16);
Chris Thomas (April 18)
Engineers: Glyn Johns & Alan Parsons (January 27 & 28); Ken Scott
(February 25); Jeff Jarratt (April 16 & 18); Richard Kush (April 16);
John Kurlander (April 18)

George: Lead vocal; slide and lead guitar (Telecaster); organ
John: Backing vocal; piano
Paul: Backing vocal; drums; bass (Fender Jazz)

"Old Brown Shoe" was written by George on piano after the group's January 26, 1969, session. In his book *I Me Mine*, Harrison states that he "began writing ideas for the words from various opposites," focusing on "the duality of things – yes-no, up-down, left-right, right-wrong, etc." This approach is evident in the song's opening lines: "I want a love that's right, but right is only half of what's wrong/I want a short-haired girl who sometimes wears it twice as long." Other opposites include pick me up/drag me down, smile/frown, love/hate and early start/late. Harrison's song is a rocking expression of the Eastern philosophy of yin-yang. It is also reminiscent of the duality found in Paul's "Hello, Goodbye."

Upon arriving at Apple on January 27, George told the group that he had written a great new song the night before, which he described as a happy rocker. Although the song was complete, Harrison had yet to come up with a title. George played his new composition on piano for Billy Preston to teach him the chords.

After the group performed some oldies and rehearsed "Let It Be" and "The Long And Winding Road," they moved on to "Old Brown Shoe." George played the song on piano, joined at times by Ringo, who was experimenting with different drum beats, and John on bass (which he had been playing while Paul was on piano for his ballads). When the performance broke down towards the end of the song, George commented, "Pianos are very difficult, aren't they?" He then picked up the tune and finished it with Ringo and John. On the next runthrough, Ringo began to find his groove, and Billy Preston added organ. During the next few takes, Paul played guitar.

The next day, George returned to the song, once again on piano, this time teaching John the chords for him to play on guitar. Paul was back on bass. After John switched to an Ominichord (an organ-sounding instrument), Preston played piano, freeing George to switch to guitar. As George wrote the song on piano and played it on piano on prior performances, he joked that he will have to learn the song on guitar. Some of George's guitar riffs are reminiscent of what he would later play when the group returned to the song in April.

On February 25, Harrison recorded demos of "Old Brown Shoe," "All Things Must Pass" and "Something" at Abbey Road. For "Old Brown Shoe," he recorded a live track of his vocal and piano and then overdubbed two lead guitar parts. This demo is on *Anthology 3*.

George taped another demo on April 16. A few hours later, the group, minus Ringo, joined him at Abbey Road for the tune's first proper recording. The backing track was completed in four takes, with George on lead vocal and slide guitar, John on piano, and Paul on drums. Paul overdubbed his Fender Jazz Bass, and George added a second guitar part on his Telecaster, matching Paul note-for-note on the bridge. John and Paul provided backing vocals and George re-recorded his lead vocal. Two days later, Harrison added a guitar solo on his Telecaster, played through a Leslie speaker and treated with ADT. He also recorded a Hammond organ part. The song was then mixed for stereo. The *Abbey Road* anniversary edition contains Take 2.

## Come And Get It (demo)

Recorded and mixed: July 24 (Abbey Road Studio 2)
Engineers: Phil McDonald; John Kurlander
Paul: Vocals; piano; maracas; drums; bass guitar

Prior to the Beatles recording "Sun King" on July 24, Paul knocked out a demo of "Come And Get It" in an hour. He sang and played the song on piano and then overdubbed his vocal and maracas, drums and bass. On August 2, Paul produced Badfinger's version of the song. The demo was first issued on *Anthology 3* and is on the *Abbey Road* anniversary edition.

## Goodbye (demo)

Paul recorded a vocal/acoustic guitar demo of "Goodbye" for Mary Hopkin's follow-up single to "Those Were The Days." This demo is on the *Abbey Road* anniversary edition.

VISIT
# www.beatle.net
# for more books by Bruce Spizer

SUBSCRIBE TO BRUCE'S EMAIL LIST

FOR MORE EXCLUSIVE BEATLES ARTICLES AND CONTENT

## THE BEATLES ALBUM SERIES ALSO AVAILABLE IN DIGITAL, HARD COVER AND SPECIAL COLLECTOR'S EDITIONS

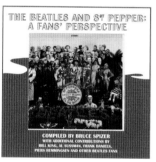

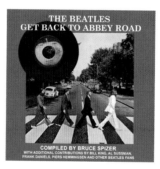

## OTHER TITLES: DIGITAL EDITIONS, FIRST EDITION HARDCOVER AND SPECIAL COLLECTOR'S EDITIONS

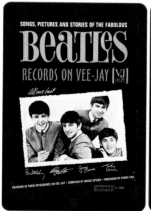

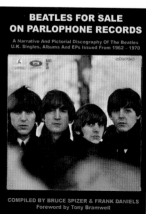